The I in Team

The I in Team

Sports Fandom and the
Reproduction of Identity

ERIN C. TARVER

The University of Chicago Press
Chicago and London

The University of Chicago Press, Chicago 60637
The University of Chicago Press, Ltd., London
© 2017 by The University of Chicago
Published 2017
Printed in the United States of America

26 25 24 23 22 21 20 19 18 17   1 2 3 4 5

ISBN-13: 978-0-226-46993-5 (cloth)
ISBN-13: 978-0-226-47013-9 (paper)
ISBN-13: 978-0-226-47027-6 (e-book)
DOI: 10.7208/chicago/9780226470276.001.0001

Chapter 3 contains material from Erin C. Tarver, "On the Particular Racism of Native
American Mascots," *Critical Philosophy of Race* 4, no. 1 (2016): 95–126. Copyright
© 2016, Penn State University Press. This article is used by permission of The
Pennsylvania State University Press.

Chapter 6 contains material from Erin C. Tarver, "The Dangerous Individual's Dog:
Race, Criminality, and the Pit Bull," *Culture, Theory, and Critique* 55, no. 3 (2014):
273–284. Used by permission of Taylor & Francis Group (tandfonline.com).

Library of Congress Cataloging-in-Publication Data

Names: Tarver, Erin C., author.
Title: The I in team: sports fandom and the reproduction of identity / Erin C. Tarver.
Description: Chicago ; London : The University of Chicago Press, 2017. | Includes
    bibliographical references and index.
Identifiers: LCCN 2016042822 | ISBN 9780226469935 (cloth : alk. paper) |
    ISBN 9780226470139 (pbk. : alk. paper) | ISBN 9780226470276 (e-book)
Subjects: LCSH: Sports spectators—United States. | Fans (Persons)—United States. |
    Identity (Psychology)
Classification: LCC GV715 .T379 2017 | DDC 306.4/83—dc23 LC record available at
    https://lccn.loc.gov/2016042822

♾ This paper meets the requirements of ANSI/NISO Z39.48-1992 (Permanence of
Paper).

To Cori, Sharon, Lizzie, Anna, Tara, Sarah,
and
all of the other sports fans in my life
who have dared to ask difficult questions about
the games that they love

Contents

Introduction: Sports Fandom and Identity

I don't remember the first time I went with my family to a sporting event. Sports were always a part of life where I grew up in south Louisiana, moving with the rhythm of the seasons, yet always in the air. I do, however, remember my early lessons in being a sports fan, following along with the cheers and songs of Louisiana State University (LSU), trying—and failing—to find the courage to be brave when I first encountered the plush tiger mascot with its terrifyingly enormous head, and experiencing the thrill of watching a young Shaquille O'Neal lumber up and down the court of the Pete Maravich Assembly Center. My most vivid childhood sporting memories, though, are not just about the games themselves, but more importantly, about becoming a sports *fan*. I remember weaving with my parents through a sea of people all clad in the same colors, making our way into the stadium or arena, learning to chant and sing at the right times and to follow the action on the field or court. By the time I was a teenager, I had also learned to disparage our rivals (and to feel a genuine distaste for them), to keep up with the details of our team's fortunes in the local paper, and to engage in analysis of and arguments about play calling. As I grew into a full-fledged fan, I began to care deeply about how "we" did from one season to the next, to understand myself as "a Tiger fan," to feel pride in that status, and to feel resentment for those "fans" whose devotion, participation, or attention during games did not match mine. And when I moved away—across the country and beyond—I took my fandom with me as a reminder of home. In learning to be a fan, in short, I learned something more than spectatorship.[1] Although the scenes of Tiger Stadium, Fenway Park, and Super Bowl Sunday were undoubtedly ones of grand spectacle, being a good fan required more of me than passive absorption. Although I was certainly not an athlete, I believed that my participation was significant—though, more often than not, the character of that significance was unclear.

To nonfans, the allegiances of sports fans can appear more than unclear; the word more often used is, in my experience, "irrational." Fans of the University of Alabama's football team exhibit a borderline religious devotion to the Crimson Tide, even if they have no academic connection to the university. In the context of professional sports, fans' devotion to individual players like LeBron James can change overnight with the whims of contract renegotiation. Beyond these problem cases, sports fandom in general invites significant interest (to put it mildly) in the outcome of *games*—and games played by others, at that. Why in the world would anyone care about the batting, tackling, or shooting fortunes of people they are likely never to meet or with whom they have very little in common? How can we make sense of fans' willingness to alter their loyalties in some cases but not others? Why does sports fandom matter so much to so many?

In this book, I argue that sports fandom, far from being inconsequential, is a primary means of creating and reinforcing individual and community identities for Americans today. Sports fandom in the contemporary United States prescribes a variety of ritualized practices that contribute not only to communities' persistence over time but also to the racial and gender hierarchies that characterize those communities. Sports fandom is, to borrow a term from Foucault, a practice of subjectivization—a means by which individuals are regulated and, at the same time, achieve a sense of their own identities. Sports fandom matters, then, because it is one of the primary ways in which we tell ourselves who we are—and, just as importantly, who we are not.

It is no accident, I argue, that fans nearly always use "we," not "they," when discussing the fortunes of their teams or that controversies over racist mascots are met with such passionate resistance by supporters of the teams that use them. Fan identity is bound up with that of the team, in at least two ways: first, it is fans' actions and devotion that creates the significance of the historically persistent team over time: there is no such thing as "the Yankees," in other words, without Yankees fans, without the opposition of Red Sox fans, without a people to celebrate the mythology of Babe Ruth, Mickey Mantle, and the iconic pinstripes. Teams need fans as much as or more than fans come to need them. Second, fans' relationships to teams and individual players are venues through which fans form, transmit, and reproduce their own senses of regional, gender, and racial identity—and this is not only true in the case of star athletes who are so-called role models. The importance of sports fandom for identity is evident in a variety of fan practices, from the ways fans

talk about their rivals to their testing of the knowledge or loyalty of their fellow fans, the demographics of fan bases of men's and women's athletics, and
the linguistic differences that emerge when (for example) fans root for white
players or black players. When they watch, follow, and consume sports, there
is much more at stake for fans than the simple outcome of a game.

There is, in truth, much more at stake for all of us. If, as I argue, many
white fans' apparent idolization of black athletes treats them more like mascots than heroes—as symbols of strength and masculinity whose power
becomes dangerous if not contained to the realm of fantasy—then sports
fandom in the contemporary United States has seriously worrying racial
implications. If sports fandom continues to be characterized by the overt
policing of gender norms and rampant homophobia, then its overwhelming popularity and influence ought to be a concern for more people than
those who count themselves sports fans. If the economics of sports fandom's
self-perpetuation demand the exploitation of athletes and the valorization of
consumerism, then ethicists, players, and nonfans alike should be urgently
concerned with understanding, critiquing, and changing it.

Despite the urgency of my task, I do not and cannot offer a universalizing
view of sports fandom as such. Sports fandom is a historically and geographically located set of practices, which are decidedly nonhomogenous. What I
aim to accomplish, instead, is a detailed analysis of the ways in which some
of the most dominant and visible practices of sports fandom in the United
States today (and particularly in the American South) function to shore up,
reproduce, and very occasionally, subvert racial, gender, and sexual hierarchies. In so doing, I will be focusing on fans of what are commonly called
the "revenue sports"—typically, football, baseball, and basketball. I will also,
more often than not, be discussing the habits and practices of white sports
fans. This focus is deliberate, but not because sports fandom is unimportant for people of color. Rather, my inquiry is focused in this way because,
as I will argue, the racialization of contemporary sports fandom demands
that we grapple with the role of the athletic spectacle, the ritual display of
black masculinity, and the instrumentalization of people of color as symbols
of power in the creation and reproduction of racial whiteness. My goals here
are thus in the spirit of Toni Morrison's call for an investigation of the role of
literary images of "blackness" in the production of white consciousness in
Playing in the Dark. She writes, "A good deal of time and intelligence has been
invested in the exposure of racism and the horrific results on its objects. . . .
But that well-established study should be joined with another, equally important one: the impact of racism on those who perpetuate it. It seems both

poignant and striking how avoided and unanalyzed is the effect of racist in-
flection on the subject" (1992, 11). In the vein of Morrison's important argument that whiteness is produced in and through its portrayals of and relation
to people of color, I will argue that white fans contribute to the reproduction
of their whiteness in and through fan practices involving their imaginative
relation to and ritualized display of people of color. Similarly, I will argue that
normative heterosexual masculinity is reproduced via the practices of sports
fandom that more or less explicitly disparage femininity and (by extension)
homosexual desire. This is not to say that sports fandom is uniformly oppressive; sports fans are not univocal, and (as I will show) there are marginal
forms of sports fandom that constitute genuine glimmers of social resistance.
But it is important that we take a hard look at the effects of hegemonic sports
fandom and its role in the perpetuation of the dominant social order.

In making this case, I draw on a variety of philosophical influences, most
notably—as my use of the term "subjectivization" suggests—Michel Foucault.
Foucault's work has been extremely important to the development of my
thinking and my conviction that the work of philosophy can (and perhaps
must) take place in the careful analysis of the history and practice of everyday features of social life. Yet this work is not, strictly speaking, Foucaultian.
I develop my own argument in this text as an intervention into the fields of
feminist philosophy and critical philosophy of race but do so in dialogue with
a host of voices. Those voices come from philosophy's canonical center and its
margins and include, most prominently, Simone de Beauvoir, William James,
Malcolm X, John Searle, and Iris Marion Young. Throughout, I also draw
significantly on the work of social scientists, most particularly sociologists
and anthropologists, as well as that of historians of sport and popular culture.
My argument is a philosophical one, as I seek to defend a historical, socially
contextualized account of selfhood, race, and gender—but in this argument, I
am not content to remain within the disciplinary bounds of philosophy or to
pledge my loyalty to any single philosophical camp.

The theoretically heterogeneous nature of my argument becomes clear
from my first chapter, in which I define the scope of my inquiry into "fans"
and situate it with reference to the existing debate in philosophy of sport on
partisan and purist sports fans. In that chapter, I conduct both a historical
investigation into the development of "sports fan" as a concept and identity
and argue for a broad theoretical understanding of what constitutes sports
fandom. Despite the thickly normative character of the "fan" concept—and
the fact that for many fans, the adjudication and exclusion of persons who
are not "*real* fans" is an important component of fandom—I claim that we
ought to understand sports fandom as inclusively as possible in order to fully

understand its effects. This is particularly important, I suggest, if we are to make salient the racializing and gendering functions of sports fan practices.

In chapter 2, which forms the theoretical basis of the rest of the book, I argue that sports fandom is a practice that facilitates the cultivation and reproduction of individual and community identities for Americans today. In making this argument, I draw on Foucault's concept of subjectivization and argue that sports fandom can be understood as a practice of subjectivization—that is, as a means by which individuals both subordinate themselves to a discipline and, at the same time, achieve a sense of their own identities. Just as a religious practitioner creates and obtains new forms of self-knowledge by participating in confession, prayer, and the observance of Lent, the sports fan comes to understand him- or herself as a particular sort of person by virtue of his or her participation in the practices of sports fandom. In particular, sports fandom is instrumental in the production of normatively masculine subjects and of subjects who understand themselves as belonging to a specific (often racialized) community or region—as an "I" who is part of a particular "we."

In chapter 3, I investigate the production of this "we" through one of the more prominent symbolic practices of sports fandom, that of the institution of mascots. I take up this argument with reference to the Native American mascot controversy and show that the usage of Native Americans as mascots by non-Native communities depends upon the concomitant instrumentalization and exclusion of non-Native persons by the "we" of the sports fan community. This theoretical conceptualization of mascots is important both because it shows the role of symbolic fan practices in social ontology and because it offers a salient example of the ways in which white communities are produced via sports fan practices that explicitly racialize and subordinate nonwhite groups.

In chapter 4, I apply my conceptualization of mascots to an analysis of white fan relations with prominent star players and argue that although such fans may root for and valorize star players of color, they often do so by treating these players as mascots. Drawing on the work of Malcolm X, I contrast white fans' hero worship of white star players like Tim Tebow with their mascotting of star players who are black or Latino men. Though both hero worship and mascotting are fantasies of identification, they are distinguished by different ways of imagining a player's relation to the community of which one is a part. To treat a person as a mascot is, I argue, to treat him or her as a symbol or object instrumentalized in the service of communal identity, even as they are excluded from full membership in it. Hero worship, in contrast, conceives of its object as "one of us" and as belonging to the community in a *representative* rather than commodified sense. Both forms of fan identification contribute to the reinforcement of white masculinity's normative status, meaning that the mere existence of cross-racial sports fandom is not necessarily cause for optimism.

I further develop the concept of mascotting in chapter 5, where I conduct a detailed analysis of the function of the mascotting of young black men in southern collegiate athletics. Despite the apparent progress of racially integrated college sports in the South, I argue that the pervasive mascotting of black athletes at predominately white institutions in this region contributes to the maintenance of a masculine white supremacist social order. The mascotting of these athletes is built upon the racist association of black masculinity with hypermasculinity, violence, and heterosexuality, which positions these black athletes both as objects of fantasy and as disposable when they are no longer useful for white fans. At the same time, the mascotting and exploitation of these athletes contributes to the reproduction of whiteness as dominant, respectable, and cultured, and the treatment of women, particularly black women, as objects of sexual exchange.

In chapter 6, I examine fan rejection of previously mascotted players and argue that fan antipathy for star players often results when players refuse the mascotting relation or act in ways that prevent them from being instrumentalized as mascots. Looking at the cases of LeBron James, Richard Sherman, and Michael Vick, I argue that black men who do not conform to fan expectations of mascots are treated as dangerous, either as criminal threats to the community ("thugs") or as a contagion that threatens to consume the healthy body of good (white) society. The ease with which players move from mascot to danger in the eyes of fans illustrates just how tenuous the relationship between white fans and black male athletes is.

In chapter 7, I turn to sports fan practices that decenter masculinity in order to argue that sports fandom need not always reinforce existing social hierarchies. I am particularly interested here in women's fan practices—both as fans of mainstream men's sports and as fans of women's sports. Recognizing that sports culture is not exclusively the domain of men will nuance and complicate our understanding of the gendering—and, as it turns out, racializing—effects of sports fandom in the contemporary United States. I argue that before we dismiss sports fandom as irrevocably hierarchizing, we should investigate forms of sports fandom that might work to destabilize rigid gender, racial, and sexual norms. Some forms of women's sports fandom succeed in deploying fandom to valorize the very forms of subjectivity that are typically excluded from or denigrated by mainstream sports culture. Women's sports fandom may not be "typical," but this is precisely the point.

Women fans and fans of women's sports *do* fandom in ways that give us reason to hope that for sports fans, all may not yet be lost.

✶

Reflecting on the role of sports fandom in my life, I am haunted by a recurrent memory of one night in LSU's Tiger Stadium in the early 1990s. The air is thick with humidity, and I am squealing with laughter as my friend—another preteen white girl—and I scream a chant that we recently learned. The chant is funny because it is transgressive. It is funny and daring because we are girls who are frustrated with being excluded from the boys' events at Sunday school, which are all adventure and competition, and angry about being expected to be nice, sweet, and content with sleepovers. The chant is funny and daring and empowering because its words—*Kill! Kill! Blood makes the grass grow!*—position us as privileged subjects whose amusement is built upon the explicit denigration and instrumentalization of others, whose prone bodies on the field remind us not of the frailty of human life but of the ease with which we could make ourselves significant, if only we managed to respond to violence, to masculinity, and to the ordinary expectations of others in the "right" ways.

I don't remember where we learned the chant, but I know that we were eventually reprimanded for using it. We had not performed our fandom appropriately. I cannot shake the feeling, however, that what was inappropriate in our chant was not the expression of pleasure at the misfortunes of our rivals or even the sense that the bodies of these men were disposable and existed for our satisfaction. Such sentiments are expressed each day by sports fans across the country. But we had made the implicit explicit, an explicitness made all the more striking and disturbing by our youth and white femininity.

I see myself in that stadium, asserting my individuality by refusing to be a lady, and cultivating my sense of belonging in the culture and traditions of south Louisiana—by calling for the blood sacrifice of young black men, their bodies broken for the glory of my home. I see myself there, and I shudder at how very entangled my subjectivity is with such horrors. I hope it is possible to do fandom differently. But we will not find out without first exposing its evils, just below the surface.

1

Who Is a Fan?

The term "fan" is shot through with values. Although this might come as a
surprise to people who are not particularly interested in sports, or to sports
fans who have not spent much time reflecting philosophically on their fandom, the concept's value-laden nature is apparent as soon as we attempt to
answer this chapter's question, "Who is a fan?" The mere act of defining our
terms, crucial in any philosophical analysis, quickly requires us to stake out
the limits of fandom—to make calls on who is in and who is outside of the
"fan" community—which, as most sports fans will tell you, is a necessarily
controversial bit of business. Proving that someone is or is not a fan often
involves parsing the smallest details of a spectator's knowledge, behavior, or
feeling, analyzing their claim to fandom with the rigor of a tax attorney investigating whether a particular lunch truly satisfies the criteria for a business-
expense deduction. Making matters more complicated is the fact that standards for the application of the term "fan" are as unclear as they are frequently
invoked. Claims about who counts as a "real fan" are common among fan
groups, but those claims are far from univocal in their content. Fans tend
to be particularly interested in, as reception theorist Daniel Cavicchi puts
it, "distinguish[ing] themselves from 'nonfan' audience members" (2014, 56),
an end that is accomplished through a wide variety of practices—including
speech, dress, collections, and travel, just to name a few. In its most exacting
forms, fandom prescribes a thickly normative testing regimen: repeated demands by one's peers for proof that one is a "real fan," distinct from a poseur,

or worse, a mere rider on the "bandwagon." Implicit in the "fan" concept, then, is a set of expectations about how one *ought* to behave as a sporting enthusiast.

The normative quality of the "fan" concept thus goes beyond the sort of normativity that is implicit in any philosophical definition. It is undoubtedly true that, as poststructuralist thinkers such as Judith Butler (1990) have pointed out, conceptual clarification always requires the assertion of some norm—as soon as I specify the referent of the term "woman," for example, I involve myself in claims about what one "must" be in order to count as a woman and the exclusion of some persons from that category. Likewise, defining even less contested terms always requires some degree of world-chopping: to define a circle is to specify the ideal type of that shape and simultaneously to say that it is *not* a square, triangle, etc. But "fan" is normatively loaded not only by virtue of the nature of linguistic distinctions or the inherently limiting character of definitions; *its specific content is normative.* "Fan" denotes a kind of spectator who is marked out from others—whose status *exceeds*, somehow, that of a mere audience member, whether for good or ill. It is a concept with a history, an "extraordinary form of audiencing" (Cavicchi 2014, 52) whose very name makes explicit its excesses; the term itself exists to mark the advent of a new—and, at least at its inception, aberrant—form of interaction with sport. As we will see, though, the implicit normative claim involved in calling someone a "fan" shifts over time, evolving from derision to legitimation; the application of the term almost always relies on a set of assumptions about respectable spectator engagement.

"Fan" is, in other words, a concept that is not value-neutral. Whereas "circle" carries norms for its application that make no prescriptions beyond how the word should be used, "fan" not only carries norms for its application but also makes implicit claims about standards of behavior. Those claims can be more or less prescriptive, depending on the extent to which one understands "norm" to indicate, on the one hand, "that which is typical" or, on the other, "that to which one ought to conform." As feminists have pointed out, however, the lines between the two senses of the word "norm" tend to be blurred in the case of human behavior, as "the typical" frequently becomes imbued with prescriptive force. For evidence of this claim, we need only reflect on the previously widespread practice of forcing all children to be right-handed because most are, the enforcement of heterosexuality on the grounds that it is "natural," or the subjection of perfectly healthy intersex children to genital surgeries simply because their genitals do not resemble those of "typical" boys or girls. Because the suspicion of abnormality is such a powerful tool of socialization, one might have expected that sports fandom would remain the

domain of social outcasts and the generally weird, given its initial association with abnormally obsessed baseball enthusiasts. Yet as "fans" grow their
numbers and sports fandom becomes more widespread, the term gains its
own prescriptive force, whose implicit claims about how sporting enthusiasts
ought to behave are evident in the epigraphs to this chapter.

With such normativity built into the concept, it is perhaps unsurprising
that virtually all of the literature in the philosophy of sport dealing explicitly
with fans is concerned with fan ethics—with what makes one a good fan,
whether it is ethical to support one team over another, and so on. The latter
question—whether it is more virtuous to be a "partisan" fan or, on the other
hand, a "purist" who values athletic excellence over arbitrary team loyalty—
has, in fact, consumed most of the existing philosophical discussion of sports
fans. While the interest in the ethics of fan loyalty is a reasonable one, it is
curious that philosophers have for the most part undertaken answers to this
question without devoting much attention to the notion of fandom as such—
without, that is, understanding what makes fans *fans*, what they do, and why
they do it. My interest here is in investigating these questions by philosophically analyzing the meaning of sports fandom, both for the sake of philosophical clarity and for the sake of showing the gravity of the ethical questions
that sports fandom ought to raise. Indeed, my view is that when we attend
to the details, meanings, and effects of sports fandom in the contemporary
United States, we will find that its normative effects—that is, the myriad ways
in which sports fandom reinforces particular judgments of value, standards
of behavior, and so on—far exceed worries about whether fans should be
partisans or purists. As I will argue in later chapters, these normative effects
move well beyond the world of sports.

For now, though, I am concerned with defining my terms, and with clari-
fying the object (and limitations) of my investigation. Contrary to a particularly popular social scientific taxonomy of sports fans (Giulianotti 2002), I
will not claim that fans' practices or emotional lives must occur along specific lines or according to particular patterns; neither will I take a stand on
whether fans must be partisans or purists. Sports fandom is discernible in a
wide range of persons, activities, and practices and can be characterized by
affective states ranging from religious devotion to jingoistic pride or a simple
desire for positive feelings. My argument will proceed in two parts: historical and contemporary. First, I will offer an analysis of the history of the term
"fan," tracing its emergence and development in relation to sport in the late
nineteenth-century United States. Second, I will, through consideration of
the contemporary theoretical discussion of sports fans and partisanship, argue for a two-pronged, broad definition of "sports fan," which is characterized

by a combination of *care* (that is, emotional investment) and *practice* (that is, some form of active engagement with the sport one watches). In my definition of "fans," not even "purist" fans are emotionally unattached, for we can see the same patterns of affective investment and semiritualized practice even in cases of fans who lack team loyalties. So, although philosophers might generally be inclined to favor "purist" sports fandom on the grounds that it is less irrational, we should note that no form of sports fandom escapes passionate involvement. Moreover, all forms of sports fandom involve some degree of repetitive practice that is worth further examination; these practices will be addressed more thoroughly later in the book. Although sports fandom is a normatively loaded concept, then, I argue in what follows for an understanding of the term that is *not* thickly normative or overly restrictive in its application. I employ a broader meaning of the term in order to carefully observe both its evolution and its wide-ranging contemporary social effects.

From Fanatics to Fans

"Fan" is so common in contemporary life—both as a term and a cultural phenomenon—that it is easy to forget that it has comparatively recent origins. Although it is difficult to mark the precise moment in which sporting enthusiasts became sports "fans," scholars generally agree that the term came into popular usage in the late nineteenth century, specifically with reference to baseball fans. The *Oxford English Dictionary* (*OED*), along with a few other dictionaries of etymology (Barnhart 2002; Hendrickson 1987), cites an 1889 issue of the *Kansas City Times and Star* as the first print usage of the word when used to refer to "a keen and regular spectator of a (professional) sport," noting that it is an abbreviation of the word "fanatic" (*OED* Online 2015a). The 1889 article cited by the *OED*, chronicling the reaction to the ouster of Kansas City Cowboys manager Dave Rowe reads as follows: "Kansas City base ball fans are glad they're through with Dave Rowe as a ball club manager." Rowe had not lasted long in Kansas City, completing only two seasons at the helm, winning only 30 percent of his games in each.[1] The "fan" reaction described in the *Times and Star* article is a familiar one: relief that team change is coming and hope for the future.

Yet the claim that this is the first recorded usage of "fans" to refer to sports enthusiasts rings false. The "fans" referenced here are devotees of the Cowboys, but they hardly seem "fanatical." Given the vociferousness with which baseball enthusiasts supported their teams in years prior to this reference—spectators at an 1883 game in Cincinnati, for example, became so furious with an umpire that the game was stopped and police called in to curtail the "rowdies [who did] not agree with all of the umpire's decisions" (*Cincinnati Commercial Gazette* 1883)—it is surprising that the paper would refer to the comparatively tame reaction of relief at the departure of a losing manager as an expression of fanaticism. Moreover, it is worth considering the quickness of the sentence above: the word "fans" does not appear in quotation marks, nor does the article offer any explanation of what it means by the supposedly novel term. It appears, in other words, that the author of the 1889 article expects his audience to know the term already and does not take himself to be abbreviating "fanatics." It appears, instead, that the author is using a term already in circulation to refer to the followers of a particular sports team.

In fact, the *OED* misses several earlier usages of "fan" in American newspapers and periodicals. At least twice in 1887, articles appear in sporting publications that demonstrate the beginnings of a move to use "fans" to describe baseball enthusiasts—as opposed to "cranks," the term that had previously been most popular. In their *Comments on Etymology* article, Popik and Cohen note that in June of 1887, the following lines appeared in an article in *The Sporting News*: "What a pleasure Billy must derive when talking to those cranks and fans who continually harped upon his managerial qualities" (1996, 3). Similarly, David Shulman cites a more thoroughly explained usage in the November 1887 issue of *Sporting Life*, which offers an account of the origins of the term:

> "It was Ted who gave the nick-name of 'fans' to baseball cranks. You never hear a man called a 'fiend' out in the Western League cities. 'Fan' is the word that is invariably used. It is a quick way of saying 'fanatic,'" explained Tom Sullivan. ("Memories of Ted Sullivan," *Sporting Life*, November 23, 1887, quoted in Shulman 1996, 328)

It is unclear, however, that "fan" was widely in usage beyond the Midwest. As Shulman notes, the 1888 book on baseball terminology, *The Krank, His Language and What It Means*, "did not include *fan*," (329) and all of the 1888 newspaper usages of "fan" appear to be confined to Kansas City, St. Louis, and Cincinnati.

This geographical confinement is consistent with the myth of the origin of "fan," circulated in various forms by former manager of the St. Louis Browns Ted Sullivan. In three different versions of the same story (told in 1896, 1898, and 1903) Sullivan claimed to have coined the term "fan" in 1883 to refer to those "cranks" who had the particularly annoying habit of behaving as though they knew more than he did and offering unsolicited advice on the management of the team (Popik and Cohen 1996, 5–6; Shulman 1996, 330). Sullivan's 1898 telling of the origin myth is particularly striking:

The word or term "fan" has passed into baseball literature and is as current in baseball phraseology as the purest word within the pages of Webster or Johnston. The technical definition of the word fan is "a person that is heavily burdened with baseball knowledge, or *so permeated is he with it that it oozes out of the crevices of his anatomy as does steam out of the pipes of a boiler.*" That is one definition, and that definition was prompted by and applied to the person that was responsible for the origin of the term.

. . . A man came into my place one day and in the presence of three or four of the Browns commenced to ply me with questions about baseball in general. He knew every player in the country with a record of 90 in the shade to 100 in the sun. He gave his opinion on all matters pertaining to ball. . . . He kept up this onslaught on me until someone came to my assistance and called him outside.

I turned to some of my players and said: "What name could you apply to such a fiend as that?"

Charley Comiskey replied: "He is a fanatic." I responded: "I will abbreviate that word and call him a 'fan.'" So when he was ever seen around headquarters, the boys would say, "the fan" was around again. (quoted in Popik and Cohen 1996, 6; emphasis mine)

By 1898, Sullivan's description of the fan is extraordinarily vivid and literary; the image he draws is one of a man possessed of encyclopedic knowledge, who is obsessive and uncontrollable. The enthusiasm of the fan is palpable and perhaps a bit dangerous, like steam from the leaky pipes of a boiler, portending explosion. Notably, Sullivan's 1896 telling of the origin myth is rather different, not only in terms of the personages involved—his interlocutor this time is Browns owner Chris Von der Ahe, not Charlie Comiskey—but also in terms of his description of the "fan" behavior: "Chris had a board of directors made up of cranks who had baseball on the brain, and they were always interfering with me and telling Chris how the team ought to be run. I told Chris that I didn't propose to be advised by a lot of fanatics . . . fans for short" (5–6). In this telling of the story, fans still exhibit a propensity for know-it-all-ness, but they are less unpredictable—meddling board members, rather than feverishly obsessive "fiends." In each case, however, what is striking is that "fan" is used at least somewhat derisively, the shortened form of the word lending an air of lighthearted joking to the underlying claim of disturbingly excessive involvement.

The ambivalence here expressed—anxious amusement at fans' investment in a game—was articulated even before the advent of the word "fan." The 1876 song "The Base Ball Fever" makes use of similarly lighthearted lyrics that describe baseball enthusiasts' love of the game as a form of contagious disease.

The song's lyrics prefigure Sullivan's image of the obsessive "fan": a person of near-frenzied enthusiasm for the game, whose inability to contain their irrational need to see matches interferes with everyday life. The irrationality of crazed fans reaches its climax in the final lines of the song, in which the narrator offers to "bet [his] Beaver" that his skills are as great as any of the ballplayers he watches on the field, his judgment having presumably been clouded by "the fever" (Angelo 1876). The puns, rhyme scheme, and piano melody lighten the mood, but the coupling of these comedic elements with a vaguely disturbing image of its narrator as feverishly delusional suggests a decided ambivalence toward this new class of sports enthusiasts, who are, for better or worse, outside the norm of previously acceptable spectatorship.

By 1888, the concern about this form of spectatorship begins to die down slightly, at least as regards typical "fans." There are still reports of fans behaving irrationally, but the indications of uncontrollable passion are somewhat less prevalent. Several innocuous uses of "fans" appeared that year: "Some Boston base ball fans gave Kelly a banquet the other night at Clark's hotel" (*Kansas City Star* 1888a); and "[The Athletics] play the neatest game in the association, and many 'fans' name them as sure pennant winners" (*Kansas City Star* 1888b). Yet, usage of "fan" is not consistent in this period. The *Sporting News* still used "fan" derisively as late as 1889, and the *San Francisco Evening Bulletin* that year observed that fans "abuse the umpire even when he is in the right" (Dickson 2011, 304). Obnoxious and even threatening behavior toward umpires was well documented as a problem during the 1880s, which was eventually remedied through the institutionalization of police presence during games. Whether "fan" was truly an abbreviation for "fanatic"—or, alternatively, a colorful way of suggesting that a particular spectator is a "windbag" (Morris 2003)—the term itself, at least in the early years of its usage, suggested an abnormal, deviant (or worse) mode of sporting engagement.

Yet by the late 1890s, we find Ted Sullivan eager to publicly claim credit for coining the term in publications read by fans, and by the early twentieth century, its meaning is broad enough that it is sometimes used as a form of self-identification. By the twenty-first century, of course, the term is extremely widely used as a self-identifier, with fully 57 percent of adult Americans claiming to be football fans (Quinn 2009, 5). The transition in the usage of "fan" from the late nineteenth century to the early twentieth is important—not because learning what "fan" originally meant will clarify the question of who "real fans" are today, but because attention to the implicit normative claims about audience behavior through the history of spectator sport highlights the extent to which the norms of sports fandom are contingent and changeable. More importantly, it also illustrates a significant shift in individuals' relations to spectator sport: fanatical concern with the outcome of games played by others comes to be associated not with mental illness or deviant behavior but with typical sporting enthusiasts. Who are we, such that we could become, or desire identification as, "fans"?

Fandom, Care, and Action

Contemporary theoretical literature on fandom is almost always concerned with fans of *teams*, rather than with individuals players on a team or with loyalty to individual athletes competing in solo sports like tennis or ice skating. This focus on teams is not altogether surprising (teams persist though the careers of individual athletes are more transient)—but this is not to say that followers of solo sports or followers of, say, LeBron James are not "fans." There are, as I will argue, a wide variety of practices and interests that make up contemporary sports fandom in the United States, and—notwithstanding sports fandom's normative character—it is not particularly useful to discredit some forms of it as illegitimate if our goal is to understand what sports fans are up to and why the normative force of sports fandom looms so large in the first place. That said, in what follows, my focus will be almost entirely on the phenomenon of *team* loyalty—in order both to situate my inquiry in relation to the contemporary philosophy of sport discussion of sports fans and to offer a particularly salient example of the topic of my investigation. Although most contemporary theorists of sport have not been primarily concerned with defining sports fans as such, analysis of what they *do* say in their ethical and analytical discussions of fan practice is useful for this purpose. I turn now to examination of four such discussions of fandom, not to accept any one of these accounts—none is, I believe, satisfactory—but in order to observe a consistent assumption about sports fandom underlying each, despite the differences in their details.

Sociologist Richard Giulianotti offers the most detailed attempt at a theoretical account of sports fandom in his "taxonomy of spectator identities in football."[2] Giulianotti defines "fan" quite narrowly, describing it as but one of the four "ideal-type spectator identities" (2015, 249). Those ideal types are "supporters, followers, fans, and *flâneurs*." Giulianotti's taxonomy of these types depends, first, on the degree of loyalty persons feel for a team, which ranges from "hot" to "cool," and secondly, on the degree to which spectators' relations to their teams are mediated by consumer practices, which range from "traditional" to "consumer" models. "Supporters" are the most "hot," and most "traditional." Supporters' allegiance to their teams is unwavering; they are "culturally contracted to their clubs" (253) such that changes to allegiance are felt to be impossible. Those relations are maintained through direct, bodily disciplines: knowing and participating in team chants at the game venue, wearing team colors, and tattooing themselves with team emblems. "Followers" differ from supporters primarily in the intensity of their felt solidarity with a particular team. Followers may have "a range of favored clubs and football people" (255), which interest them for a variety of reasons. The "fan," in contrast, has a very strong sense of loyalty but "experiences the club, its traditions, its star players, and fellow supporters through a market-centered set of relations" (256). Giulianotti distinguishes fans and supporters by suggesting that fans have a "non-reciprocal" relation of intimacy with the club and its players, by which he seems to mean that fans feel themselves attached to an entity that bears no direct relation to them because they do not attend games or participate in the "subculture" of supporters—often because they do not live near the team. Consequently, fans' abilities to buy pay-per-view access to games and to demonstrate loyalty through consumption are important for maintaining their sense of relation to the team. Finally, *flâneurs* have the "coolest" sense of allegiance to their teams, favoring one team over another on aesthetic grounds, or because it is fashionable. Affiliation, for these spectators, is again mediated primarily through consumption— and the less effort involved, the better. Giulianotti suggests that contemporary televised sporting broadcasts are "tailored toward a flâneur-type experience," since they "[distill] entire matches or tournaments into 100-second transmissions of blinding, aestheticized action" (258). The motivations of each type of spectator are different, Giulianotti suggests, ranging from a sense of obligation to the club (supporter) to the desire for sensation and excitement (flâneur).

There are, I think, at least two problems with adopting this taxonomy when discussing sports fans. The first is that as "ideal-types," these divisions do not exist in any pure form in the real world; it would be difficult indeed to find any significant number of sports spectators whose engagement with their team falls exclusively within one of these categories. For example, it is easy to imagine that a "supporter" who wears team colors, gets team tattoos, and goes to all of her team's games when she is in town would be fairly dependent upon consumption for her relation to the team (where will she get the team paraphernalia that she wears?) and might likewise be forced to simply watch recaps on television, if (for example) she falls ill or encounters other barriers to in-person participation. These behaviors involve quite a bit of consumption, despite the fact that, in Giulianotti's taxonomy, "traditional" modes of relation are described as diametrically opposed to consumption. In reality, fan experiences and practices vary with changes in individuals' lives, including the financial, community, and geographic resources available to them. For this reason, the taxonomy does not seem particularly useful for explaining the lived experiences or social effects of actually existing fans.

The second problem is that this taxonomy tacitly valorizes certain forms of spectator engagement over others without argument. Though Giulianotti does not directly suggest that one form of spectatorship is better than another, the language he chooses makes it difficult not to infer as much. Consider his description of "fans":

> Fans refer to stars by first name, discuss their private lives and traits, collect biographical snippets, surround the family home or workplace with their images, and perhaps even fantasize about a loving, sexual relationship with their objects of affection. Star footballers, like other celebrities, are rarely in a position to reciprocate. . . . Consequently . . . for such public relations, football players and club officials are trained to draw upon an ever-expanding reservoir of clichés and dead metaphors to confirm typified public constructions of their personality. (2015, 256–257)

Leaving aside the fact that not even "supporters" have truly reciprocal relationships with the athletes for whom they cheer—making it unclear why "fans" are singled out in this regard—Giulianotti's description of these fans is almost openly disparaging. Fans are described not only as delusional, starry-eyed women (the gendering of the description is unmistakable); they are also responsible for the increasingly vacuous quality of sporting broadcasts, since players and club officials must appeal to their desire for personality over the hard facts of sport. Likewise, Giulianotti's depiction of flâneurs is clearly unflattering; in his conclusion, he writes, "I shall avoid treating the reader as a flâneur and providing a highlighted recapitulation of arguments" (259). Flâneurs are shallow, lacking the ability to genuinely engage. Followers at least appreciate the sport, it seems, but are not loyal in the way that genuine supporters are. Despite Giulianotti's apparent valorization of some "types" of spectatorship and disparagement of others, it is by no means obvious that one of these forms of engagement is more "authentic" than another or that they even constitute genuinely different forms of engagement with teams in practice, given the resources available to different individuals. The tacit hierarchy of spectatorship activities Giulianotti assumes exacerbates the problem of type idealization. In the end, we are left with caricatures of spectator types that represent few if any actual spectators—and which are thus not particularly useful for understanding what sports fans are up to in their practices of fandom.

Although Giulianotti's taxonomy of spectator identities is not particularly illuminating as a taxonomy, it is useful in giving an idea of the range of activities that constitute fan practice and in displaying the centrality of loyalty or attachment for such practices. The centrality of this affect in sports fandom is also evident in the debate over partisanship in the philosophy of sport. Many years prior to Nicholas Dixon's influential article "The Ethics of Supporting Sports Teams" (2001), R. K. Elliott argued that "ordinary" fans' mode of watching sport—that is, watching sport with a specific "rooting" interest, rather than from the detached perspective of a neutral, aesthetic observer— added a depth and beauty to the experience that would be missed by those with no loyalty to either team (1974, 110). Elliott's claim is significant not only because it reinforces the notion that typical sports fandom is characterized by team loyalty but also because it suggests that such fandom has implications for the creation and perception of meaning and value.

Contemporary opinion on this loyalty is divided. Nicholas Dixon famously argues in favor of a position he calls "moderate partisanship," in which a fan is loyal to a particular team but moderates her loyalty to the extent that she will withdraw her support for cheating or other ethical violations (2001, 149). Despite the objections of some of his interlocutors, Dixon argues that loyalty to a team is not only permissible but positively virtuous—just as is loyalty to a family member. In contrast, he considers the attitude of a fan who has no such loyalty but is a "purist," that is, one who "supports the team that . . . exemplifies the highest virtues of the game." Although some suggest that the purist's position is more ethically defensible by virtue of being grounded in true sporting value, Dixon argues that the purist's changeable team affiliation is suspicious and that "he barely qualifies as a fan at all" (153). Stephen Mumford strenuously disagrees, claiming that purism is more defensible than partisanship. According to Mumford, the purist's loyalty does not shift with the excellence of play; rather, the purist has no preference for the winner of a given contest at all. True purists, according to Mumford, appreciate the game itself and have no vested interest in its outcome. This outlook is the "better" one, insofar as partisans' experience of the game is substantially colored by their desire for one team to win—so much so that partisans can be said not to "see" the same game, as they tend to miss significant features of it, especially the failures or missteps of their own teams (2012, 13). Other philosophers of sport agree with Mumford, at least in part. Randolph Feezell and J. S. Russell argue that Dixon's argument against purism is unconvincing. Although Feezell argues for a position he calls "moderate purism"—an appreciation of the game at times expressed in the desire for some particular team to win, moderated by the knowledge that it is unhealthy to be invested in something so trivial (2013, 88–89)—and Russell (2012) suggests that there is no ideal fan position at all, the two agree that partisan loyalty is neither intrinsic to being a fan nor a particularly desirable feature of it. Both, rather, argue that we should strive to be good fans by reflecting on the values that we endorse through our fan practices and allegiances.

When attempting to answer the question of what a fan *is*, it is useful to consider the various descriptions of sports fandom we have encountered thus far. Each one, from the 1880s "crank" to the eighth-grader's idealized Mets fan in the epigraph to this chapter, Dixon's moderate partisan, and Mumford's purist, shares two common characteristics: *caring* about a sport that they observe—that is, having some degree of affective investment in it—and engaging in some kind of *activity* through which that care is expressed, cultivated, or enhanced. Although the objects of that affective investment and the types of activity used to express or cultivate it may take a variety of forms, in each case, we have both a *feeling* component and a *practice* component. Normative claims about what makes a "good" fan turn on specific beliefs about the proper content or expression of these components. For the eighth-grade Alex, fans are characterized not only by team allegiance but by a practice of knowledge acquisition. In this view, the feeling might be important, but it must be verified through practice to count as legitimate. Fans demonstrate their loyalty to the team, and perhaps also to the game, by knowing as much as possible about it.[3] For Giulianotti, affective loyalty to the team is cashed out in specific actions: it is demonstrated and reinforced through participation in chants, the wearing of certain clothing, and sometimes, the tattooing of one's body. For Mumford, the affective component is not loyalty to a team but love of the sport as such, which can be demonstrated in interest even in those games in which one has no personal stake. Though the specific content of "fan" changes, what remains constant in the normativity of its application is the requirement that fans both feel a connection to their team or sport and put this felt connection into practice. The combination of these two dimensions distinguishes fans from persons who merely attend or happen to watch sporting events.

Team loyalty offers an especially obvious example of this combination of care and action. If I am loyal to you, I feel some combination of connection and obligation to you, and this feeling must be accompanied by some practice (I keep my vows, I come to your aid, etc.) in order to be deserving of the term. Fans who are loyal to a specific team feel connection and obligation to it—they often feel themselves to be part of it, as indicated by the ubiquity of "we" discourse, and do not change their affiliation in the face of losing games or seasons. Loyal fans likewise engage in some form of practice or other: they cheer for their teams or wear team colors or perform any of the range of activities already mentioned. Yet loyal fans are not the only ones engaged in the combination of care and practice. A purist who spends hours following basketball, who knows the history of the game, who welcomes every opportunity to watch, surely exhibits a caring devotion to the game, even if she or he has no chosen team. The purist's *practice* may take different forms than that of the partisan—they probably do more knowledge acquisition and less face painting—but this element will still be present. Likewise, the purist's affective attachment is particularly striking when we consider that the object of his or her practical devotion is "just a game," which has ostensibly no meaning outside of the game itself.

That these two components jointly characterize sports fans is perhaps most evident when contrasted with the characteristics of nonfans. Anyone who has watched sporting events with an audience of mixed levels of sporting enthusiasm will likely have observed a difference between the general comportment of fans and nonfans toward the games in question. I experienced a particularly striking example of this when taking two different groups of students to see Atlanta Braves games in the 2014 and 2015 baseball seasons. The first was a group of international students who had never seen a baseball game; the second was a group from my Philosophy of Sport course, almost all of whom had attended a baseball game previously. Some of the latter group identified as baseball fans and some did not, but all identified as fans of some sport. Both groups of students were jovial and enthusiastic about the experience of being at the ballpark. They took photos and participated in "the wave." But whereas the latter group of students were clearly invested in the game—demonstrated in various ways, as they brought baseball gloves, cheered for well-executed plays, groaned at bad swings, and resisted the idea of leaving early despite bad weather and a looming deadline to get back to campus—the former were not. Although this nonfan group participated in some practice components of fandom (participating in the "wave," clapping for the home team, attending the game itself), they did so, unsurprisingly, without any accompanying emotional investment. Though they generously listened to my explanations of the game, they were much more interested in watching the constantly changing big screen for new images of people dancing in the stands or embracing for the "kiss cam" and in cheering for the "Home Depot Tool Race," a sort of sideshow act that occurs between innings featuring runners dressed in oversized tool costumes.[4] While it is undeniable that the Tool Race and the stadium's big screen are entertaining, they are not part of the game as such. Moreover, while fans may, like mere spectators, enjoy entertaining distractions, these spectacular features are not central to fans' enjoyment of the game itself. Fans are distinct from nonfans in *caring* about what happens in the game and engaging with it actively.

Of course, among fans, there is significant disagreement about how much care is required and how it ought to be demonstrated, and individual sports fans tend to have strong opinions about whether other fans of their acquaintance perform their fandom in acceptable ways. This fact is, I have suggested, an unsurprising feature of a category that is fundamentally normative in nature. To be a "fan" is to be a special type of spectator. Given the shift in the connotations of the term from negative to positive, there are bound to be disagreements about the standards one must embody in order to merit the term. Though I will not take a particular normative stand on the specifics of fan behavior, it is crucial to note that fans are distinguishable from mere spectators. I have argued that this distinction hinges on fans' combination of *care about* and *practice in relation to* a sport or team.

Narrow versus Broad Definitions and the Normativity of "Fan"

This book is primarily about partisan fans, specifically those fans who are loyal to a particular team. It is concerned with fans whose fandom is displayed not only through knowledge but through the participation in rituals like tailgating, face painting, cheering, posting on fan message boards, jeering rivals, wearing team colors, reading columns, decorating one's house or work space with team paraphernalia, and developing social bonds with other fans. It includes fans whose affective relation to their teams ranges from love to filial loyalty, anger, a nebulous desire for domination, and demoralized embarrassment. I am, then, using a broad definition of "fan," in an effort to include as many different modes of invested sports spectatorship as possible. I do not restrict fandom to those persons who feel or perform their fandom in specific ways—and in particular, I do not restrict it to those who possess some indefinable quantum of sports knowledge—since, as Paul Snowdon points out, "one's level of competence and understanding do not . . . determine the importance in one's life of things," including, perhaps most especially, sport (2013, 79). As it is precisely the importance of sports fandom in the lives of contemporary American sports fans that I aim to explain, it would be particularly unproductive to limit my inquiry only to a specific subset of those fans.

The reason that I will be principally interested in fans who are loyal to a specific team is that this form of fandom—besides being nearly ubiquitous in the United States today—offers perhaps the most salient example of the combination of emotional investment and practice that characterizes sports fandom. Although it is certainly true that purist sports fans do engage in both (and I will discuss some examples of this type of engagement in chapter 2), partisan fans' practices tend to be more organized and ritualized and, concomitantly, their affective relations to the sport or team heightened. It may be, as well, that the regularity with which partisan fans follow one specific team enhances their experience of fandom and deepens its significance. In his sociological study of sports fans, Kevin Quinn compares this phenomenon to the experience of religious participants: "Going to church becomes more meaningful as church attendance becomes more frequent. Similarly, the time that a fan spends following the local team today results in greater enjoyment when following the team tomorrow" (2009, 105). In both cases, the significance of one's devoted practice is dependent not only on familiarity or repetition of engagement but a continuous object of devotion; just as religious devotees who typically attend a Baptist church will not find a Mosque or Unitarian church an adequate substitute, sports fans' experiences of fandom are typically enhanced by continued exposure to and engagement with a single team (106). Examination of those experiences, how they become significant, and how they affect both fans and nonfans will be my concern in the next six chapters.

Despite my primarily being concerned with partisan fans, the comparatively broad understanding of sports fandom in what follows is particularly important because of the normative character of the "fan" concept. Ironically, the ethical questions that sports fandom raises (or should raise) and sports fandom's normative effects as a cultural practice tend to be obscured when more narrowly normative theoretical definitions of "fan" are assumed: if we restrict fandom to those persons who attend games and paint their faces, or who know the names of a particular number of players on a team, or who feel a particular way toward umpires who make calls that are unfavorable to "their" teams, we may miss, just for example, the practices of many women fans of the University of Mississippi, whose game-day rituals include proper dress and food preparation, the standard fan greeting of "Hotty Toddy!" and the strategic placement of Confederate-inspired décor, including the Confederate battle flag and images of the former mascot, the genteel plantation owner "Colonel Reb." Sports fandom in the contemporary United States—particularly in the South—is such a deeply engrained cultural practice that its manifestations often extend beyond narrowly defined conceptualizations of fandom. Noticing such practices as these is crucial for recognizing the variously normative effects of sports fandom that exceed the sporting context—including, as I will show in subsequent chapters, the racial and gender values fandom is used to reinforce, the behaviors and practices it prescribes, and the sense of identity it helps to build. It will, accordingly, be crucial to take seriously the extent to which sports fandom and its effects extend well beyond the field or arena.

Beyond the range of practices in contemporary sports fandom, there is another reason to take a broad view of what fandom means: to put it simply, the typically narrow outlook of those defining "real fans" takes too much for granted. Attention in this chapter to the historical development of the concept of fans makes this taking-for-granted particularly salient. Not only is it the case that contemporary fan debates about who "counts" as a real fan often make use of arbitrary distinctions (why, we might ask Alex the Mets fan, should we require that fans name four members of a team, not three or eight?); these contemporary debates presume fandom as a normative ideal, rather than as an aberrant—and potentially disturbing—mode of spectator relations. That it was not always so, that "fan" has shifted so much in connotation in the last century and a half, is obscured in typical engagements with the normative character of "fan" as a term. The shifting status of "fans" and fan behavior is crucial information with which to engage if we are to understand both the force of sports fandom in contemporary life and how and why sports fandom comes to be so important for both individual and community identity.

Sports fans have existed since the late nineteenth century, but neither their habits nor their emotions nor their cultural positions have remained constant. Contemporary sports fans, likewise, make up a motley crew of partisans, purists, trivia mavens, strategists, and simple flag wavers. If anything can be said to unite this group, it is that their fandom involves both *care* and *practice*. As further investigation of such caring and practice will require attention to their details in concrete social contexts, we now move to examination of the rituals, symbols, and disciplines of sports fans. Along the way, we will find that sports fandom's normative effects are not limited to implicit claims about fan behavior. Rather, sports fandom exerts normative force well beyond the sporting arena. Sports fandom, then, is not only a normative concept; it is, as a practice, a means of creating and reinforcing social norms and values.

Sports Fandom as Practice of Subjectivization

Popular culture is produced by the people out of the products of the cultural indus-
tries: it must be understood, therefore, in terms of productivity, not reception. Fans are
particularly productive.

JOHN FISKE (1992, 37)

We must cease once and for all to describe the effects of power in negative terms: it "excludes," it "represses," it "censors," it "abstracts," it "masks," it "conceals." In fact, power
produces; it produces reality; it produces domains of objects and rituals of truth. The
individual and the knowledge that may be gained of him belong to this production.

MICHEL FOUCAULT (1995, 194)

Though there are many ways to be a sports fan, the practice itself is always, to
some extent, demanding. It requires emotional investment, at times leaving
fans anxious or emotionally drained, and usually requires a sense of solidarity with a group of people with whom fans may have nothing in common.
Fandom also demands continual engagement and sometimes a serious time
commitment to something that looks very much like work. Fans may read
about their teams and sports, memorize statistics, spend money to collect
sporting paraphernalia, travel to see their team or sport, learn and perform
cheers, or endure harsh weather conditions to attend games. Moreover, fans
exert social pressure on one another to perform their fandom in acceptable
ways or to cultivate increasing levels of devotion, ensuring fandom's normative force. It is true, of course, that sports fandom is often accompanied by
inherently pleasurable activities, like drinking alcohol, eating, and socializing, but as leisure activities go, sports fandom itself requires (or minimally,
invites) a striking level of effort.

Why do so many people in the contemporary United States put forth this
effort? Why not, for example, just go straight for the drinking, eating, and
socializing, since these are pleasurable on their own? It is clear that sports
fandom is meaningful to sports fans, that it "gives" them something; without
such a payoff, it would indeed be a curious choice of activity. One can begin
to get a sense of what that payoff might be by perusing images of sports fans
who attend a sporting event at the moment of a team's victory: every face
in an expression of absolute joy. The pleasure of victory is, one might imagine, no small motivation to endure the work of sports fandom. Scholars and

fans alike have described this pleasure as akin to religious ecstasy. In their book *All Things Shining*, Hubert Dreyfus and Sean Dorrance Kelly describe the Dionysian experience of being a fan caught up in the pandemonium of a live sporting event thus: "There is no essential difference, really, in how it feels to rise as one in joy to sing the praises of the Lord, or to rise as one in joy to sing the praises of the Hail Mary pass, the Immaculate Reception, the Angels, the Saints, the Friars, or the Demon Deacons" (2011, 192). The comparison to religious experience is, of course, no accident. Like devoted communicants, Dreyfus and Kelly suggest, fans in the throes of sporting passion are possessed as if by something outside of themselves. Although it is quite difficult to point to the cause of this possession, "something overwhelming occurs. It wells up and carries you along as on a powerful wave" (199). Dreyfus and Kelly argue that sport is appealing to fans because it offers such feelings to an increasingly secularized population.

This feeling of possession, or of intense, frenzied pleasure, is one that is no doubt familiar to many devoted sports fans who have had the experience of being present at the sacred space of the home field or court. For those who are not familiar with this experience, it must suffice for the moment to offer a few observations. First, as previously noted, fans at a sporting event (and even those watching at home) do not, on the whole, watch as mere observers or spectators. Although contemporary sporting events do themselves occur in the midst of spectacle, and often "license passive watching" (Izod 1996, 184), committed fandom is characterized by care about, and active engagement with, the game itself and the rituals and practices that accompany it. This engagement is the result of deeply felt allegiance to a team, which is, as Stephen Mumford (2004) puts it, in significant respects analogous to those allegiances one might feel to one's spouse or family. When this form of investment is multiplied in a group—as it is in any collective experience of sports fandom, but particularly in the context of a live sporting event—the effect is an emotional scene that has virtually no equal in contemporary life. Fans shout, wail, leap from their seats, cover their faces in horror, hug and kiss strangers in moments of unmitigated joy, crumple in despair, scream loudly and long enough to lose their voices and give themselves headaches, and spread their arms wide while tilting their faces to the heavens. Otherwise rational persons (some of whom are even employed as professional philosophers) find themselves moved to tears and unable to suppress the urge to throw their hands overhead at the sight of a perfectly executed touchdown pass, completed just as time in the game expires.

The fact that nearly every sports fan has had such euphoric experiences at one time or another leads some scholars to suggest that these experiences are, in fact, the sole or primary end of sports fandom. Randall Collins, for example, has argued that the purpose of sports fandom is nothing other than "the experience of the peaks of ritual emotion" (2004, 59). A more popular explanation is that sports fans value not only the collective emotion they feel but, more importantly, the opportunity to feel an enhanced sense of self-worth by identifying with the victory of their teams. This phenomenon is known as "basking in reflected glory," or "BIRGing" for short (Cialdini et al. 1976; Dalakas, Madrigal, and Anderson 2004). When fans identify with a team, the theory of BIRGing suggests, they gain the ability to feel that team's victories as their own and thus to feel personally gratified, euphoric, prideful, and so on, when their team does well. Though the glories and accomplishments are, strictly speaking, not their own, fans are able to feel themselves warmed and aglow by virtue of their emotional association with the team. Like orbiting satellites, fans of successful teams beam with such a vivid sense of self-satisfaction that they appear—at least to themselves—to be one with its source. Their glory, however, is no more their own than is the moon's light.

While it is undeniable that BIRGing offers real incentives to sports fandom, BIRGing, on its own, does not adequately explain why fans do all that they do—nor, for that matter, why anyone would be a fan of a perennially unsuccessful team. Moreover, the idea that sports fandom's principal upside is BIRGing leaves completely unexplained the phenomenon (uncommon though it may be) of purist fans, who dedicate time and effort to following a sport with no glory to be had. If a fan is missing either team loyalty or team success, BIRGing should not be available. Yet a great many fans are followers of notoriously unsuccessful teams (fans of the Chicago Cubs and the New York Jets come to mind), and at least some fans have no affiliation at all. More importantly, though, many of those fans whose teams are successful exhibit a dedication to their teams and practice their fandom to extents and in contexts that are not reducible to simple BIRGing. What are we to make, for example, of a fan's dedication to learning individual pitching statistics in the baseball off-season? How do we explain a fan's stubborn resistance to leaving an outdoor game in subzero temperatures, even when her team is losing? Why would a fan burn the jersey of a player he formerly loved when that player signs a contract with another team? We need an explanation of the practices and disciplines of sports fandom that is capable of explaining why fans would engage in the everyday (noneuphoric) practices of fandom at all.

In this chapter, I argue that the everyday practices of sports fandom constitute a key means of cultivating and reproducing individual and community identities for Americans today. Sports fandom in the contemporary United States involves fan engagement in a variety of practices (some rigidly ritualized, but others more diffuse and variable) that assist its practitioners in constituting a coherent sense of self. Importantly, the self made knowable through these practices of sports fandom is one whose relation to the wider social world—in terms of that self's regional, gender, and racial identity—is clear. In making this argument, I employ a concept articulated by Michel Foucault: subjectivization. Subjectivizing practices are means by which individuals both subordinate themselves to a discipline and, by virtue of it, achieve a sense of their own identities. So, for example, a religious practitioner creates and obtains new forms of self-knowledge by participating in confession, prayer, and the observance of Lent, just as a student creates and obtains new forms of self-knowledge by subjecting herself to the rigors of the comprehensive examination process of her graduate program in philosophy. The individual "receives as his status his own individuality" (Foucault 1995, 192) in and through these disciplines. The disciplines through which individuals gain such self-knowledge call to mind, for Foucault, the dual meaning of the word "subject." One may be "subject" to a law, state, or moral order, in the sense of being governed by or obligated to it. One may also be a "subject" in the philosophical sense of being an "I"—the first-person subject of a life. Foucault argues in *Discipline and Punish* (1995) that one of the distinguishing features of the modern era is the extent to which the latter sense of "subject" is dependent on the former. It is by being subjected to particular rules, disciplines, and power relations that we come to understand ourselves as particular kinds of subjects.

Foucault reserves his analysis for genealogical investigations of particular phenomena, including the organization of prisons and schools. I do not offer a comparable genealogical analysis here, and neither do I represent my claims as thoroughly Foucaultian. However, I adopt from Foucault the concept of subjectivization because it is particularly useful for understanding what sports fans "get" from their fandom. Sports fandom is understandable as a practice of subjectivization, I will argue, because the sports fan comes to understand herself as a particular sort of person by virtue of her participation in these practices, which enable their subjects to imbue their lives and self-concepts with new layers of meaning. Examination of the most typical practices of sports fans, including knowledge acquisition, outward demonstrations or performances of fandom, and participation in fan discourse, shows that these details of everyday fandom are not extraneous additions to fandom but central to its function. Sports fandom matters to fans, then, not merely because the moment of victory is pleasurable. More than this, sports fandom, in its everyday details, is one of the primary ways in which fans tell themselves who they are—and, just as importantly, who they are not.

The Everyday Disciplines of Sports Fandom

When I was a teenager in Baton Rouge, Louisiana, I spent nearly every fall morning before school the same way: reading the sports page of the local paper while eating cereal and drinking coffee. The fact that it was fall was significant, as the sports page was nearly consumed with coverage of the LSU football team. My family had managed to get season tickets to LSU football games when I was thirteen years old, the year that Gerry DiNardo was hired as head coach, and fans across south Louisiana hoped for redemption from an embarrassing decade of play under the previous coach, Curley Hallman. During the fall of my high school years, I lived from Saturday to Saturday, counting the days until the next game or dwelling on the last. My morning ritual with the sports page punctuated that time with a predictable rhythm: on each day of the week, a different type of coverage. Some days focused on reports from team practice, down to notes on what levels of padding the players wore, others on a special human-interest story about an individual player; Sunday was devoted almost entirely to full-color images of the game and excruciatingly detailed recaps—which, of course, I read despite having watched the game the previous day. Beyond this reading, I engaged in a host of other fan practices: I recorded the scores of each winning game on a poster in my bedroom; I collected LSU paraphernalia (sometimes bits and pieces that I found discarded in the stadium); I learned the lyrics to the alma mater and all of the marching band's fight songs and sang them loudly in the stadium; I watched reports about the team on ESPN and listened to the local radio station; I continually looked for new ways to adorn my body with LSU's colors or logos, from nail polish to temporary tattoos and hair dye. All of this consumed a significant amount of time and energy. It was important to me. But if someone had asked me at the time why it was important, I don't think I could have offered anything approaching a clear explanation.

Of course, no one did ask—and they did not ask because this behavior was not exactly abnormal. My sports fandom was perhaps a little more involved than that of most girls, but it was not very far out of the ordinary for sports fans from my region more generally. Sports fandom was and is important to a majority of the population in south Louisiana, and for most folks, this is simply a fact of life. The sort of habitual and ritual practices of sports fandom in which I was involved, in other words, were a point of connection with my surrounding community. Though many of my classmates did not read the paper, and though I did not have access to some of the same sports fan practices as they did—my family, for example, did not participate in the days-long tailgating that remains a hallmark of many of the LSU faithful—we engaged in overlapping sets of practices that bore a kind of family resemblance to one another and that marked us as LSU fans. Fans throughout the United States engage in similarly related fan traditions, which mark them as fans of their team (or, in the case of sports purists, as fans of some specific sport).

Looking more closely at the various forms these fan practices take is instructive. Although it is tempting to focus only on the ecstatic emotional experiences of sports fandom, we should not forget that for the devoted sports fan, they are but one component of fandom, even if a rather important one. I will divide the everyday disciplines and practices of sports fandom into three broad categories—which have overlaps, but which are distinguishable both by the types of activities they involve and (as I will show) their concomitant effects. The first category is broadly associated with *knowledge acquisition*— for example, reading and watching reports on away games, coaching changes, player news; learning historical and contemporary statistics associated with a team's performance; analyzing and evaluating play selection and arguing with other fans about game strategy. Other sports fan practices are more broadly understandable as *performances*: fans decorate their homes, cars, or even bodies with the markings or colors associated with their teams; they learn to chant, cheer, and sing in the correct ways; they learn to feel and express loathing for specific team rivals. When focused on these performance components of fandom, we could say that fandom is an activity analogous to the cultivation of virtue in the Aristotelian sense: a being-at-work that is accomplished over a lifetime. For some, indeed, it is more than a lifetime—as contemporary "coffin manufacturers even produce 'caskets in the colours of Alabama, Auburn and Georgia, as well as Tennessee' for that final touchdown" (Burstyn 1999, 19). One is a fan in this sense by virtue of her deliberate, repetitive participation in the mundane details of fan life—and, perhaps, death. The third major category of fan practice I will refer to as *fan discourse*. Sports fans make use of specific discursive patterns when talking about their teams. A prime example of this is the explicit utilization of "we" discourse and the centrality of the community in fan language. Fans tend to speak of "their" teams using "we," not "they." This is perhaps unsurprising, given the affective responses of "BIRGing" discussed earlier. Yet the use of "we" discourse and the enforcement of discursive norms of the local fan community are not limited to "BIRGing," as we will see. In what follows, I will discuss examples of practices in each of these categories and argue that each one contributes to the production and reinforcement of a particular sense of self. In particular, I will argue that by engaging in such practices, fans cultivate knowledge of themselves—sometimes as masculine, sometimes as southern, sometimes as morally superior, but always as a self with a clear connection with some group whose social import exceeds the individual.

The Will to (Sports) Knowledge

In 1859, before the institution of organized professional baseball leagues in the United States, and nearly thirty years prior to the advent of "fans," Henry Chadwick, a cricket enthusiast, invented the baseball "box score" (National Baseball Hall of Fame 2015). The box score made it possible to track, through a simple coding system, the record of each hit, run, and out of a baseball game—and the performance of the individual players involved. Although newspapers printed the final scores of games prior to the advent of the box score, they left out significant details. The box score made it possible not only to see a quick recap of the progression of an entire game but also to track the performance of individual players. The latter feature, some speculate, may have been the whole point. Chadwick was not only a sportswriter; he was also something of a moralist, who was so concerned to encourage good behavior (i.e., the avoidance of drinking and gambling) and "to reform the morals of baseball players by assigning responsibility for their actions" that he devised the box score as a means to record and publicize each defensive player's responsibility for the outcome of each turn at bat (Rayman 2005, 107). Reading the box score, for example, will tell us which players worked together to throw a runner out or whether a run scored because of a particular player's mistake. The box score makes knowable the details of the game down to judgments about whether the shortstop *ought to have* made a catch, but did not[1] and which pitcher was ultimately responsible for a certain runner's being on base.

The box score thus made new forms of knowledge possible. It became possible to know the record of individual players' performances, to conduct statistical analysis of them over time. It became possible to know, for example, an individual pitcher's earned run average—that is, the average number of runs opposing batters scored against him, excluding those that resulted from some kind of error on the part of a defensive player. Such knowledge, moreover, allowed fans to assess the objective merits of a particular players compared with others: how frequently did they score runs, and how frequently did they err defensively in the field? The knowledge produced by the box score had, in fact, the potential for perpetual expansion. Players and teams could be compared across time and space, enabling a kind of parallel competition in statistics even when competition on the field was impossible.

It is certain that these new forms of knowledge—and their continued expansion in baseball and, later, in other sports (the passer rating in football; free-throw, three-point, and field-goal shooting percentages in basketball)—had significant effects on the habits, training, play, and goals of individual athletes. As Joshua Rayman has argued (2005) these effects are examples of what Foucault would call disciplinary power. Such forms of knowledge have the effect of individuating athletes from the team, of making them conscious of their status as individuals and in relation to other players, and consequently, of encouraging the internalization of the drive to improve one's individual statistics. This internalization is key, since, for Foucault, what distinguishes disciplinary power from authoritarian-style power is that it is effective by working from "below" rather than from "above"—that is, by, over time, habituating individuals into monitoring and policing their own behavior, rather than having to be coerced through threats or other external forces. The paradigm case of disciplinary power is that of the panopticon: a circular prison in which cells are arranged around a central tower, which may or may not be inhabited by a guard, such that each prisoner is fully visible at all times yet unable to know when he or she is being watched. In this arrangement, Foucault writes, prisoners' behavior is constrained not by force but by their visibility, which "assures the hold of the power that is exercised over them. It is the fact of being constantly seen, of being able always to be seen, that maintains the disciplined individual in his subjection" (1995, 187). Importantly, in contexts other than prisons, such "subjection" to constant visibility is not always felt as oppressively restrictive by those who are subject to it. In schools, for example, children who know that their daily accomplishments of staying seated in their desks and raising their hands to speak will be recorded with gold stars on the teacher's chart internalize those norms and conform to them as much as possible—not because they feel threatened, but because they want to be recognized as a "good boy" or "good girl." Similarly, athletes who know that the details of their every play on the field are visible and recorded for posterity regiment themselves to be as efficient, powerful, and flawless as possible. Chadwick's invention of the box score, and the similar mechanisms of increased knowledge production around athletic statistics that followed it, was thus effective in precisely the way that he intended.[2]

What Chadwick did not intend, and could not have envisioned, was that this expansion of knowledge forms would likewise have disciplinary effects on sports spectators and, in fact, would give birth to the very concept of the sports *fan*. Recalling Ted Sullivan's description of the man who led him to coin the term "fan"—a man who "knew every player in the country with a record of 90 in the shade to 100 in the sun" and who was so "heavily burdened with baseball knowledge, or so permeated . . . with it that it oozes out of the crevices of his anatomy as does steam out of the pipes of a boiler" (Popik and Cohen 1996, 6)—it becomes clear that the idea of the sports fan as a repository of sports knowledge is substantially dependent upon the recording and compilation of individual sporting statistics. Although the amassing of such knowledge was, initially, an oddity worthy of a special moniker, and though even managers did not make substantial use of statistics for some time,[3] as sports fandom became more popular, knowledge acquisition became normative for those who would claim the title "fan." The potential for fan knowledge acquisition proliferated alongside the expansion of forms of knowledge of sports and athletes, exploding in the twentieth century not only through growth in sports reporting in print media but through the advent of television sports broadcasts, the ever-expanding roster of cable sports networks, and the rise of Internet sports media, which often promise their readers more objective sports knowledge, unfiltered by team administrations or official spokespersons, on whose good graces traditional media depend.[4] This expansion in available sports knowledge brings with it a call to know more.

In accordance with the normalization of knowledge acquisition among sports fans, the possession of such knowledge is an important criterion used by fans to differentiate themselves from mere spectators. This practice of differentiation, according to media scholar John Fiske, is ubiquitous in all sorts of fan communities, from sports fans to Star Trek fans. Drawing lines to make clear who is or is not a "real" fan, according to Fiske, is a means of reproducing "popular cultural capital," which confers a sense of enhanced social status and the "esteem of one's peers in a community of taste" (1992, 34). Importantly, such popular cultural capital is available even to those persons who do not have access to "official cultural capital"—say, the education or background required to have access to the privileges of mainstream social prestige. In other words, though fans may or may not have the background to move comfortably in culturally legitimated social spaces like art galleries, wine tastings, or fine dining restaurants, their membership in a fan community can provide an alternate means of access to a form of elite social status. "Fans discriminate fiercely," Fiske writes. "The boundaries between what falls within their fandom and what does not are sharply drawn. . . . [F]ans may argue about what characteristics allow someone to cross [the line] and become a true fan, but they are clearly agreed on the existence of the line" (34–35). In order for fandom to retain its normative status, there must be criteria according to which one's success or failure to follow its norms is judged. Without this criterion, it would be much more difficult for fans to use their fan status to obtain social capital—or, as another pair of scholars has pointedly put it,

"If all were welcome to the club . . . it would lose its exclusivity and thus its weight" (Markovits and Albertson 2012, 124).

Although knowledge is not the only criterion that sports fans use for assessing legitimate fandom, it is a crucial component. A study of Pittsburgh Steelers fans, for example, found that fans disparaged persons they deemed "'fair-weather' fans" for three main reasons: "attending games and favoring the Steelers only when the team is doing well; failure to attend during cold or unpleasant weather, and knowing little about the playoffs" (Cottingham 2012, 176). These fans believed that "real" fans would go to games and root for the Steelers in adverse conditions—including during losing seasons and when the temperature dropped well below freezing—and would understand the structure of the NFL playoff system. Persons who did not meet these criteria were subject to "moral disdain" by other fans (175). Similarly, a study of fantasy sports participants found that sports fans who participate in fantasy leagues are highly motivated to demonstrate their high social status by acquiring sports knowledge, sometimes "repeatedly checking Web sites for statistics on several different players, bordering on the compulsive." In contrast, "individuals who are less well informed are often openly ridiculed" (Davis and Duncan 2006, 253). Sports fans learn to make these status distinctions among themselves on the basis of sports knowledge early in their fan lives. Recall eighth-grade Alex's visceral reaction to his classmate Jillian's profession of fandom: "I hate when girls say they are fans of a team. *They don't know anything about it*" (Markovits and Albertson 2012, 206; emphasis mine).

Since sports fans often use their knowledge to demonstrate their legitimacy, knowledge acquisition becomes, for many, a central component of the discipline of fandom. What is crucial to note, however, is that this equation of the acquisition of detailed sporting knowledge with "proof" of fandom is almost always gendered masculine. We get a clear indication of this in Alex's suspicion of Jillian's claim to be a Mets fan: he assumes that because she is a girl, Jillian will not have adequate knowledge to "count" as a genuine fan. He likewise assumes that he is in a position of epistemic authority, and thus that he can function as a legitimate arbiter of fandom by giving Jillian a test to prove her status. Alex is far from alone in making such assumptions and demands. Women sports fans—and even women who are professional sports journalists—almost universally report having their sporting knowledge questioned. Joanne Gerstner, a sports journalist, recalls a particularly vivid experience:

> People call the sports desk and I answer, [and] then they ask for someone from sports. I tell them that I can help them, and they say, "No, no, I want

someone from sports." One guy called in asking how many championships Michael Jordan has won. . . . I gave him the answer, and he wanted to be put on the phone with a guy to "verify" my answer. Sometimes I just said that I was the secretary and passed the phone to someone else. (quoted in Markovits and Albertson 2012, 207)

Even women at the highest levels of sports journalism face challenges with being taken seriously as authorities on sports. Veteran ESPN anchor Linda Cohn, one of the most recognizable figures in sports media, describes the exacting standards for women's sporting competence thusly:

Let's just say I'm hosting *SportsCenter* on ESPN and a baseball score comes in and it's 14–7. . . . And I'm kidding around and I say the Red Sox beat the Yankees by a touchdown, just for a joke, which is done all the time. You can bet there would be phone calls and email. "Doesn't she know sports? What is she talking about?" I've been at ESPN for 16 years and been in the business for over 20. But even at this stage in my career, I can't say that. (quoted in Markovits and Albertson 2012, 177)

Women's competence as knowers is, as feminist epistemologists have pointed out,[5] regularly called into question. But in the context of sports fandom, their outright *in*competence is frequently presumed from the outset—and so, too, is their status as legitimate fans.

As in other examples of what feminists call "epistemic injustice" (Fricker 2009), women fans' testimony is regularly discounted unless corroborated by a man. In this case, though, the "corroboration" takes a specific form: a proof of one's fan competence that can only be demonstrated by passing tests like the one Alex gave Jillian. Such knowledge tests are a frequently reported experience for women sports fans, and they are nearly always "administered" by boys or men. When I conducted an informal poll of my friends on a popular social media site, self-identified women sports fans reported being quizzed on sports knowledge from the insultingly mundane ("Do you know who is out there playing right now?") to the hyperspecialized ("record [of wins and losses] between teams, total number of Super Bowl wins, number of players who are left-handed . . . Any random stat that the asker knows the answer to") (Facebook, Inc. 2015). Others, like Jillian, reported being asked to name a certain number of players on the team, to recite trivia about particular star players, to identify a particular hand signal used by a referee, or to explain a particular rule of the game. Sports journalist Dana Wakiji recalls a similar "testing" experience:

I remember one time I was at some bar or whatever and there was this football game, and the guys were so condescending and were like, "Ohhh, well . . .

really, you know about sports? Well, can you tell me what a nickel defense is?" and I'm like, 'Yes, it's an extra defensive back. You wanna know what a dime defense is? Would you like me to break down the left wing lock?" (quoted in Markovits and Albertson 2012, 207–208)

Throughout Markovits and Albertson's study of female sports fans in the United States, women fans report a similar sort of feeling: "on a constant and perpetual probation with men regarding sports . . . they always have to prove themselves . . . operat[ing] with a severe credibility deficit and with virtually no legitimacy" (208). Though some women are able to obtain at least temporary legitimacy as fans by "passing" such knowledge tests, the prospects for their long-term acceptance look grim. As a woman named Anna, who has served as the commissioner for her own fantasy football league for ten years, put it, "I know there's no winning, because usually more tests are on their way" (Facebook, Inc. 2015).

In truth, men and boys do tend to have a greater volume of a certain kind of sporting knowledge than women. I say "a certain kind" to draw attention to the fact that there are a wide variety of knowledge forms, and that the form of knowledge in which men appear to have a demonstrable advantage is only one sort—namely, propositional knowledge.[6] That is, men tend to have knowledge of sports that can be expressed in propositional form: "Iverson had 38 points, 12 assists, 5 steals and only 4 turnovers" (Davis and Duncan 2006, 253) or "Jim Kelly was the Bills QB vs. Troy Aikman in Super Bowl [XXVIII]" (Facebook, Inc. 2015). A few studies have suggested that male fans of sports are, on the whole, more knowledgeable than female fans (Dietz-Uhler et al. 2000; Gantz and Wenner 1995; Markovits and Albertson 2012). At least one has shown that men who are fans have substantially more knowledge about sports than women who are fans—knowledge here assessed by the ability to accurately answer test questions about things like the rules of specific games or the meaning of in-game abbreviations such as "In baseball, what does ERA stand for?"—even though women fans' self-assessment of their knowledge is not substantially different from men's (Dietz-Uhler 2000, 223). A study of undergraduates at the University of Michigan produced similar results when it asked men and women to name as many members as they could remember of famous historical and contemporary teams (Markovits and Smith 2007), as did a study of schoolchildren in Germany. In the latter, "Four-to-six-year-old boys not only knew the various teams' names, the colors of their jerseys, and the names and numbers of their key players but also the different strategies played by different teams, as well as the historical dimension of games that happened when these boys were much younger and

could not possibly remember in an active way or even preceded their birth"
(Markovits and Albertson 2012, 31). The girls in this group were not so preco-
cious in their sports knowledge. The suggestion that male fans, on the whole
"know more"—that is, know a greater number of facts about sports—than
female fans appears to be more than mere stereotype.

It is, however, far from obvious that this implies that women are on some
objective measure less real fans than men. As I argued in the previous chapter, if our goal is to understand what sports fandom does for fans, it is more
productive to pay attention to the various practices through which fans live
their fandom than to make normative judgments about which practices are
more legitimate, or more central to fandom, than others. Taking the norms
of fandom for granted—especially those norms deployed by fans to exclude
others from the realm of legitimacy—would leave us much less well placed to
understand how those norms are used to produce particular forms of identity. The norms associated with knowledge acquisition, and their uneven deployment across genders, exemplify the sort of practice that should not be
taken for granted as normative but investigated in the details of its usage.
In fact, it is crucial to note this gender difference—and the concomitantly
gendered practice of "testing" fellow fans—in order to observe a key way in
which sports fandom functions as a subjectivizing practice. Specifically, the
practice of knowledge acquisition in sports fandom is a means of reinforcing
the gender binary and reproducing entrenched power relations characterized
by masculine domination. Through the dual disciplinary practices of continuous knowledge acquisition and the administration of informal "testing,"
these boys and men use their sports fandom both to create and reassert their
own masculinity and to keep girls and women subordinate—either excluded
as outsiders or dependent upon masculine approval for legitimation as fans.
These mechanisms, in other words, function to reproduce masculinity as a
gender identity characterized by domination or mastery and by its hierarchical relation to femininity.

To see why, we need to consider briefly what kind of thing normative
"masculinity" is. It is impossible to point precisely to masculinity *as such*,
since (as Beauvoir put it in her classic investigation of femininity) it does
not exist as an essence in any Platonic heaven. Even if we grant that males
and females exist as unproblematically natural kinds (a claim put into serious question by some twentieth-century feminists), this does not tell us anything about the essence of masculinity or femininity—as there are, at least
in ordinary ways of speaking, "masculine" women and "feminine" men. The
fact that masculinity and femininity as descriptors do not necessarily track
sex differences suggests that they are not so much contained within organ-

isms as they are descriptions of particular ways of living and moving in the world. As Judith Butler puts it, the things we call "gender" are performative enactments: "the repeated stylization of the body, a set of repeated acts within a highly rigid regulatory frame that congeal over time to produce the appearance of substance, of a natural sort of being" (1990, 45). "Masculinity," in other words, is the sort of phenomenon that is produced over a lifetime of having one's behavior policed, corrected, and encouraged—"earrings aren't for boys"; "suck it up, son"; "good hustle, champ"—and internalizing the imperative to repeat the normatively sanctioned behaviors. Such repetition is key, not only because these behaviors become habitual, but also (and more importantly) because it is only through repetition that gender can give the reassuring appearance of stability. Continuous gender performance—from dress to movement, speech patterns, and interactions with others—is crucial both for individual subjects to be consistently understood by others and to be knowable to themselves.

What, then, are the enactments associated with masculinity today? Though it is impossible to make a final or universal declaration of those behaviors that are definitively masculine—the instability of the category precludes this possibility—we can say, provisionally, that normative (heterosexual) masculinity prescribes, among other things, those acts associated with domination or mastery (particularly bodily domination or mastery) and those associated with the subordination of nonmasculine persons. This emphasis on mastery, domination, and the subordination of others is unequivocally opposed to vulnerability, passivity, or weakness, which are, in the view of normative heterosexual masculinity, feminine. Being an adequately masculine man requires, as William James put it, "strenuousness" (1987, 1287)—powering through difficulty in order to achieve mastery of one's circumstances. It also requires, as the accusatory colloquialism "Who wears the pants in this family?" suggests, the specific mastery of women, whose subordination functions as its own justification. Each of these categories of action is, as I will argue, cultivated through the practices of knowledge acquisition in sports fandom.

First, considering the association of domination or mastery with normative masculinity, it is easy to see why sports in general are typically gendered masculine. The traits, dispositions, and actions typically associated with domination—such as, for example, competitiveness, aggression, and control—are required and reinforced by athletic competition. Moreover, such traits are expressed in explicitly embodied ways by athletes: aggression and competitiveness when displayed by football players looks rather more physically menacing than the same traits when expressed by investment bankers; it is for this reason that people often suggest that professional athletes are *hyper*masculine. It is not difficult to imagine, then, why sport is such a deeply gendered domain in our contemporary context, why athletic competition is almost universally gender segregated, why men's teams are regularly treated as the most (or only) important ones, or why male children grow up playing and following sports at much higher rates than their female peers. If sports participation cultivates traits required for normative masculinity, and if normative masculinity also depends for its existence on its distinction from femininity, then the inference that secure (normative, heterosexual) masculinity requires participation in sports is but a short trip away—particularly in a world with fewer and fewer accepted means of explicitly excluding women.

Yet successful participation in sports is not always open to those desirous of performing normative masculinity. Very few have the skills or physical gifts to excel as elite athletes—or even as moderately successful amateurs. Sports *fandom*, however, offers a means of sports participation that is widely accessible, even to people with severely limited physical capabilities. This participation, of course, takes a variety of forms—including not only the disciplinary practices with which I am presently concerned but also fantasies of identification with individual athletes, to which I will return later. The disciplinary practice of knowledge acquisition, however, is uniquely effective as a masculinizing practice because it enables *both* the expression of mastery *and* the facilitation of homosociality (or what is sometimes referred to as "male bonding") that more or less explicitly subordinates women. The memorization and recitation of propositional knowledge about sports—particularly knowledge of the details of individual players' performance—positions the knower as powerful, and as dominant, in at least two ways. In the first place, the knower becomes like the guard in the tower of the panopticon: seeing all, aware of every move of the individuated subjects who do not see him yet modify their behaviors because of their internalization of his anonymous gaze. The sports fan thus occupies a position of disciplinary power over those whom he could not hope to overpower through physical force. In the second place, the knower of sports facts, insofar as he is successful in disciplining himself to remember and use them effectively, positions himself as *in command of those facts*—they are at his disposal; he can recite them at will; his mind is a veritable storehouse of the truth of sports. In this way, the sports fan gains dominance by the metonymic substitution of his mastery of sports knowledge for mastery of the field of play.

The display of sports knowledge is useful, moreover, for reinforcing one's normative masculinity in the view of other men—which is sometimes accomplished through the more or less explicit exclusion or subordination of women. The traditional social relations between men, which many theorists, following Eve Sedgwick (1985), have referred to as "homosocial," typically involve "men's striving and competing for prestige and approval within their peer groups" (Nylund 2004, 148). That prestige and approval often depend on bonding and competing (or bonding *through* competing) in an exclusively masculine space, which, at least tacitly, requires the exclusion of women and of men who are viewed as insufficiently masculine. As David Nylund (2004) has argued in his study of sports talk radio, talking about sports with other men—particularly in competitive contexts, in which conversation partners may be publicly approved or ridiculed, depending on the quality of their insight—is a key site of homosocial bonding. In fact, this particular avenue for homosocial bonding seems to have grown more important in the contemporary world, as more and more women enter the public sphere and the dominance of normative masculinity seems increasingly precarious. As a result, participation in explicitly masculine sports culture becomes increasingly urgent, since it "functions to assuage men's fear of feminization in current postmodern culture" (149). Fans who are men and boys practice this competitive homosocial bonding through "displaying a strong knowledge of player statistics" and ridiculing those less informed in contexts such as fantasy sports participation (Davis and Duncan 2006, 253), sports talk radio, and everyday sports talk among peers.

The effectiveness of this form of sports participation as a homosocial institution is, however, in question when women enter it. In this light, the apparent ubiquity of the practice of subjecting women sports fans to knowledge tests becomes more explicable: the outcome of testing requires women either to be symbolically excluded from the realm of sports fan participation (if they fail the test) or to be cast in a position of subordinate dependence on provisional approval for inclusion (if they pass). But the interaction of the test itself also institutes a clearly hierarchizing power relation, as Foucault argues in his analysis of the examination as a disciplinary mechanism. Like the panopticon, the exam renders each student individuated and knowable; it "enabled the teacher, while transmitting his knowledge, to transform his pupils into a whole field of knowledge" (Foucault 1995, 186). The lack of reciprocity in the examination relationship, however, is more powerful for being only implicit in its assertion. Whereas explicit assertions of authority would be highly visible, and thus more obviously resistible, in the disciplinary power of the exam, power

> is exercised through its invisibility; at the same time it imposes on those whom it subjects a principle of compulsory visibility. . . . Their visibility assures the hold of the power that is exercised over them. It is the fact of being constantly

seen, of being able always to be seen, that maintains the disciplined individual
in his subjection. . . . [T]he examination is, as it were, the ceremony of this
objectification. (187)

Though women sports fans are not (usually) in an explicit, continuous peda-
gogical relationship with those men who test them, the scene of the sports test
shares much in common with Foucault's description of the exam. In being
subjected to tests of their sports knowledge, it is the woman sports fan, not
her interlocutor, who is on the spot—she is made hypervisible to the group
of assembled men (tellingly, each story of such tests that I have come across
took place in public), obligated to provide an answer, rendered an object of
knowledge for both the questioner and anyone in his audience.

The questioner, for his part, is thus able to count his "pupil" as yet another item of knowledge—not only as an individual who may or may not
count as a "real fan," but perhaps also as a confirmation of (or more rarely, an
exception to) the principle that "women don't know anything about sports."
The man who gives sports knowledge tests thus reiterates his normative masculinity not only by symbolically guarding the homosocial space of sports
participation; he does so by reasserting his command of facts—by knowing
both his and his interlocutor's relative statuses as knowers and as fans—and
more importantly, by enacting a more or less explicitly hierarchizing relation
with the feminine. One woman fan I spoke with understood her experience
of being subjected to knowledge tests in terms that drew clear attention to
their importance in shoring up the questioner's masculinity: "I think [men]
tend to think trivia knowledge is more important than I do. I can be a Dallas Cowboy fan (and am) without knowing the passing statistics for every
quarterback since Don Meredith. I think their trivia knowledge is another
measuring stick—if you get my drift" (Facebook, Inc. 2015; emphasis mine).
The masculine "measuring stick" on symbolic display is all the more powerful
for the asymmetrical structure of the knowledge test, which, ironically, allows
the questioner to reassert his manhood without subjecting it to exposure. Yet
the sports fan who administers such knowledge tests is not, for all his posturing, straightforwardly sovereign over the interaction, nor is he free from the
machinations of gendered power. Paradoxically, his sense of self—his identity
as a fan, his masculinity, his place in the social order—is dependent in significant ways upon his continual striving for expanded sports knowledge and
upon the repeated rehearsal of the scene of the knowledge test.

In submitting to the rigors of knowledge acquisition, then, sports fans (especially men sports fans) gain more than entertainment; they gain a particular kind of self—one whose legitimacy, moral superiority, and normative sta-

tus is consistently reiterated. The deeply gendered character of this particular fan practice makes its specific subjectivizing stakes evident, though this is not to say that sports knowledge acquisition is always or only masculinizing. Rather, the subjectivization accomplished in and through this practice *normalizes*[7] masculinity: it creates an idealized norm to which individuals strive to conform and in relation to which they can be judged, ranked, rewarded, or excluded. Those who submit themselves to the discipline of sports knowledge acquisition may submit themselves to a kind of hierarchizing judgment, but they do so with tacit promise of increased proximity to normative masculinity (even if only by provisionally gaining its imprimatur) and the concomitant ability to distinguish themselves from those others who are not as successful as practitioners of the discipline.

Hearts on Sleeves: Ritual and Public Performances of Sports Fandom

Beyond the cognitive practices of knowledge acquisition, sports fandom prescribes for its practitioners a variety of public performances, which range from highly formalized rituals to everyday habits and disciplines. Much has been written about the ritual of game attendance—in which fans wear special clothing, attend a mass gathering full of call-and-response-style cheers, stand and sit at regular intervals, and sing songs celebrating the glories of the object of their devotion.[8] Such rituals are no doubt worthy of analysis, and I will, in what follows, argue that they are important elements in the cultivation of specific forms of sports fan subjectivity. But less attention has been paid in previous investigations to the public performances of sports fandom that occur in less regimented or ritualized contexts—the collection and display of clothing and décor in team colors, the usage of bodily markings and manipulation (e.g., tattoos) to declare one's fandom, the incorporation of team logos or colors into weddings or funerary articles—or to the relation between these more mundane, ephemeral, or solitary performances of sports fandom and the large-scale community ritual. In this section, I will analyze examples of both forms of sports fan performances and argue that they function, for contemporary Americans, as practices of self-cultivation—specifically, as a means of creating a sense of self that is grounded in its relation to a particular community. Importantly, however, these fan performances do not merely link individuals with a fully formed, preexisting community; rather, such performances are often centrally instrumental in the constitution and reproduction of those communities. Insofar as other modes of regional or community identification—such as unified religious or political life—have waned in recent years, sports fandom comes to occupy an increasingly prominent place in the continuation of these group identities. Sports fandom, then, helps to constitute both individual subjects and the community in relation to which those subjects know themselves.

In his now-classic study of nationalism, *Imagined Communities*, Benedict Anderson argues that the idea of a "nation" and national identity becomes of crucial importance once previously prominent modes of group identification are no longer available. Whereas phenomena like religious identity once united wide swaths of the globe—such that believers could conceive of themselves as united with other Christians or Muslims worldwide—the replacement of religious and sovereign power with nation-states increased the importance of conceiving oneself as united with one's countrymen via some ineffable essence: the German spirit, the American way of life, and so on (Anderson 1991). Without hierarchical heads of empires to grip people's imaginations, nationalist self-concepts depended upon a vivid notion of citizens' relations with their fellow citizens. In significant respects, then, the "nation" (composed, it is worth remembering, of millions of people who do not know one another at all) *is* this "imagined" community. Something very similar, I argue, occurs in the local and regional communities of the United States, where the images of communal or regional life are likely to be more salient than those of the nation as a whole. This is particularly true in the American South, where the sense of distinction from the rest of the nation looms large in the cultural imaginary. Yet, as previously prevalent methods for cultivating a sense of community or regional unity evaporate—as, for example, the Christian church loses its cultural hegemony; globalization moves jobs and workers far from home, increasing the heterogeneity of previously homogenous groups; and changes in civil rights law (e.g., antimiscegenation and antisegregation laws) prohibit juridical means of ensuring a sense of cultural unity—new means are needed to cultivate a sense of communal identity. One of the primary means of accomplishing this is the performance of sports fandom.

Beyond participation in the large-scale, formalized rituals of game attendance, fans incorporate the accumulation and display of team symbols into both their everyday lives and moments of intense personal significance. Innumerable fans, for example, make use of team symbols, colors, and songs in their weddings. Some, like San Francisco Giants fan Diana Eaton, who married on a yacht in the cove overlooking the Giants' stadium, wearing hints of the Giants' orange and black, prior to a reception replete with baseball and Giants imagery and featuring a guest book fashioned from a Giants' home plate, make this incorporation of sports fandom comprehensive (Eaton 2012). Birth announcements, likewise, are a popular venue for the display of sports fan imagery and symbols. In 2011, one Pittsburgh-area hospital took this practice a step further by covering each infant housed in its neonatal unit with a "Terrible Towel," a yellow rag waved by Steelers fans during games. Parents of the newborns were, it seems, generally approving; one father told reporters that his newborn daughter "can choose her religion, but she can't choose what team she likes" (Chase 2011). Team affiliation, moreover, carries through for many fans till death and beyond. Increasingly, fans are not only buying caskets featuring team colors or logos but being buried in their team jersey, surrounded by mourners who respect their wishes to come in the team colors (ESPN 2012). In one case, a Steelers fan named James Henry Smith, who died after a long fight with cancer,

> requested that he and the people at his funeral experience his Sunday after-noon ritual of watching the Steelers. The funeral home was transformed into Smith's living room. Smith was put in a reclining chair and wore Steelers pa-jamas, Steelers slippers, and had his legs covered by a Steelers blanket. Guests sat around Smith's body and watched a tape of a Steelers' game. (Kraszewski 2008, 138–139)

Though the incorporation of sports fandom into these moments of great sig-nificance is quite striking, it is important to remember, as one family member of a recently departed Dallas Cowboys fan suggested, that their inclusion in such momentous events reflects the centrality of that fandom in the mundane details of everyday life: "It was such a big part of her life, why not be a part of her send-off, too?" (ESPN 2012). For every sports-themed wedding, funeral, or birth announcement, there are innumerable bedrooms and offices deco-rated in team paraphernalia, dogs named after favorite athletes, tattoos com-memorating hockey championships, and fight songs installed as cell-phone ringtones. The public—and private—performances of sports fandom touch every corner of contemporary American life.

The diffusion of such practices throughout fans' lives gives an important indication of their function: the performances of sports fandom are practices of self-cultivation—specifically, they enable fans to cultivate a robust sense of themselves as individuals belonging to a particular community. To make sense of this claim, it will be useful to recall that, as I argued in the previ-ous section, fandom is a practice of differentiation—of marking oneself as distinct from ordinary spectators—and that it thus involves taking a kind of quasi-moral stance toward the subject. This is not to say that sports fans always operate with a list of rigid behavioral commandments, but rather, that they, as Foucault puts it in another context, "comply more or less fully with a standard of conduct . . . [and] respect or disregard a set of values" (1990b,

25). That conduct and those values function to position sports fans as *fans*, to be sure, but they also—as in the case of sports knowledge acquisition and the normalization of masculinity—have important effects for sports fans' subjectivity beyond the narrow confines of sport. The performance elements of sports fandom are able to function in this way because they offer an immediately tangible means to cultivate one's sense of self and place in the larger social order, by incorporating reiterations of that identity in virtually any feature of everyday life.

Practices of this sort are not new; as Foucault points out, all moral systems incorporate, to varying degrees, "code elements" and "elements of ascesis" (1990b, 31)—that is, a set of rules as well as a set of practices through which an individual attempts to mold himself or herself into a certain kind of ethical subject. The latter set of practices receive most of the emphasis in many moral traditions, including Christianity, in which the precise moral code is less important than a continual working on oneself, which can be fulfilled in a wide range of exercises that facilitate both self-knowledge and self-transformation (30). Such practices can take a variety of forms, depending on the tradition— ranging from the Christian practices of confession and fasting to the more comprehensive methods advocated by Roman emperor and philosopher Marcus Aurelius, which included everything from physical exercises to meditations and specific types of interpersonal correspondence (Foucault 1988, 51). Importantly, Foucault argues, these practices of self-cultivation are not carried out in isolation but in relation to a larger community and often making use of existing social structures—meaning that although the focus of such practices is *self*-knowledge and *self*-care; these always occur within a certain set of social or moral relations.

Sports fandom, in its performance elements, constitutes a set of practices that offer fans just this sort of self-knowledge and self-care. The difference, however, is that these practices are aimed not at the cultivation of a subject who is especially moral in the generic or religious sense but who is a good— which is to say, legitimate or authentic—member of a particular community. Those communities are often regional, but may also (I will suggest) be marked by race or class. The incorporation of fan practices throughout one's life, both in formalized ritual and less structured, individuating settings, enables one to know oneself—and more than this, to actively cultivate one's identity—as a member of that community. To illustrate this, I want to examine two particularly salient examples: sports fans who are displaced from their hometowns and use their fandom to maintain their regional identity, and University of Mississippi fans who use their fandom to cultivate a form of subjectivity characteristic of the genteel white South. Sports fandom becomes an important practice of self-cultivation in both of these contexts, I will suggest, because previously used methods of self-cultivation are no longer available to the subjects who undertake them.

If one pays attention to sports fans on any college campus with a student population of diverse geographical origins, one will notice the wide variety of team loyalties there represented. Students who are far from home wear their home team's colors or logos and make a point to watch its games, sometimes in the company of other students from the same town or region. These students engage in a behavior familiar to many displaced sports fans who deliberately maintain—and sometimes increase—their investment in their home team after moving away from it. Communications studies scholar Jon Kraszewski offers an analysis of one such group of displaced fans in his article "Pittsburgh in Fort Worth" (2008), in which he follows a group of Pittsburgh Steelers fans, all of whom have relocated, for one reason or another, from western Pennsylvania to Fort Worth, Texas. The fans in his study regularly frequent a Steelers bar in Fort Worth to watch games, talk about the Steelers, wear their Steelers gear, and eat foods associated with western Pennsylvania in the company of other Steelers fans. For these fans, Kraszewski writes, "sports do not offer simply a substitution for old forms of community; they become metonyms for home" (141). Steelers fans were able to experience themselves as members of their former community through all of the attendant practices of Steelers fandom—including the consumption of pierogies and Iron City beer (both associated with western Pennsylvania), waving "Terrible Towels," discussing the team, and engaging in a rivalry with Dallas Cowboys fans at the same bar. Thus, Kraszewski suggests, "the bar hosting the fans becomes a stage for fans to perform former home identities, and the television screen becomes one part of the mise-en-scene of this performance" (147). Persons who had previously been displaced and disconnected from their former communities regain, through sports fandom, "the idea of permanence and geographic origins" (155) in the face of the impermanence that characterizes other features of their lives.

What makes this type of practice work for displaced fans is that sport has, in the contemporary United States, "become embedded in local culture" (Kraszewski 2008, 146) and thus helps constitute a particular understanding of what it is to be a member of that local community. They do so not merely because they are associated with that community through effective marketing[9] but because sports fan practices *give* them this significance, insofar as they are used as practices of subjectivization. Thus I would like to expand on Kraszewski's claim to suggest that it is not only displaced fans who use their sports fandom as a means to cultivate a stable sense of identity; displaced fans, rather, offer a particularly salient example of this practice because there are fewer avenues for such self-cultivation open to them. Whereas fans of a team who remain in that team's region have other practices of subjectivization available to reinforce a sense of the coherence and stability of a local identity—they may interact with others in community groups or get involved in local politics, all while experiencing the local geography of the region— displaced fans do not. Yet, even local fans, who increasingly live lives disconnected from their neighbors, and in increasingly heterogeneous locales, can find in the performances of sports fandom a clearly useful means of reinforcing their sense of belonging in this particular community. The collection and display of team symbols, the participation in formalized sporting rituals, and the incorporation of team imagery into momentous or sacred events has the effect of declaring—for oneself and for others—a truth about one's identity or origins and asserting a settled position about one's relation to the larger community. It also, importantly, *contributes to the constitution of the very community of which these individuals are a part.* Since, as Anderson suggests, the existence of a community as such depends upon the symbols, imaginations, and (I would add) practices that allow its members to conceive of themselves as belonging to it, these practices of subjectivization are crucial for the creation and reproduction of the community thereby represented.

The self-cultivating practices of a particularly prominent group of fans of the University of Mississippi football team offer further illustration of the role of such practices in the reproduction of identity—in this case, the identity of the genteel white South.[10] The University of Mississippi, or "Ole Miss," as it is known colloquially, has long been associated with the white southern aristocracy, and for good reason. It was Ole Miss that James Meredith integrated under the protection of National Guard troops by becoming the first black student to enroll in 1962. Twenty years later, the university's student body remained only 7 percent black (Stuart 1982); today, black students make up approximately 15 percent of the student body—despite the school's status as the flagship university of a state whose total population is 37 percent black (Pettus 2014). Beyond the demographics of the student body, the symbols and ethos of the athletics program have clear linkages to southern whiteness— and the history of white supremacy. The university adopted "Rebels" as the nickname for its athletic teams in 1936 and shortly thereafter began using a mascot known as "Colonel Reb . . . represented as an older, white gentleman with a mustache and goatee, dressed in a black suit and planter hat, symbolizing a genteel Southern aristocrat, if not a plantation slave owner" (King and Springwood 2001, 131). In 1948, as segregationist "Dixiecrats" were gaining political popularity in the South, "droves of students from Ole Miss attended the Dixiecrat convention in Birmingham, Alabama, when the Confederate flag and the song 'Dixie' were adopted as official symbols of the party"; the same year, the Confederate flag and "Dixie" began to be associated with the football team, as fans waved the flag and the band played the nostalgic anthem as a kind of unofficial fight song (Newman 2007, 267). Until very recently, the Confederate flag, "Dixie," and the Colonel Reb mascot were ubiquitous at Ole Miss football games, with the mascot being officially changed in 2010, and (one version of) "Dixie" discontinued by the chancellor in 2009 in response to some students' propensity to substitute a chant of "The South will rise again" for the last lines of the song (Associated Press 2009). In 1997, the school banned large sticks at football games in an effort to keep fans from bringing Confederate flags into the stadium—but as the Mississippi state flag includes the Confederate cross, it has never entirely been eliminated.

The aristocratic, genteel character of the white southern identity celebrated by many Ole Miss fans is evident not only in the image of Colonel Reb—which appears all over "The Grove," Ole Miss's popular tailgating area, despite having been officially discontinued by the university. The perception in the state of Mississippi is that Ole Miss is for elites, whereas Mississippi State is associated with the working class, and this is not without reason. Graduates of Ole Miss include Senators Trent Lott and Thad Cochran, both of whom were cheerleaders during their time as students (Travis 2007, 316), and the university's colors, crimson and navy blue, were chosen explicitly because they were those of Harvard and Yale, respectively (OleMissSports 2016a). As a more conspicuously visible marker of elite class status, traditional tailgating and game attendance rituals at The Grove are decidedly formal in comparison to most sporting events: women are perfectly coiffed, usually in dresses and high-heeled shoes; men come in slacks and button-down shirts, sometimes with jackets and bow ties; the innumerable tents set up to house lavish spreads of food often feature floral centerpieces and chandeliers. All of this is part of a long history of self-styled cultural elitism at Ole Miss, which grew particularly acute in response to the establishment of Mississippi State in the late nineteenth century, after which the Ole Miss newspaper began referring to students at its in-state rival as "farmers, rednecks and cowpunchers," and at rivalry games, Ole Miss students taunted Mississippi State students with jeers like "Hay-Peas-Beans-and-Squash! A&M Cow-Pullers! Yes, by Gosh!" (M. Butler 1997). Prior to the university's withdrawal of support for Confederate symbols, between the various markers of white southern gentility and Confederate and segregationist imagery, it was difficult not to see in Ole Miss sports fandom what Joshua I. Newman called "the foremost apparatus for promulgating Mississippi's symbolic technologies of racism among its elite class" (2007, 265).

Yet it is not at all clear that post–Colonel Reb, post–Confederate flag Ole Miss fandom is entirely divorced from the reproduction of white southern aristocracy. For one thing, these symbols have not been expunged from Ole Miss fan practices, despite their officially being jettisoned from the university. And the Ole Miss teams remain, officially, "the Rebels"—though represented, as a result of a somewhat incredible compromise, not by Colonel Reb, but by a black bear named "Rebel." The Ole Miss fight song retains an explicit linkage between the football team and pride in the South, not only pride for the state of Mississippi or the university as such: "Rebels, you're the *Southland's* pride." The alma mater maintains a similar theme, with imagery that evokes an explicitly nostalgic picture of the genteel South:

> Way down *south* in Mississippi,
> There's a spot that ever calls,
> Where amongst the hills enfolded,
> Stand old Alma Mater's Halls.
> Where the trees lift high their branches,
> To the whispering *Southern* breeze,
> There Ole Miss is calling, calling,
> To our hearts fond memories.
> (OLEMISSSPORTS 2016b; emphasis mine)

Moreover, all of the ostentatious markers of southern aristocracy remain in The Grove, maintained by an overwhelmingly white fan population, in the context of a state with one of the largest (and poorest) black populations in the nation. In spite of the university's official efforts to eliminate explicit references to the Confederacy, it remains entirely plausible to claim, as Newman did in 2007, that "Whiteness is not only performed at Ole Miss; it is spectacle" (266).

Such spectacular performances function, again, both to make a claim about one's identity and, at the same time, to give shape to its meaning. It is perhaps illuminating to consider the report of James Meredith's return to Ole Miss in 1982 to give a speech commemorating the twentieth anniversary of the university's racial integration. According to observers from the *New York Times*, "As [Meredith's] talk ended, he was applauded by most of the audience of blacks and whites, but a group of about 100 whites walked out. Outside the chapel they chanted the Ole Miss 'Hotty Totty' [*sic*] song, a familiar verse heard at impromptu gatherings" (Stuart 1982). "Hotty Toddy" is a common chant recited by Ole Miss fans at sporting events. In response to a leader's calling, "Are you ready?" the assembled crowd replies, rhythmically:

> Hell yeah! Damn Right!
> Hotty Toddy, Gosh Almighty,
> Who the Hell are We? Hey!
> Flim Flam, Bim Bam,
> Ole Miss, By Damn!
>
> (OLEMISSSPORTS 2016a)

The origins of the chant are unclear, but the story of its recitation in defiant response to a speech calling for the fulfillment of the promise of racial integration at the University of Mississippi is striking, to say the least. In this context, the chant makes a specific claim about the identity of the fans, and of Ole Miss, properly speaking: "Who the hell are we? . . . Ole Miss, By Damn!" By employing the chant in oppositional response to Meredith, the chanters invoke not only the specter of competition (and perhaps the violence of football) but their own status as the proper (white) embodiment of the University of Mississippi. Moreover, insofar as Ole Miss represents the state's—and region's—elite, the chanters figure themselves as the proper embodiment of Mississippi or the South as such. The chant here functions, in other words, as a reiteration of segregationist white supremacy and of the chanters' identities as both racially and regionally normative, against the invading otherness represented by Meredith and his call for further racial progress.

This is not to claim that every instance of the "Hotty Toddy" cheer constitutes support for white supremacy. It is, however, to attend to the history of explicitly racist practices of community cultivation out of which contemporary Ole Miss fandom—and, in truth, Southeastern Conference Football fandom more broadly—emerged, to note the white supremacist soil in which it took root and flourished, and to suggest that many contemporary Ole Miss fan practices, minimally, contribute to the reproduction of a particularly racialized southern identity. Though those practices have changed in significant ways in recent years, it is crucial to recognize the ways in which they evoke a newly Disney-fied, whitewashed genteel South, which ignores the history of oppression and violence on which the elegance and manners of The Grove was built. We must ask, moreover, what forms of subjectivity are produced when overwhelmingly white fan bases in states featuring intensely racialized class stratification and segregation now cheer for overwhelmingly black teams as they compete in violent sports. We must ask whether southern football pride has in fact become a metonym for pride in the southern white aristocracy, as a mode of the further entrenchment of its power, or as a "rebranded" southern pride in which "we can [have solidarity] and can't really be criticized for it" (Curtis 2011). Both of these questions will be considered in detail in chapter 5. For now, it must suffice to note that the practices of Ole Miss fandom offer a means not only of evoking nostalgic imagery but of ritualistically reproducing white Southern aristocracy, when more direct and explicit means have been legally proscribed or rendered taboo in good society.

In both cases I have examined here—that of displaced sports fans and Ole Miss football fans specifically—sports fandom, both as formally ritualized and in everyday life, contributes to the constitution and reinforcement of identity. That identity is both individualizing, insofar as it creates subjects as knowable to themselves and others in particular ways, and creative of communities and groups, which are usually regional, and sometimes racialized. The formation and reproduction of group or regional identity is, in fact, significantly dependent upon these fan practices, as they remain, in the contemporary United States, one of the primary means available to constitute clear group identities. In this light, the claim of Gottfried von Herder that "Everyone loves his country, his manners, his language, his wife, his children; not because they are the best in the world, but because they are absolutely his own, and *loves himself and his own labors in them*" (quoted in Viroli 1995, 122; emphasis mine) is particularly striking when applied to the performative practices of sports fandom. The pseudonationalistic pride of sports fandom occurs not only when fans bask in reflected glory; Ole Miss football need not win championships for fans to draw meaning, identity, or pride from it. Rather, the regional (and sometimes racial) community of sports fans is constituted by the labors and practices of the sports fans themselves, who actively create and re-create its meaning, its boundaries, and its place in the world. In loving the team, then, fans love themselves—both as individual subjects made knowable through the practices of fandom and as members of a group whose value is reproduced in large measure *through* those practices.

Fan Discourse: We're Number One!

Closely related to the performance elements of sports fandom is participation in sports fan discourse. Beyond the normative masculine performance of simply talking about sports (and reciting sports facts), there is a particular mode of speech that is nearly universal among partisan fans: a pattern of reference to a team that I will call "we" discourse. Fans frequently speak of "their" teams using "we," not "they." This is perhaps unsurprising, given the affective responses we discussed earlier in the chapter: fans do not glory or wallow in the joy or despair they feel for others; they are so moved *for themselves*. Interestingly, social scientific research of the BIRGing phenomenon suggests that fans are more likely to use we discourse to refer to their favored team when that team has just won than when it has just lost. In some circumstances, fans even switch from "we" to "they" or some other third-person mode of description when moving from discussions of team victories to discussion of a defeat (Cialdini et al. 1976). This practice of dis-identification in the face of defeat is the opposite of "basking in reflected glory" and is consequently referred to in the literature by an equally stomach-turning acronym: "CORFing"—"cutting off reflected failure" (Wann 2006). Fans may CORF by changing their discursive practices or by avoiding the sorts of performance elements of fandom discussed in the previous section; in either case, fans who CORF effectively dissociate themselves from the poor performance of the team, most likely to preserve the positive feelings that BIRGing brings. Yet here, too, BIRGing alone is not sufficient to explain the discursive patterns of all fans, as "highly-identified" fans maintain we discourse even in cases of team defeat.

In one particularly illustrative example of the phenomenon of we discourse, scholars of sports rhetoric Kenneth Zagacki and Daniel Grano conducted an analysis of the discourse on sports talk radio engaged in by fans of the LSU Tigers. Even in the face of a terrible season, the explicit identification of individuals and the local community with the team did not always abate—though it did more often find expression in anguished cries like "*We're* the laughingstock of the nation and the SEC" (2005, 50; emphasis mine). In some cases, such fans not only reiterated their we discourse but expanded its scope to facilitate the continuation of pride in it. Zagacki and Grano describe what happened over the days following a particularly embarrassing defeat for the Tigers:

[The radio host] Hanagriff responded by shifting to one of Louisiana's premier football teams: "Well, at least West Monroe got the state some pride this past weekend." He was referring to a nationally-ranked high school team that had won a contest a few days before. . . . Other fans on this program and throughout the week also shifted focus from the humbling defeat by anticipating the upcoming spring baseball season, during which it was expected the perennially successful LSU baseball team would compete for its fifth national championship. Apparently, in the midst of the present "debacle," the fans needed to acknowledge, in a highly public manner, the praiseworthy accomplishments of other LSU athletes and other Louisiana football teams, whose efforts were noticed as a way of restoring the callers' self-esteem and also of holding the LSU football team and university officials to the highest standards of the proud tradition. (50)

For several of these callers to the radio show, their "we" explicitly includes the historically persistent LSU team, including long-dead heroes and athletes from decades prior. For them, the radio call-in show provides a means to publicly and directly perform their identification with a group that spans wide swaths of time, including both the good and the bad. Although some of this does look like classic BIRGing, other features of the fan discourse do not appear reducible to it. Many fans, for example, explicitly rebuked their peers for their apparent willingness to CORF by "booing" in response to poor play: one caller "suggested that if people were going to boo at Tiger Stadium, they were not 'real Tiger fans' and needed to go to the University of Alabama where, ostensibly, less loyal fans likewise presided" (53). This fan, like others we have encountered, suggests that the differentiation of "real fans" from others is of paramount, quasi-moral importance and offers condemnation of illegitimate fans—in the form of the claim that they belong at the University of Alabama—on the basis of the impropriety of their discourse vis-à-vis the team. Marci Cottingham documents a similar instance of discursive policing and moralizing in the case of Pittsburgh Steelers fans: after watching a play in which the Steelers' quarterback failed to complete a pass, one fan in the stands "shouted an obscenity and expressed frustration at the quarterback's poor play. A middle-aged fan in front of us turned around and asked him if he realized how hard it was to throw a football in freezing weather and under those circumstances" (2012, 177). In pointedly questioning the disgruntled fan, the middle-aged fan clearly indicates both disapproval of that fan's speech and perhaps also of that fan's willingness to CORF.

In addition to explicit we discourse, then, partisan fans employ discursive practices that are aimed at distinguishing themselves as particularly devoted fans of their team. These include the contrast of themselves with "fair-weather" or "bandwagon" fans—such as, for example, the woman who called in to an LSU fan radio show to proclaim, "No matter what any other LSU fans may think, the 'Bengal Belles' are always in total support of the LSU team, no matter what happens. We have an undying support of them" (Zagacki and Grano 2005, 56). Other fans introduce themselves, in person or on social media, with declarations of their team loyalty, often making use of terms like "die-hard," "born and bred," or "life-long" to describe their continued allegiance. Here, as in the case of the collection and display of team symbols and colors, fans discursively reiterate their identification with the team and with the community it represents. Taking the panoply of explicitly self-identifying fan practices and discourse together at once, it is striking how urgently and how frequently fans engage in this reiteration.

The propensity of fans to tell, again and again, the narrative of their sporting allegiance, mirrors Foucault's analysis of confessional practice—the practice of reporting the most minute details of one's life not only to priests but also to doctors, teachers, and even ourselves. The rise of this impulse to tell the details of our lives, Foucault claims, produces a new form of selfhood in modern Europe. In *The History of Sexuality*, volume 1, he writes:

> The confession became one of the West's most highly valued techniques for producing truth. We have singularly become a confessing society. The confession has spread its effects far and wide. It plays a part in justice, medicine, education, family relationships, and love relationships, in the most ordinary affairs of everyday life, and in the most solemn rites; one confesses ones crimes, one's sins, one's thoughts and desires, ones illnesses and troubles. . . . [T]he obligation to confess is now relayed through so many different points . . . that we no longer perceive it as the effect of a power that constrains us. (1990a, 59–60)

We now love so much to confess, Foucault argues, that we find it necessary to produce more and more opportunities to "express" ourselves. We even perceive, in some cases, that our rights to tell the truth about ourselves are under threat and our discourse is repressed, and we conceive those who reveal the most to be the most liberated and the most authentic. Whereas in centuries prior, no one would bother recalling or recording the minutia of their lives—since this was reserved for the lives of personages of importance, like royals—in the modern world, even the humblest members of society are encouraged to keep journals, to record their thoughts, to submit themselves to thorough examination (Foucault 1995, 191). This sort of writing, along with the other forms of confessional practice that call forth the same discursive ethos (including, for example, the religious practice of confession and the taking of patient histories in medical practice), is radically *individuating*, according to Foucault. Like the power of panopticism in the exam, the confessional structure of modern society—which, as some have argued, has reached previously unforeseen intensity in the age of Facebook and microblogging—produces subjects who understand themselves as particular types of individuals in and through the self-knowledge they produce through their confessional practices.

To be able to label myself as a sports fan, and in particular, as a fan of a particular team, is to operate in this confessional structure. I tell you my sporting allegiance, and I have told you a truth about myself. Perhaps more importantly, I have told myself, again, who and what I am. Even when the explicit structure of the confession is not present, sports fandom provides a means to tell ourselves who we are—by wearing team apparel or team colors, by engaging in team rituals, by literally impressing its marks on our bodies.

This desire for classification, for a clear sense of identity, is as evident in the popularity of online quizzes that ask us to contemplate (and share with our friends) which Golden Girl we would be as it is in variations on the fan construction "I bleed purple and gold" and the ubiquitous fan habit of identifying oneself as part of the "we" that makes up that team. The metaphor of blood and the deployment of the first-person plural have the double effect of conveying an inner, hidden, essential truth about oneself and explicitly situating that truth in relation to a collective. Paradoxically, then, although the effect of sports fan discourse is in large measure individuating, insofar as it allows fans to claim for themselves a distinct identity, that identity never occurs in isolation. Fan discourse produces a subject who knows him- or herself *in relation*, a self who occupies a specific place in the social milieu—in short, an "I" who is part of a particular "we."

The I in Team: The "We" of Sports Fandom

The "we" of sports fandom is manifested, as I have argued, in several different ways and contributes to the production of subjects who are variously gendered, regionalized, and racialized. The practices of sports fandom contribute to the production and reproduction of these identities in the contemporary United States by habituating individuals into particular patterns of self-knowledge and interaction with the surrounding social world. Ironically, this habituation is demanding of sports fans and requires increasing expansion (particularly for men and boys, for whom the imperative to increase sports knowledge is especially acute), devotion, and consumer activity—though this demand is felt not primarily as a set of oppressive regulations but as a desire that must be pursued, shared, displayed, and talked about. Sports fandom has, then, undergone a drastic change since its inception in the nineteenth century as aberrant behavior, not only becoming de rigueur in many parts of the country, but insinuating itself throughout the identities, the lives, and, as we have seen, the deaths of its practitioners. In this respect, sports fandom may be described in terms that Foucault once used to describe sexuality:

> Through a reversal that doubtless had its surreptitious beginnings long ago . . .
> we have arrived at the point where we expect our intelligibility to come from
> what was for many centuries thought of as madness. . . . Hence the importance
> we ascribe to it, the reverential fear with which we surround it, the care we
> take to know it. Hence the fact that over the centuries it has become more
> important than our soul, more important almost than our life. (1990a, 156)

Though it is certainly true that sports fandom has not replaced sex as "the secret" of an individual's identity, it does, I have argued, work to produce individuals who find in it their own intelligibility, their own meaning, and their very selves. Lest we think this too large a claim, it is important to remember the extent to which sports fandom, in the contemporary world, is bound up with the normative gender regulations that govern modern sexuality, the familial and social bonds that connect the individual to her surrounding community, and—as I will argue in the following chapters—the racializing narratives that justify and reinforce white supremacy.[11]

Sports fandom's effects on these major organizing and hierarchizing features of contemporary life certainly explain its import to sports fans. But more than this, its subjectivizing effects suggest that it has import—and perhaps quite significant import—to more than mere individuals. Rather, sports fandom's reach into myriad practices that sustain gender, race, class, and region as we know them means that its objects are not merely individual subjects but whole populations and communities. Insofar as the everyday practices and meanings of sports fandom contribute to the meaning and retrenchment of race, to the regulation of gender and sexuality, and to the cohesion of regions and classes, it not only constitutes selves but contributes to the regulation and normalization of whole populations. As such, we must attend closely to it—not only to understand those individuals who call themselves sports fans, but to understand American identity today.

3

Putting the "We" in "We're Number One": Mascots, Team, and Community Identity

The residents of Ossining pride themselves on living in an "ethnically diverse" community. One of the threads that bind the community is attending Ossining schools and representing the Ossining Indians. I feel that the use of the Indian mascot unites Ossining.

. . .

The Forrest Hills Board of Education voted 5–0 on July 19 to retain the Anderson High School Redskins mascot, because of the overwhelming support shown by students, parents, teachers and members of the community. It was made clear to the board that the Redskins mascot *belongs to the students and alumni of Anderson, and that it will not be given up because of pressure or intimidation from outside groups such as the American Indian Movement.*

LETTERS TO THE EDITORS OF THE WESTCHESTER, New York
Journal News and the *Cincinnati Post* by supporters of Native American mascots[1]

Partisan sports fans, I have argued, use their fandom to cultivate and reproduce their own identities, not only as individuals, but as members of a larger, socially significant community—as an "I" who is part of a specific "we." Yet, the "we" of sports fandom does not obviously precede the practices of fandom. Though fan groups are often regionally based, the "we" of sports fandom is not reducible to region, as the fracturing of certain communities into rival fan bases makes clear: fans of the Chicago Cubs and the Chicago White Sox may live in the same city but do not constitute a coherent "we"; neither do fans of the Mets and the Yankees or fans of the rival Louisville Cardinals and Kentucky Wildcats basketball teams. Such intraregional divisions result, of course, from fans' partisan loyalty to different players and teams, but they are also often indicative of different conceptualizations of the communities that those teams are supposed to represent. Such cases make salient the extent to which partisan sports fans use their fandom to create and reassert the characteristics of the "we" to which they are loyal. How this happens, however, is a complex affair. In order to use their fandom in this way, sports fans need to identify both with "their" team and with the larger community that it is supposed to represent—which is no small task when we consider the innumerable differences between fans and the players who make up their teams, the diversity of the communities to which those teams belong, and the innumerable changes to both community and team that occur over fans' lifetimes. Engaging in partisan sports fandom, in other words, requires that fans adopt a complex set of symbolic practices that enables them to identify the athletic activity of strangers as meaningful for them and their community. Putting the "we" in "we're number one" involves, as I will argue, fan investment in socially potent symbols—and most notably, in the type of symbols we know as "mascots."

Although the adoption of sports team mascots has been a ubiquitous practice in the United States for some time, little philosophical work has addressed mascots' general significance or symbolic or social functions. The vast majority of the theoretical work that exists on mascots—in either philosophy or the social sciences—is focused on the question of Native American mascots and takes up the task of defending the claim that the usage of Native American mascots is indefensibly racist. This conclusion is, I believe, the correct one. However, the vast majority of scholars who have defended the claim that such mascots are racist have done so without significant attention to the symbolic function of mascots as such and their import to the broader social practices of sports fandom. There are good reasons for this omission. One can, of course, offer compelling arguments that demonstrate the racist status of Native American mascots insofar as these are instances of the dissemination of stereotypical or derogatory images of Native Americans, as Ward Churchill (2003) and others have done, or demonstrate the psychological harm caused by these images for Native persons, as Fryberg et al. (2008) have done. Such work is important and arguably correct in its assessment of the imagery of Native Americans that sports teams with Native American mascots reinforce. What this work does not do—indeed, does not aim to do—is to explain what is different about the usage of such images of Native Americans *as mascots*, as distinct from their usage in film, books, and so on. I will argue in what follows that an account of this specific ill—that is, the specific problems of using Native Americans as *mascots*—requires a fuller account of the function of mascots as such.

Now, to be fair, it's not true that no one in the anti–Native mascot camp has considered this problem. Those who have done so, however, have often been arguing from highly contestable or even false premises, which do not systematically investigate the usages or functions of actually existing mascots. As a result, it is not difficult to multiply defeating counterexamples when we are faced with such arguments. It is not, for example, defensible to argue that Native American mascots are offensive because they equate Native Americans with animals, when we observe that a majority of mascots simply are not animals. Likewise, it is not defensible to argue that Native American mascots are offensive because mascots are inherently trivializing, when we observe how many mascots there are that express deliberate valorization of the communities they represent (e.g., the Irish, the Packers, the Metropolitans, the Canadiens, or even the Rebels). If we are going to reject team names like "the Redskins"—and I think we should—then let us do it on sound grounds. The grounds we need require a philosophical investigation of the use of mascots as such—its purpose and function as a symbolic practice existing within a particular social/historical context.

In what follows, I will argue that mascots function as signifiers that draw into an artificial unity (1) a variety of teams existing over a period of time and thereby (2) a community of individuals who are thus able to *use* that team as their own symbolic locus of unification. My argument will proceed as follows: first, I will clarify my usage of the term "mascot" and analyze some data on actually existing mascots in order to explain why we ought to reject the dominant arguments against Native American mascots. Next, drawing on the thought of John Searle, I will suggest that mascots are better understood as contributing to the constitution of something than merely describing or symbolizing it. Third, through a brief historical investigation of the evolution of professional sports mascots, I will argue that the unification of teams and their concomitant communities is accomplished by appeal to a symbol that facilitates a particular fantasy of collective identity. Thus the usage of Native American mascots is racist, I will argue, not only because it involves stereotypical portrayals of Native Americans, but (more specifically) because it treats Native persons *simply* as a means to symbolic unification—and not, importantly, as members of the community they thus serve. In other words, in these cases mascots *work* as unifying signifiers precisely by being the *purely instrumental facilitator* of a group's collective fantasy of itself.

This robust account of the symbolic function of mascots will serve two purposes in my argument. First, it will enable me to offer a particularly striking example of the extent to which the practices of sports fandom are not innocuous but are often complicit in the maintenance of white supremacy. The example of Native American mascots is an important instance of the racializing effects of sports fandom, particularly for the white communities who use them. The usage of Native American mascots by non-Natives involves a specific form of racist practice, which also characterizes *other* elements of sports fandom that I will discuss in subsequent chapters. Second, and just as importantly for my larger purposes in this book, my account of the historical development of mascots and their key function in the social ontology of teams will enable me to offer an account of the means by which sports fans use their fandom to contribute to the constitution and reproduction of identities—including their own, that of the team, and that of the local community.

Terminological Clarifications and the Problems of Previous Accounts

In this section, I want to offer some terminological clarifications and set out some data that support the claims I have made about the inadequacy of previous accounts of mascots. First, when I refer to mascots, I have in mind a collection of related practices, some of which could be called by different names, depending on one's particular purposes. Often, for example, people distinguish between a team's nickname—say, the "Tigers"—and its mascot— say, "Mike the Tiger." Or, more controversially, we might distinguish between the nickname, "Illini," and the mascot, "Chief Illiniwek." There are good reasons for making this distinction. One might argue, as the NCAA did, that the portrayal of Chief Illiniwek by a white student "playing Indian" is more ethically objectionable than the simple use of a nickname associated with Native Americans (NCAA 2005). However, I will not maintain this distinction here. The reason for this is twofold: first, in most cases, it is quite tricky to maintain a clear dividing line between nicknames and their idealized material instantiations. On what side of the boundary, for example, do official team logos bearing physical representations of the nickname fall? The second, more important reason is that (as I will argue) these practices of naming and physically representing a name have, in the case of sports fandom, the same symbolic function and effects. Thus, statements against the usage of Native American imagery by sports teams have treated "mascots," "images," "iconography," "nicknames," "symbols," "logos," "personalities," and "artifice" as equivalent and as subject to the same censure (NAACP 1999; National Congress of American Indians 1993; US Commission on Civil Rights 2001; Five Civilized Tribes Intertribal Council 2001; American Psychological Association 2005). Whether a name is spelled out on a uniform or symbolically instantiated by a plush representation, the ostensible purpose is to represent the particular team with which it is associated. Following both pragmatic and post-structuralist accounts of meaning, then, I am suggesting that we understand names and mascots as part of a constellation of practices that give rise to a particular social effect—and thus that they are not meaningfully distinct for my present purposes (even if there may be other purposes for which such a distinction could be usefully maintained). So, unless I note otherwise, when I refer to a team's "mascot," I am referring both to its nickname and to the various forms of iconography that represent it (whether in two-dimensional depictions, human or humanoid costumes, or uniforms symbolic of it). I am choosing to foreground the *mascot* feature of these practices, rather than the nickname, the colors, or something else, because it makes these practices salient as a system of symbols that relies on *idealized representations* of the things they purport merely to signify, which, I will suggest, is important for their functionality.

Second, I am following Paul C. Taylor in using "racism" in a broad sense that includes any form of disregard for persons of a particular race. Defining racism in this way, according to Taylor, includes "the withholding of respect, concern, good-will, or care from the members of a race" (2013, 32), leaving open the possibility that such withholding may be intentional or unintentional and located primarily in the consequences of actions and practices or in the consciousness of individual agents. I thus allow that racism may take a variety of forms and be a characteristic of a variety of entities, including "people, actions, beliefs, practices, institutions, and attitudes" (34). Consequently, in order to demonstrate that the usage of Native American mascots is racist, I do not believe that I need to show that, say, a particular fan of the Atlanta Braves intends to ridicule Native Americans when she or he performs the "Tomahawk Chop." It will, instead, be enough to show that the usage of the "Braves" mascot (including the "Tomahawk Chop" and other associated symbolism) involves disregard for Native Americans.

Finally, throughout this book, I use the phrase "white supremacy" not primarily to refer to groups like the Ku Klux Klan but instead to "the system of domination by which white people have historically ruled over, and, in certain important ways, continue to rule over, non-white people" (Mills 1997, 1–2). Following philosophers of race like Taylor and Charles Mills, I use this term to describe the taken-for-granted pattern of unearned social privilege that white people continue to enjoy in the contemporary United States, which operates "independently of the ill will/good will, racist/antiracist feelings of particular individuals" (36). The fact that this racial hierarchy is *not* strictly dependent upon the beliefs or feelings of individual persons is significant, for to acknowledge complicity in "white supremacy," on these terms, is not to accuse individual white persons of being white supremacists in the manner of David Duke. Rather, because "white supremacy" indicates the fact that white persons are privileged economically, socially, and symbolically over nonwhite persons—such that white persons on the whole have better life chances and are culturally represented in more favorable terms than nonwhite persons—complicity can occur unintentionally. Indeed, as Mills and others point out, the prevalence of white supremacy paradoxically has the effect of rendering their privilege invisible to most white people. Though there certainly are explicitly racist white supremacists around today, much of my discussion of white supremacy in this book will not focus on them but on the everyday means by which sports fans unthinkingly reinforce white privilege and the concomitant disregard for or denigration of nonwhite persons.

With these terminological clarifications in mind, I will briefly address the data behind my rejection of at least some of the arguments that have been made about Native American mascots to date. To compile this current data, I examined the mascots used in the four major professional "revenue sports" leagues in the United States: the National Football League, Major League Baseball, the National Basketball Association, and the National Hockey League.[2] When looking closely at the types of professional sports mascots currently in use, it is clear that although one might suggest that nonhuman animals constitute a plurality of mascots today (depending on our classificatory schema), this menagerie is, to the contrary of claims made by some of the most well-known opponents of Native American mascots (King and Springwood 2001, 55–56), far from the majority.[3] Indeed, nonhuman animals represent less than one-third of all major league sports mascots in the United States (see table 1). There are, in fact, more human figures used as mascots— even excepting the special case of Native American mascots for comparative reasons—than there are animals. Although this ratio does differ from sport to sport, even football, which has the highest percentage of animal mascots, features animal mascots for slightly less than 50 percent of its teams. It is thus difficult to sustain the claim that Native American mascots simply treat Native Americans as animals—or, at least, it is difficult without significant supplemental argumentation.

It is also important to consider the breakdown of the types of persons who are used as mascots. Philosopher Peter Lindsay has argued that when humans who are not Native Americans are used as mascots, these references are to specific human groups that do not exist any longer (such as Vikings) and thus can be trivialized through their use in sports (2008, 212–213). Lindsay claims that Native Americans are thus mistreated by being implicitly relegated to this "trivial" class of persons when they are used as mascots. Here again, I do not think that this claim on its own is defensible when considering the sheer number of mascots that explicitly *do* represent actually existing persons and do so in an plainly valorizing way: this is especially true in the case of the category of persons who are known by their location—such as the Islanders, the Mets, etc.—and ethnic groups other than Native Americans such as the Celtics, and the Canadiens.

Still, the content of the symbols, figures, and persons used as mascots *does matter*. One would have to engage in some fairly serious philosophical ob-

TABLE 1. Types of Mascots in Major US Professional Sports Leagues, 2013

Major sports combined

Animals	40
Persons by occupation	30
Persons by location	11
Natural objects/phenomena	12
Human-created objects	7
Native Americans	5
Clothing color	4
Mythical persons	4
Supernatural beings	3
Arts	3
Other ethnic groups	2
Individual names	1
Total mascots	**122**

Football

Animals	15
Persons by occupation/activity	8
Mythical persons	3
Native Americans	2
Human-created objects	1
Persons by location	1
Individual names	1
Supernatural beings	1
Total mascots	**32**

Baseball

Persons by occupation/activity	9
Animals	8
Persons by location	5
Clothing color	3
Native Americans	2
Mythical persons	1
Supernatural beings	1
Natural objects/phenomena	1
Total Mascots	**30**

Basketball

Animals	8
Persons by occupation/activity	8
Human-created objects	5
Natural objects/phenomena	4
Persons by location	2
Arts	2
Ethnic groups	1
Total Mascots	**30**

Hockey

Animals	8
Persons by occupation/activity	5
Natural phenomena	5
Persons by location	3
Human-created objects	2
Natural objects	2
Native Americans	1
Supernatural beings	1
Clothing color	1
Arts	1
Other ethnic groups	1
Total Mascots	**30**

tuseness not to notice that choices of mascots are not arbitrary and that only certain sorts of things seem to *work* as mascots. In order to make sense of this, though, we will have to do two things: first, we will need to understand *what it means* for a mascot to "work"; second, we will need to examine the content and context required for this "working." In the next section, I will address the first of these two issues.

The Signifying—and Unifying—Function of Mascots

In *The History of Sexuality*, volume 1, Foucault concludes that, far from being a natural kind, "the notion of 'sex' made it possible to group together, in an artificial unity, anatomical elements, biological functions, conducts, sensations, and pleasures, and it enabled one to make use of this fictitious unity as a causal principle" (1990a, 154). Foucault's claim is that the rise of certain medical and psychiatric practices produces a category of knowledge—sex—that comes to be understood as the unitary point of origin from which an incredible variety of disparate phenomena supposedly proceed. Although there is not a science of mascots, their function as signifiers, as I will argue, is quite like that of "sex." Or, perhaps better, a mascot is the principle means by which a "team" is unified and figured as a unitary point of origin.

This is perhaps a counterintuitive claim, so let's analyze an example: the New York Yankees. First, it's important to note that, today, that which is signified by the term "New York Yankees" is more complex than it initially appears. We will, of course, want to say that it signifies a baseball team located in the Bronx, being composed of a particular set of individuals, perhaps including a manager and front office organization. But once we begin to enumerate the necessary constituent parts of the Yankees, we run into problems. Let us consider, for example, when Alex Rodriguez was finally released from his contract—did the Yankees still exist? Yes, of course; even if A-Rod had been a necessary feature of an adequate extensional definition of the Yankees up to that moment, the act of his release rendered the meaning of "the Yankees" unequivocally distinct from him.

Yet, the meaning of "New York Yankees" is further complicated when we consider that its meaning is not merely limited to isolated instances of time. Rather—and just as importantly for fans—the "New York Yankees" is an entity that persists over time, despite innumerable personnel changes. Thus fans and commentators are able to "follow the Yankees," to track the evolution of "their" performance, to expound upon the significance of "their" leading the all-time series against "their" rivals, the Boston Red Sox. And yet there are significant respects in which there *is not a team "there"*: rather, there are innumerable teams over the course of years. For not only is there not the same team year to year; "there" is often not even the same team from one month to the next (or even, arguably, one play to the next). Still, as Stephen Mumford puts it, the allegiance of sports fans depends on "the endurance of its intentional object," the team, despite the fact that it is quite difficult to specify "what the endurance of its object consists in. Even a gap in existence seems to be no insurmountable obstacle to [a team's] identity" (2004, 188). Although we might be inclined to point to legal conventions like franchise or charter to ground team persistence and, thus, the intentional object of fan devotion, this, too, is problematic. It is unworkable, first of all, because fans are not devoted to franchises as legal entities; often, in fact, fans have an overtly hostile relationship to the ownership and bureaucracy of the team. Even when fans have warm feelings for their ownership or franchise, it is by virtue of their love for the team, not vice versa. Second, and more pressingly, there are problem cases that illustrate the implausibility of the claim that a team's persistence consists in its franchise or legal structure. The Cleveland Browns, for example, have been composed of two distinct ownership organizations and

franchises—between which there was even a gap in existence—but are nevertheless conceived of by Browns fans as a single team to which they have never
stopped being devoted.[4] How, then, does the notion of a team—with lifetime
records, championships won, lifelong fans, and so on—function?

Mumford argues that teams are "social substances," by which he means
that their identity is "to a degree conventional and conspiratorial." In other
words, teams exist over time to the extent that enough of the surrounding
community of observers treats them as such. Thus, Mumford argues, "one
of the components that are constitutive of the substance and its persistence
through time is the intentional allegiances of which they are the object"
(2004, 191). In other words, although the practices of sports fandom require
an intentional object toward which fandom (or, to use Mumford's language,
"allegiance") is directed, that intentional object is significantly constituted *by*
sports fandom. However, Mumford claims that there must be "at least some
metaphysical grounding" for the agreement by sports fans that there is a sin-
gular team "there"—but grants that specifying this grounding is indeed quite
dicey: there seem to be no necessary or sufficient conditions for identity of
teams *other* than this agreement. Still, Mumford argues, *something* must persist in each case that will "persuade enough people that the conspiracy is sufficiently rational" (192).

Specifying the "something" whose persistence grounds the identity of the
Yankees involves us in a ship of Theseus–esque puzzle that will be insoluble
as long as we assume that a team is like an artifact, or even like a "substance,"
however social that substance may be. If, however, we allow that a team may
not, strictly speaking, be an object, but instead a name for a certain pattern
of relationships, then the problem may be more manageable. In his book *The
Construction of Social Reality*, John Searle argues that many features of the
social world are simply the product of "collective intentionality." These "social facts" are dependent upon individuals sharing "we intentions," which can
range from "we are executing a pass play" (in football) to "we are having a
cocktail party." In every case, the social fact created—whether it be playing
football or having cocktails—is dependent for its existence, in part, on the
collective agreement of the individuals involved (1995, 26).

One might draw on this argument to claim that the underlying metaphysical essence of the Yankees is the collective intentionality of the players—that
is, their "we intentions" to be a team together. But, while it is surely correct
that such collective intentionality on the part of the players is a necessary
condition for being *a* team, it is certainly false that their collective intentionality is enough to make them *that team*, the Yankees. You and I may collectively intend to play together as the Yankees, but while we may form a team,

we lack the relevant agreement from our wider social milieu to make us part of the team that included, at various points, Babe Ruth, Mickey Mantle, and Reggie Jackson. This is because *that team* is an example of what Searle calls an "institutional fact"—a collectively imposed function that is dependent upon collective agreement for the function to be possible (1995, 41). Institutional facts, like the value of money and scoring points in football, depend upon a collective agreement about "status-functions" of certain phenomena. Such facts, according to Searle, depend upon an agreement of the form "X counts as Y in [context] C" (46) for their existence, since, apart from such an agreement, there is nothing about the exchange of bits of paper or the carrying of a ball across a line that makes them significant—and, indeed, apart from this agreement there is no such thing as "money" or "points" at all. Thus, institutional facts or objects are fundamentally patterns of interaction, regulated by collective agreement about the *status* of a certain phenomenon: namely, that it (X) will have a particular function (Y) in some specified context (C). In the same way that collective social agreement governs when and where the utterance of certain words will result in my being married, it is collective social agreement that governs the continued existence of the Yankees and their persistence over time. There is no way to be "married," just as there is no way for Ruth, Mantle, and Jackson to be members of the same "team," apart from the agreement that makes these functions possible.

Whether this agreement is *rational* or not is perhaps as difficult a question in the case of money as it is in the case of sports fandom. In each case, we seem to be involved, as Searle puts it, in a kind of circular justification: the Yankees exist because people believe that they do. I take no position here on the rationality of the agreement, because it seems to me irrelevant. Even if we grant that the collective intentionality of fans or money-users is entirely self-referential, this will not change the status of Babe Ruth or a hundred-dollar bill or, importantly, the real consequences that would follow our attempts to will ourselves to be Yankees or a person's thieving of such a bill. Still, it is perhaps more difficult to imagine why we might collectively agree to the existence of the historically persistent Yankees than to the value of money, since the functions made possible by *this* institutional fact are more saliently useful than those made possible by a professional baseball team.

Answers to this "why" question need not, however, take the form of rational justifications. Sports fandom is decidedly a-rational. Allegiances to sports teams, like allegiances to friends and family members, are, even if rationally justifiable, primarily *felt*, or in Mumford's words, experienced as "emotional attachment" (2004, 184). For this reason, it is unclear why such emotional attachments would need to be metaphysically grounded in a way that is "rational"—they might just as well, I think, be grounded in vague feelings of connection or heritage, or even in the felt imperative to follow social convention. In fact, the motivation required for treating a team *as a team* may very well be precisely affective and caught up with the desire of fans to identify with (or against) its fortunes. Mumford even admits that such fantasies of identification are a key feature of allegiance to a sports team when he writes, "Part of the object of the allegiance is the supporters themselves: They support an entity of which they are a part" (193). However, Mumford suggests that this interesting feature of sporting allegiance is a consequence of his account of the identity of sports teams, rather than a constitutive feature of them. But if we take seriously the extent to which fan behavior *is* constitutive of a team's identity (as Mumford suggests), we will have to acknowledge that such behavior need not be (and often is not) motivated by the rational appeal to a metaphysical grounding but could instead be motivated by an affective attachment that need not be particularly rational. If this is true, then I think we must ask *not* "to what are fans becoming attached" but rather "*what are the mechanisms whereby fans become* attached" to a team, such that there could be "a team" *there?*

Returning to Searle's description of the mechanism involved in the collective imposition of status functions is helpful here. Status functions (which, again, take the form "X counts as Y in C") are dependent not only upon collective intentionality but also upon *language.* In order for X to "count" as Y in some context, the members of the relevant group must agree to collectively represent it in the same way. As Searle puts it, "Physically X and Y are exactly the same thing. The only difference is that we have imposed a status on the X element, and this new status needs *markers*, because, empirically speaking, there isn't anything else there" (2004, 69). These markers can be words or word-like symbols, Searle claims (75), but in every case, such "collective representation . . . requires some vehicle. Just scrutinizing or imagining the features of the X element will not do the job" (74–75). Considering our previous examples of Ruth, Mantle, and Jackson illustrates why we need such markers. These players do not share any intrinsic features that obviously make them members of the same team; though they shared we intentions with their own teammates from time to time, they never shared such we intentions as a group, since they never played together. Yet, it is undeniable that they "count" as members of the historically persistent team, the Yankees. That they function as such is only possible because of a linguistic practice that marks them with this status.

A mascot is just such a status-marking linguistic practice. The function of a mascot, I think, is to facilitate the collective agreement and attachment of fans. In so doing, these markers draw together disparate persons, events, plays, losses, wins, riots, championships, ticket sales, and so on, into an artificial unity—a team—that is then, in Foucault's language, understood as that which *underlies* all of these things, or is their causal origin. The institution of a mascot (as name and symbol) is a discursive practice that makes possible the sense of the numerical identity of a team and thus contributes to the constitution of it. Mascots, then, both represent *and help to bring about* that which is represented. Importantly, they need not do this through literal speech acts—symbols such as colors or animals or Yankees pennants can work just as well.

Moreover, the unifying signification of mascots is not carried out in isolation but is more or less explicitly connected to the identification of a team with the community it represents. That is, the unification of disparate entities and phenomena into the historically persistent "Yankees" *facilitates* the identification of the Yankees with individual persons from New York. It is by subsuming the multiple and changing individuals who make up these teams into the symbol of the team that I, as a fan, am able to identify with their fates. Thus the secondary function of the team-constituting institution of mascots is, I think, the identification and unification of a group of people (fans) who conceive themselves as related *to one another* at least in part because of their relations to that team. In other words, mascots work not only to constitute a team but also to enable the self-identification of a *fan base*, which is a particular sense of collective or communal identity. Thus, when the symbol of the mascot draws together innumerable elements into a supposedly unitary "team," it does this, I think, for a larger purpose: facilitating the sense of a larger artificial unity: the community.

In order to investigate the connections between the unification of a team to the unification or identification of a larger community, I want to examine one more example, this time one that is closer to home for me, as a native of south Louisiana: the LSU Tigers. In the case of the Tigers, we have the same major symbolic elements as the Yankees: individuals subsumed to a larger symbol in order to reiterate the existence of a continuous historical entity (here, LSU football). This subsumption was dramatically illustrated in the Tigers' ritual introductions on the Jumbotron preceding each 2012 home game in Baton Rouge's Tiger Stadium: as each starting player's name was announced (to the cheers of the 90,000 assembled Tiger faithful), a video image of him in LSU uniform, yellow helmet and all, appeared on the large screen. As though the uniform were not enough to enact his rebirth as one "Tiger" among many, the image of each player's face was, for a moment, digitally altered to appear with disturbingly realistic stripes, yellow eyes, and a catlike version of his own visage (LSU Starting Lineup Video 2012). The individuals in question were able to become meaningful as representatives of the fans in the stands, or *as local heroes*, precisely by being dramatically brought under the sign of the mascot.

The local pride that is fostered by such symbolic unifications by mascot should not be underestimated. The everyday dealings of hometown or regional teams are reported on in excruciating detail in local papers; devoted fans discuss the fortunes of "their" teams using the pronoun "we," not "they"; the cities and supporters of rival teams are mocked as unsavory in some way or another (Zagacki and Grano 2005). Moreover, teams' fan bases are overwhelmingly localized: fans tend to form allegiances to teams local to their hometowns—which are stable in cases where individual persons move away, but which do not always survive the relocation of the *team* to another locale. In other words, as social scientists who study sports fandom have suggested, one of the primary functions of contemporary sports fandom is to foster a sense of community belonging in an increasingly fragmented metropolis (Hognestad 2012; Danielson 1997, 5). My claim, then, is that this communal "we" that is fostered, encouraged, and performed by the nearly ubiquitous fan chant "We're number one" is itself facilitated by the institution of mascots— apart from which it would be much more difficult to find a "we" to identify with at all.

But what is it about the mascot that makes this "we" workable? In other words, what is it about mascot symbols that enable them to function in this doubly identifying way? If successful mascots have served to facilitate the unification of a team and its concomitant community, we should be able to articulate *what is necessary* in order for a particular signifier to be able to work as a mascot—but we should not necessarily expect that those conditions of efficacy require anything like rationality, strictly speaking. Because the meaning and effectiveness of a signifier is ultimately dependent upon its context—meaning that symbols work differently at different times—my investigation of the conditions of mascots' efficacy will proceed historically.

Mascots' Evolution and Efficacy

In a 1907 article, a sports reporter for the *New York Times* wrote, "Local patriotism, as manifested in baseball, is a strange, irrational pastime. The crowd of local patriots have no hesitation in violently applauding this season as a native the same player whom last year they violently hissed as an alien enemy" (quoted in Danielson 1997, 9). This turn of phrase illustrates what a good mascot must do: it must be powerful enough to make friends of my enemies and to make family of strangers. We must, somehow, come to feel that

the honor of *our community* is at stake in the batting, tackling, and shooting
fortunes of people who may have minimal knowledge of our geographical
origins, our traditions, or even our language.[5] What kinds of symbols can accomplish this? If we look at our contemporary classes of mascots all at once,
I think that we will be at a loss to explain the panoply of figures there represented. Instead, I think it will be more productive to again take a hint from
Foucault and recognize that when we are dealing with discursive practices,
we should not expect univocal explanations or historically neutral or static
phenomena. So, in a Foucaultian spirit, I want to do a brief historical analysis
of professional baseball and football[6] mascots in the United States, paying attention to the moments of discontinuity and division rather than continuity
and unification.

When we view professional baseball and football teams and their mascots historically, it is striking how very little continuity there is between the
earliest forms of mascots or team names and the most recent (see tables 2
and 3). It is, in some ways, difficult to imagine how the images of red stockings (1869), on the one hand, and diamondbacks (1998), on the other, could
be equally (or even similarly) effective as unifying signifiers—or it is at least
difficult to imagine this at their advent. One could easily imagine a signifier
like a red stocking *becoming* culturally meaningful given time and agreement
in usage; a pragmatic account of meaning should expect no less. The story
is more complicated, however, when one considers a context in which these
signifiers are new.

The earliest such signifiers—such as the Athletics, Redcaps, and Brown-
stockings of nineteenth-century baseball—are purely descriptors of the team,
in either its location (the Philadelphia Athletic Club) or apparel. This trend
was largely repeated in professional football, with the addition of names that
simply reflected the occupation of its athletes or the sponsoring business entity. Significantly, though, these teams were not simply members of a glorified
beer league; they were professional teams, generating enough fan loyalty to
support a business—and ultimately, a big business, that was organized into
the revenue-generating machines of Major League Baseball and the National
Football League. And yet such teams did generate such fan loyalty and identification by, apparently, asking fans to identify with the color of a sock.

But this isn't quite true, of course: the name, and the uniform, in these
early cases, is almost incidental—and it is so precisely because the work of
unification it must perform is already supported (or, perhaps, accomplished)
by other means. Who is that team? Well, they're the team from the Philadelphia Athletic Club, from Cincinnati, from the Panhandle Railroad, or
from the Jefferson Park neighborhood. In these early cases, the naming looks

TABLE 2. Baseball Mascots Chronologically, with Developments in Racial Segregation and
Professionalization

1860 Philadelphia Athletics	1894 Sioux City Cornhuskers	**1921 Minor league draft**
1869 Cincinnati Redstockings	1899 St. Louis Perfectos	**instituted**
1870 Chicago Whitestockings	1900 Cleveland Lake Shores	1932 Brooklyn Dodgers
1870 National League founded;	**1900 American League founded**	1936 Boston Bees
segregation instituted	1900 St. Louis Cardinals	1936 San Diego Padres
1871 Boston Redstockings	1901 Baltimore Orioles	**1947 Reintegration begins**
1876 Boston Redcaps	1901 Boston Americans	1961 Minnesota Twins
1882 New York Gothams	1901 Chicago White Sox	**1965 Amateur draft instituted**
1883 Boston Beaneaters	1901 Cleveland Blues	1965 Houston Astros
1883 St. Louis Brownstockings	1901 Washington Senators	1969 Kansas City Royals
1885 New York Giants	1902 Chicago Cubs	1969 Montreal Expos
1885 St. Louis Browns	1902 Cleveland Broncos	1969 Seattle Pilots
1887 New York Metropolitans	1903 Cleveland Naps	1970 Milwaukee Brewers
1887 Pittsburgh Allegheneys	1903 Los Angeles Angels	1972 Texas Rangers
1888 Brooklyn Bridegrooms	1903 New York Highlanders	1977 Seattle Mariners
1890 Chicago Colts	1907 Boston Doves	1977 Toronto Blue Jays
1890 Cincinnati Reds	1908 Boston Red Sox	1993 Colorado Rockies
1890 Philadelphia Phillies	1911 Boston Rustlers	1993 Florida Marlins
1891 Brooklyn Grooms	1911 Brooklyn Trolley Dodgers	1998 Arizona Diamondbacks
1891 Pittsburgh Pirates	1912 Boston Braves	1998 Tampa Bay Devil Rays
1894 Detroit Tigers	1913 New York Yankees	2005 Washington Nationals
1894 Grand Rapids Rustlers	1915 Cleveland Indians	2008 Tampa Bay Rays

Note: Includes mascots of NL and AL teams (current and defunct) as well as professional teams later
admitted to MLB. In cases where a team uses the same name as a previous one and is in the same locale, I
have used the earlier date.

much more like a constative. It is, largely, merely significant of what is already
"there": a group of people united by living together in a particular locale. Indeed, in these early days of professional baseball and football, many players—
even professional ones—were literally *from* the cities and neighborhoods for
which their teams were named. In such cases, the team's being *that team* is
not dependent upon the standard institutional fact rule, "X counts as Y in C."
Even though the team is a social fact characterized by collective intentionality, it is precisely the sort of case that Searle describes thusly: "the 'rule' does
not add anything but a label, so it is not a constitutive rule" (1995, 44). Names
of this sort are simply labels for preexisting characteristics, meaning that being identified with *that team* is simply a matter of sharing those characteristics (notably, local origins). Given this reality, it is not difficult to imagine
fans developing an attachment to or identification with a team. This sort of
identification is of a piece with other familiar forms of local pride.

What seems quite different, however, is the "irrational" local patriotism
documented by the 1907 *Times* reporter—the sense of a community whose
boundaries and kin are being constantly remade by changes in contract and

TABLE 3. Football Mascots Chronologically, with Developments in Racial Segregation and Professionalization

1901 Columbus Panhandles	1924 Buffalo Bisons	1936 Pittsburgh Americans
1901 St. Louis Cardinals	1924 Cleveland Bulldogs	1936 Rochester Tigers
1902 Toledo/ Kenosha Maroons	1924 Columbus Tigers	1937 Cincinnati Bengals
1905 Detroit Heralds	1924 Frankford Yellow Jackets	1937 Los Angeles Bulldogs
1906 Canton Bulldogs	1924 Kansas City Blues	1940 Pittsburgh Steelers
1910 Rochester Jeffersons	**1925 Red Grange signed**	1944 Boston Yanks
1915 Staten Island Stapletons	1925 Detroit Panthers	1944 Brooklyn Tigers
1916 Akron Burkhardts	1925 Kansas City Cowboys	**1946 Reintegration begins**
1916 Muncie Flyers	1925 New York Giants	1946 Buffalo Bills
1916 Providence Steam Roller	1925 Pottsville Maroons	1946 Chicago Rockets
1918 Akron Pros	1926 Akron Indians	1946 Cleveland Browns 1946
1919 Green Bay Packers	1926 Brooklyn Lions	Los Angeles Dons
1919 Racine Legion	1926 Buffalo Rangers	1946 Miami Seahawks
1920 APFA (later NFL) formed	1926 Duluth Eskimos	1946 San Francisco 49ers
1920 Buffalo All-Americans	1926 Hartford Blues	1949 Chicago Hornets
1920 Chicago/Decatur Staleys	1926 Los Angeles Buccaneers	1952 Dallas Texans
1920 Cleveland Tigers	1926 Louisville Colonels	1953 Baltimore Colts
1920 Dayton Triangles	1926 Racine Tornados	1960 Boston Patriots
1920 Hammond Pros	1927 New York Yankees	1960 Houston Oilers
1920 Rock Island Independents	1928 Detroit Wolverines	1960 Titans of New York
1921 Chicago Bears	1929 Boston Bulldogs	**1962 Washington Redskins**
1921 Cincinnati Celts	1929 Minneapolis Redjackets	**integrate**
1921 Cleveland Indians	1929 Newark/Orange Tornadoes	1963 Kansas City Chiefs
1921 Detroit Tigers	1930 Brooklyn Dodgers	1963 New York Jets
1921 Evansville Crimson Giants	1930 Portsmouth Spartans	1965 Atlanta Falcons
1921 Louisville Brecks	1932 Boston Braves	1965 Miami Dolphins
1921 Minneapolis Marines	**1933 Segregation instituted**	1967 New Orleans Saints
1921 Tonawanda Lumbermen	1933 Boston Redskins	1976 Seattle Seahawks
1921 Washington Senators	1933 Philadelphia Eagles	1976 Tampa Bay Buccaneers
1922 Ban on use of college	1933 Pittsburgh Pirates	1995 Carolina Panthers
players)	1934 Detroit Lions	1995 Jacksonville Jaguars
1922 Milwaukee Badgers	1934 St. Louis Gunners	1996 Baltimore Ravens
1922 Oorang Indians*a*	**1936 First NFL draft (1936)**	1999 Tennessee Titans
1923 Duluth Kelleys	1936 Boston Shamrocks	2002 Houston Texans
1923 St. Louis All-Stars	1936 Cleveland Rams	

Note: Includes NFL teams (current and defunct), plus teams from AFL II, AFL IV, AAFC and APFA (each of which featured teams later incorporated into modern NFL). In cases where a team uses the same name as a previous one and is in the same locale, I have used the earlier date.

*a*Only team with Native American mascot to feature Native American players.

sock color. This change in sports fandom, it seems to me, reflects changes in the development of the cultural practices of sport—and marks the emergence of true *mascots* as we know them today. As baseball and football become increasingly professionalized, and their athletes commodified, the teams involved become increasingly heterogeneous and decreasingly identified with their locales through birth or background. This is displayed prominently in table 2, where increasing professionalization and commodification of baseball and football are marked by the advent of organized professional leagues, restrictions on players eligible to be treated as professional, the institution of drafts, and the advent of the highly publicized signings of "star" athletes. In concert with these developments, players are traded or accept lucrative contracts far away from their childhood homes. Competition between proliferating leagues (not to mention teams) drives this diaspora of athletes *and* desire for a hometown team that will still, somehow, inspire civic pride. Along with increasing professionalization and commodification, then, we see the emergence of names—of mascots—that conjure increasingly powerful, even fantastical, images. Who are we? We are the Broncos! We are the Yankees! We are . . . the Indians.

Even these more fantastical images, of course, are of various types. At times, as in the case of the Yankees, these images are simply idealized images of the community itself. The community cloaks its athletes in a vision of itself or of its proudest moments, and they *become* Texans, or Patriots, or Yankees, no matter their personal origins. And, importantly, the projection of this idealized image allows these teams to *represent the community itself* in this idealized way.

But other symbols are of an apparently different sort. The Tigers, the Spartans, the Falcons, the Tornadoes, the Jets, the Vikings, the Astros, the Rockies —these images are, I think, fantastical images of power, force, and legendary or even superhuman capability. These images are the stuff of dime novels and Hollywood films, larger-than-life embodiments of daring, danger or might itself, even though they refer, literally, to entities or objects whose actual existence is (or was) far more mundane. The vagaries of actual existence, truthfully, are not the point in the case of these mascots. It does not matter whether individual Norse men were fearsome in battle, or even whether they wore the famous horned helmets—just as it does not matter whether actual Tigers or Falcons pose a physical threat to humans, as we destroy their habitats, nor whether the machinery of a jet engine (short-lived as it is) is a worthy model for the bodies of our athletes. What matters, instead, is the collective fantasy of power or aggression that they inspire—the sense that we, too, become fearsome or daring when identified with them. This class of cases involves the invocation of ideals associated not with a specific feature of the community itself but with the force of winning in competition—and this is the class to which Native American mascots belong. As Laurel Davis points out, "Native Americans are stereotyped as wild, aggressive, violent, brave, stoic, and as having a fighting spirit, traits commonly valued in athletics" (1993, 12).[7]

In a third class of cases of long-standing team names (such as the Reds, the White Sox, or the Red Sox), the unifying signifier *becomes* a mascot, insofar as it conjures images of the heroes of yore or the "tradition" of the community that was their home. In each of these three cases, though, it is important to note that the literal content signified by the mascot is important *only* to the extent that it conjures an image of the community as ideal, powerful, historically significant, or some combination of the three. Some images simply will not do—feminine figures, for example, are apparently unworkable, as are any other images tainted in the cultural imagination as weak; also unworkable, in many cases, is a mascot from a team's previous location, particularly if it is too evocative of that region or its people. The important thing, in each case, is that the content of the mascot image matters, *not* because its adopters have substantial interest in the literal thing or person signified by them or because it makes a rational appeal to some metaphysically grounded continuity, but to the extent that the adoption of this mascot can produce a strong enough image to serve as an *instrument* of unification whose meaning is not limited to its literal referent.

One might suggest, at this point, that the fantastical images of communal identity that I have described here are not, in fact, nearly so important as the marketing strategies employed by the owners of these professional teams, whose financial goals are achieved precisely by inciting the sort of brand loyalty evinced by dedicated sports fans. There is a vast literature on marketing and the commodification of identity, which has established the significant role of advertising and the fetishization of capitalist consumption in the reproduction of contemporary subjectivities (Hebdige 1979; McCreanor et al. 2005; Croghan et al. 2006). In such accounts, the commodification of sports works precisely to make a "'consumer' feel like a 'fan' . . . through consumer goods." It is, in other words, "through consumer goods that the 'fan' can increase their knowledge, and more importantly, display their commitment . . . and [thus] feel increasingly integrated within their chosen supporter community. For crucially, this is what the contemporary sport venue sells" (Crawford 2004, 81). Thus, one might argue, once we have reached the level of cultural practice operative in professional sports team mascots in the United States, what might appear to be the identification of a community—say, in "Red Sox Nation"—is only a very successful branding campaign. The "metaphysical grounding" in such a case would thus be nothing more than the skill of professional marketers, who dupe individuals into believing that their own identities are at stake in the support of a particular team—which is to say, a particular business.

There is clearly a significant marketing element in the production and consumption of mascots (and thus, of sports teams), and nothing in my argument is meant to reject the notion that the identity of contemporary teams and their concomitant fan bases are inextricably bound with their places in the capitalist economy. On the contrary, I have suggested that the advent of increasingly fantastical mascot images is largely necessitated by the community fluctuations occasioned by the increasing commodification of professional sports and athletes. However, accepting this claim does not imply that we necessarily accept that mascots are reducible to ad campaigns. Indeed, it seems to me that a sufficiently robust account of the effects and functions of mascots must not accept such a reduction. Reducing mascots simply to effective branding fails to explain the difference between fan loyalty and simple brand loyalty—why, that is, even the most loyal purchasers of Coca-Cola or Budweiser do not tend to think of themselves as members of a community or act as though the product they consume is integral to their identities in some way. Moreover, simply writing off mascots as marketing tools and sports fans as dupes does not address the specific content of that marketing or the fantasies that make it compelling. In other words, even if it is true that mascots are examples of effective marketing (and again, I do not deny that they are), leaving the analysis here fails to explain the specific character of fan involvement—an involvement that is, again, in large measure constitutive of the entity (or "team") being marketed. Although it is crucial to recognize the role of consumption in the practice of sports fandom, then, a robust account of mascots requires *both* attention to the *content* of the mascot images that facilitate communal identification *and* a recognition of the active role of sports fans in adopting mascots—and thereby, communities. I have attempted to do precisely this by offering a historical analysis of the advent and content of mascot images that takes the fandom activity of community constitution and identification seriously.

The Instrumentalization of Native Americans as Mascots

I have argued that mascots are unifying signifiers that facilitate the constitution of historically persistent teams and, in so doing, enable the identification of a community with its team. Historical analysis reveals that the content of the mascot image must be sufficiently powerful (in at least one of three ways) to make this latter unification possible. We are now, finally, in a position to return to the question of Native American mascots. Keeping in mind the function of mascots, and the means by which this function is accomplished,

I want to conclude by articulating why the mascotting of Native Americans is so deeply troubling.

Following the implications of my argument, the use of Native Americans as mascots is the usage of Native American persons as instrumental facilitators of a fantasy of communal identity. This usage is facilitated through a fantastical caricature of "the Indian" that "works" as an image of the second type I describe above—an image of power and violence. Rather than functioning as an idealized image of the actual community it represents, "the Indian" as a mascot reduces innumerable peoples, families, and cultures to a fearsome symbol that may be adopted purely to foster a sense of the community it represents as powerful and daring—as the star of its own Hollywood film. The realities of the lives of actual indigenous people are immaterial to this usage; this fact is made disturbingly vivid by the performance of rituals like the "Tomahawk Chop" by a sea of mostly white, foam tomahawk–wielding fans to the tune of a caricatured Native drum beat. These images are certainly, as Churchill, Fryberg et al., and others have pointed out, stereotypical and degrading, and their effectiveness as mascot images seems dependent upon the reiteration of these stereotypical images (it is difficult to imagine portrayals of, say, contemporary life on the reservation as effective mascots). We could, in fact, stop here, and note that the proliferation of these derogatory images, despite the protestations of Native American groups, involves a clear disregard for a group of persons based on their race—and thus constitutes a racist practice. As I suggested in the beginning, however, I think that there is a particular ill associated with using these images *as mascots*, and to understand why, we must recognize what the usage of such images in this context implies.

More than treating Native American persons as inconsequential or reducible to a simple stereotype, their mascotting requires the tacit exclusion of actual indigenous people, for their inclusion could disturb their effectiveness as a symbol that facilitates the unification of a (white) community to which they, decidedly, *do not belong*. In other words, although Native American mascots are, in significant respects, "like" mascots of Vikings or Astros (insofar as they are figured as images of human power), their insidiousness lies in their peculiar combination of instrumentalization *and* exclusion. The usage of "the Indians" or "the Redskins" as a unifying signifier requires *both* the reduction of actually existing persons to an image capable as serving as the medium of a fantasy of communal identity *and* the elimination of these actual persons from the community so constituted, lest they disturb the fantasy—or, more pressingly, pose a threat to the community instrumentalizing them. Ironically, that is, the figure of "the Indian" as a powerful image requires envisioning actual indigenous persons as literally powerful, violent, threatening, or intimidating *to those treating them as mascots*. This is the image of Native Americans as savage threat to white civilization that must be eliminated—unless their power can be contained and harnessed for "our" own purposes. The use of Indian mascots, in short, involves the tacit reiteration of a sentiment that has more or less explicitly characterized white supremacy: these people exist *for us*.

The extent to which indigenous peoples are *purely* instrumentalized by Native American mascots is made more salient when we consider the racialized limits of the teams and communities they serve to constitute and the surrounding cultural context that makes their caricatured images effective. The Boston Braves, the first professional team in the United States to make use of a Native American mascot, did so in 1912—forty-two years after the "gentleman's agreement" that institutionalized racial segregation for the National League and only twenty-two years after the massacre at Wounded Knee. The few Native American athletes who were allowed into the league during this period faced significant racist taunting, including "war whoops . . . [and] ki yis" from fans, "silly poetry . . . [and] hideous looking cartoons" from the local sports media, and the nearly ubiquitous nickname of "Chief" from their teammates (Vascellaro 2011). Their status as racially marked outsiders was made consistently clear, even as fantastical images of that marking were being used as symbols for the team and community that denied them full membership. Similarly, the NFL's oldest Native American mascot still in use today—the Washington Redskins—was adopted in 1933, the year that racial segregation was instituted in professional football.[8] Prior uses of Native American mascots in professional football included teams named after existing baseball franchises (the Cleveland Indians and the Boston Braves) and, in one notable case, a "publicity stunt" team made up entirely of Native players who toured the country for the explicit purpose of drumming up sales for the owner's dog kennel business (Pro Football Hall of Fame 2013). Even the leader of this "all-Indian" team, Jim Thorpe, who went on to be named the greatest athlete of the twentieth century in 1950 after success on a handful of other professional football teams and the 1912 Olympics, was treated more as symbol than man. Thorpe's 1953 *New York Times* obituary, for example, opens, "Jim Thorpe, the Indian whose exploits . . . won him acclaim as one of the greatest athletes of all time, died today in his trailer home" (*New York Times* 1953). In both football and baseball, athletes of Native descent, even when they were stars, were not so much integrated as tokenized, caricatured, and themselves treated as mascots. Native American mascots reached their peak of new usage, then, during a period of de jure white supremacy and in tandem with a host of other practices that enforced the secondary status of actual Native Americans.

Continuing this trend today are the NFL's Washington Redskins—ironically, the last team in the league to racially integrate, in 1962 (T. Smith 2012)—whose team owner Dan Snyder continues to insist that "Redskins" honors Native Americans, while refusing to meet with actual Native Americans who dispute that characterization (Cox and Maske 2015). Opponents of the activists who speak out against the Redskins mascot, more often than not, express—more or less explicitly—views like those of one particularly open author of a letter to the editor of the *Washington Post*, whose argument is based on the claim that the name "never held any such weight or meaning *for me*. . . . As for whether the Redskins name marginalizes Native Americans, that battle was lost to the U.S. government and non-natives' greed more than a century ago" (*Washington Post* 2015; emphasis mine). The message here is quite clear: Native Americans are not part of this conversation, because white views and feelings are the important ones, this matter having long been settled. Beyond the Redskins, whose mascot is the frequently singled out among other Native American mascots for its usage of a slur, teams and communities all over the United States continue to instrumentalize fantastical images of Natives while, as Paul Taylor puts it, "continuing to treat Indian tribes as wards of the state" (2013, 145).

With mascotting's combination of instrumentalization and exclusion in mind, it is perhaps telling that one of the most frequently cited arguments made in favor of the continued usage of Native American mascots is the importance of upholding a team's, or a community's, traditions (Callais 2010, 72–73; Silva 2007, 253; L. Davis 2002, 14). Opponents of Native American mascots should take these declarations seriously because, however irrelevant they may appear to the ethical question of the usage of such mascots or to the general argument about the harmfulness of demeaning imagery, they contain a tacit admission of the role of such mascots for the teams and fans that support them. Specifically, they contain the tacit admission that mascots are crucial for the perception of continuity and persistence of a particular community and that this continuity and persistence is (felt to be) of greater importance than any harm that might be experienced by those who are instrumentalized to serve as mascots. In short, such admissions make salient the extent to which Native American mascots are more revealing of the white communities that use them than the Native ones they purport to "honor."[9] The treatment of Native Americans as mascots is racist, then, not only because it involves (or indeed, requires) the proliferation of stereotypical and degrading images of Native Americans. The mascotting of Native Americans, in addition, instantiates the *particular* ill of instrumentalizing the persons caricatured by mascot images, treating them as worthwhile only insofar as they are effective as unifying symbols for someone else's community. Treating Native Americans as mascots is thus racist in two ways at once: it disregards Native persons by withholding respect and concern for them by portraying them with demeaning stereotypes, *and* it further withholds respect and concern by treating them not as full members of the community but as a means to that community's ends.

Native American mascots are racist in a way that is not reducible to other instances of negative stereotyping. To understand why, we must first make sense of what mascots in general are and how they function. Mascots, I have argued, play a constitutive role in the identity of historically persistent teams and, by extension, in the identity of the communities that those teams represent. The usage of Native Americans as mascots is the reduction of persons to this constitutive role, which requires their concomitant instrumentalization and exclusion from the community that so instrumentalizes them. Native American mascots are thus not merely racist; they are racist in a way that exceeds the racism of the mere stereotypical imagery that they use.

If we accept this argument for the particular racism of the usage of Native Americans as mascots, I think we will have to ask further, perhaps more difficult questions about our contemporary practices of sports fandom. This pure instrumentalization of persons by sports fandom, this mascotting, is not, I think, limited to literal mascots. More reflection is needed, I will argue, on the status of many fans' relationships with athletes today, particularly athletes of color. When we feel, as fans, that athletes *owe us something*; when we glory in a player's power but are angered by his expressing political opinions, experiencing personal turmoil, or otherwise indicating full humanity; when our relationship to athletes is governed by a sense that they exist *for us*, our fandom is dangerously close to mascotting. As I will argue in subsequent chapters, we must attend to other features of the practices of American sports fandom and the relationship between that fandom and the reproduction of normative whiteness—and ask whether certain forms of fandom invite or ensure its perpetuation. This is not to say that sports fandom *as such* is necessarily ethically suspect. The communal identity that is created and fostered by sports fandom may be valuable. But we must ask its price and on whose backs it is bought.

Hero or Mascot? Fantasies of Identification

It is undeniable that racial integration has changed sports in the United States—and that it has changed sports fandom. Fans today cheer for teams of athletes who may or may not look like them. Whereas previous generations of white fans explicitly viewed the success of all-white teams as a testament to the continued greatness of whiteness in the face of the increasing threat of racial integration and miscegenation (Borucki 2003), contemporary white fans—even in parts of the country characterized by open racial tension— exhibit an apparently "color-blind" fandom. These shifts have led some thinkers, like Claudio Tamburrini, to suggest that sports are a force for good in the contemporary world—and in particular, that they may be a means of racial uplift. Sports have played an important role "in the re-appraisal of ethnic minorities" by the dominant white culture, Tamburrini claims, which had previously only admired sports heroes having the "characteristics—racial, social, cultural, and economic—of the dominant groups in society" (1998, 43). The spread of sports competition and the integration of professional leagues has disrupted this entrenched pattern, leading some to believe that race relations are improving and that sports fandom is a key mechanism for continuing that trend. If white fans can learn to cheer for and identify with players of color, so the thinking goes, can the end of racialized oppression be far behind?

In order to answer this question, and to get a clearer sense of the extent to which racial integration of sports might be a boon to antiracist social change, we need to better understand what fans do when they cheer for or identify with individual players. I have argued that sports fandom in the contemporary United States is a central means by which individuals cultivate and reproduce their own identities. The ability of sports fans to use their fandom in this way is driven in part by fans' relations of identification with individual athletes: such identification is necessary in order for athletes' endeavors to be meaningful to individual fans as "enlarging" their sense of self or as mattering to them at all. Yet it is not clear that all forms of fan identification with athletes have the same structure or the same effects. This is evident in the ethical debate about whether athletes are, or should be, role models. If fans of a particular team can feel the success of its members as their own but view themselves as specially connected to *some* of those members as role models, then their identifications with individual members of their teams are functioning differently in different cases. In fact, I will argue, fan identification with individuals varies substantially in its forms, which carry radically different meanings. This is true, I will claim, not only in the obvious cases of star versus nonstar players. Rather, forms of fan identification with star players vary in ways that call into question Tamburrini's claim that sports is a means of mitigating racial oppression. In other words, all fan devotion is *not* created equal.

In what follows, I analyze examples of fan identification with a range of star players and argue that two common forms of fan identification—hero worship and what I will call mascotting—are distinguished by different conceptions of a player's relation to the community, and that these relations are often racialized. To treat a person as a mascot is, I will argue, to instrumentalize them in the service of communal identity, even as they are excluded from full membership in it. Hero worship, in contrast, conceives of its object as "one of us," as belonging to the community in a *representative* rather than commodified sense. Qualitative differences in white fans' relations to major white stars and major black and Latino stars put this contrast in stark relief. The frequent racialization of the hero worship versus mascotting dichotomy is also evident in the differences between white Anglo and Latino fan receptions of the same Latino (particularly Dominican) players. This is not to say that white fans only engage in hero worship of white players or that they only mascot players of color. It is, however, to argue that white sports fans' rooting for and valorization of some individual players of color is not, on its own, enough to suggest that contemporary sports fandom is antioppressive or even ethically neutral. Rather, closer examination of white fans' relations to players of color gives reason to be concerned that sports fandom in the contemporary United States is a highly visible and influential site of the reinforcement of white supremacy.[1]

In order to make this argument, I will first briefly examine the most commonly discussed form of fan identification with individual players: the role model. An analysis of role models is useful insofar as it enables us to conceptualize the imaginative projection in which fans engage when they identify with individual players. Following philosopher of sport Randolph Feezell, I refer to this projection as the "lusory attitude." I will argue that hero worship and mascotting deploy different forms of the lusory attitude, which are characterized by different fan approaches to the "we" that is supposed to be symbolized on the field or court. I will support my claims by analyzing fan responses to major star players. First, I analyze mainstream white fan response to Tim Tebow as a paradigm case of hero worship and argue that Tebow is valorized precisely because he is conceived as representative of the good character of white masculinity, of white evangelical Christianity, and of a nostalgic idealization of small-town America. Next, drawing on Malcolm X's *Autobiography*, I argue that paradigm cases of mascotting involve the instrumentalization of men of color by white fans—either as nonthreatening "pets" or as vehicles for the vicarious experience of forbidden pleasures associated with aggression, sexuality, violence, or animality. The contrast between hero worship and mascotting is particularly visible, I argue, when we note the differences between white and Latinx[2] fans' reactions to baseball stars like Pedro Martínez and Manny Ramírez—and the commonalities between Latinx fan descriptions of Martínez and Ramírez and white fan descriptions of Tebow. Finally, I will end the chapter by examining the case of Michael Jordan, perhaps the most likely candidate for an example of a black man who was the subject of hero worship by white fans. I will conclude, however, that even Jordan was the subject of mascotting, his athletic greatness "safe" enough—that is, not "too black"—to command the devotion of white fans. Although it may certainly be true that some white fans root for players of color in ways that are not reducible to mascotting, the prevalence of the mascotting of black and Latino players by white fans suggests that cross-racial fandom is not necessarily cause for optimism. Rather, the contrast of hero worship and mascotting is indicative of the fact that the "we" of sports fandom is highly racialized and hierarchizing.

Role Models, Imagination, and the Lusory Attitude

In a 1993 Nike commercial, basketball star Charles Barkley famously declared, "I am not a role model. I am not paid to be a role model. . . . Just because I can dunk a basketball, doesn't mean I should raise your kids." Barkley's remarks—and his refusal to embody the image of athletic virtue demanded of him—sparked a firestorm of controversy, as public figures ranging from Vice President Dan Quayle to Barkley's rival Karl Malone claimed that Barkley's response was some combination of morally blameworthy and willfully ignorant. Penning a response of his own in *Sports Illustrated*, Malone wrote,

"Charles, you can deny being a role model all you want, but I don't think it's your decision to make. We don't choose to be role models, we are chosen. Our only choice is whether to be a good role model or a bad one" (Malone 1993).

The question of whether star athletes are or should be role models, and to what extent being a role model confers special obligations on athletes, has subsequently become a popular topic among philosophers of sport. Interestingly, much of the ensuing controversy—in the case of both philosophers and the general public—has resulted from, as Randolph Feezell points out, the equivocation of several senses of the term "role model." One can be a role model in the normative sense—that is, one may be a person who is *worthy* of emulation, either with regard to a specific role (e.g., as a basketball player) or more generally, as a good person. Alternatively, one may be a role model in a purely descriptive sense, insofar as one is *actually emulated* by some individual in one way or another. At the root of Barkley's disagreement with Malone seems to be the running together of these descriptive and normative senses of the term. Barkley maintains that he is not a person worthy of emulation in the wider moral sense, and thus that people ought not look to him as a moral exemplar. Presumably what follows from this, and from his reminder that he is not paid to be such an exemplar, is the claim that he is under no special obligation to behave in a certain way off the basketball court. Malone, on the contrary, suggests that Barkley is a role model in the descriptive sense of the term, which he takes to imply an obligation for Barkley to behave well—to be a "*good* role model." In his book *Sport, Philosophy, and Good Lives* (2013), Feezell convincingly argues that there is no good reason to believe that Barkley's being a role model in the purely descriptive sense implies that he is a role model in the normative sense or that he ought to be—beyond fulfilling the general moral obligations shared by all persons. But why, then, are these equivocations made with such frequency, and why is the revelation that sports heroes might not be worthy of emulation in the broader moral sense disappointing?

Feezell's explanation for this phenomenon is useful for my purposes insofar as it identifies the unique structure of the "role model" relation in sports fandom. Outside the sports context, few would agree that an unknown stranger's choice to admire or emulate you confers upon you a special obligation to be worthy of their emulation. This would be particularly unlikely if the person in question not only had never met you but knew very little about you beyond your job. It must be the case that there is something unique about the sports fan context that makes this sort of equivocation persuasive. Feezell's explanation, in part, is that when fans identify with athletes, or think of them as role models, they aren't actually engaged in identification with or emulation of an individual person. Rather, they are absorbed in an engagement with what Feezell calls a "lusory object." "Lusory," a term Feezell borrows from the famous theorist of play, Bernard Suits, refers to the characteristic of having "'meaning or significance [that] cannot be understood independent of' a particular game's rules, conventions, and goals" (2013, 149). When we adopt the "lusory attitude," according to Suits (2005, 52), we engage in a kind of make believe, bracketing the "real" world and entering into a world in which certain things and acts have significance that they could not have apart from a game. For example, a line on the ground is just that unless I have, with a group of eight other people, adopted the lusory attitude necessary for playing baseball—at which point it becomes the base path I must run on or be called out. In fact, the lusory attitude is necessary for the very concepts of "outs," "runs," "bases," and so on to be meaningful. Similarly, individual objects— bats, goals, and for Feezell, even star players—have the meaning that they do only as a result of our adoption of the lusory attitude.

What this means, for Feezell, is that when fans identify with or admire a player, they are doing something rather different from identifying with or admiring a human individual. In order for the events and persons on the field to be meaningful in the way that they are, fans, like the players they watch, must adopt the lusory attitude: fans must, in significant respects, enter the game itself. When this happens, Feezell writes,

> The person who is a husband and father becomes a "center-fielder," "clean-up hitter," and a "clutch player" who often hits home runs of "Ruthian proportion" in the Little City where his extraordinary achievements are cheered and admired. It is a failure of our language, or rather our linguistic sensitivities, that we refer to the person qua father and husband, with the same name as the lusory object whose athletic deeds, at times, seem to be almost superhuman. . . . When we refer to our favorite sports hero[es] . . . [w]e are projected into their stories, and we make them our own. (149–150)

This imaginative projection is crucial in order for the hero to be a hero for fans at all. Fans, after all, know almost nothing about sports heroes beyond what they see on television—which is itself typically packaged in neat, familiar narratives, allowing its stories and images to be more easily identifiable. When consuming such images and narratives, fans fill in the gaps by imagining themselves in the position of their favorite players, making diving catches, or knowing just when to shoot the jumper. The players they identify with are thus more like "imagined objects or fictional characters in a drama . . . than persons whose lives outside of sports are either exemplary, noteworthy, or even interesting" (150). The fictive, or lusory, world of sports heroes, then, is in significant respects a product of fan involvement—and it is for this reason that fans experience such outsized disappointment when their heroes do not behave in ways they expect.

Feezell's claim that admiration of sports heroes is not actually admiration of or identification with actual persons but rather with lusory objects dovetails nicely with my description of sports fandom as a practice of subjectivization. The reiteration of and identification with particular narratives of heroism and virtue is a practice of fan discourse that has the effect of giving shape to a particular kind of "I" who understands him- or herself as part of a specific "we." Whether one is rooting for a player, hoping for his failure, explicitly emulating her, or expressing disappointment at his off-the-field conduct, one is engaged in a practice of subjectivization. The practice of identifying with individual players, as Feezell suggests, involves imaginatively projecting ourselves into their narrative, but it also involves the tacit reiteration of our own identity as part of a particular "we" whose valor is at stake on the field. By identifying with such players' successes and failures, fans draw on and reproduce normative conceptualizations of the character and limits of their own communities. Yet, as I will argue, the specifics of fan identification vary and entail different uses of the "we"—which may or may not include the players representing it.

Hero Worship

The 2011 ESPN documentary *Tim Tebow: Everything in Between* offers a carefully curated look at the details of the life of Tim Tebow, a Heisman Trophy winner and former quarterback for the University of Florida, in the months preceding the NFL draft. At the time of the documentary's production, Tebow was already a larger-than-life figure: as the quarterback of a national championship team from the football-crazed American South, Tebow had considerable star power. Beyond this, though, he was beloved across the country for other reasons: Tebow was an outspoken evangelical Christian, the son of Christian missionaries, and known to drop to his knee in visible prayer after successful plays. Perhaps just as importantly, Tebow was a strikingly attractive young white man with a radiant smile. We are given a sense of his star power as the film opens: the camera follows Tebow after the Gators' second national championship, and it seems that no one who comes in contact with him can contain their excitement—from the narrator who intones, "What he did, and the way he captured a nation . . . I don't think we'll ever see anything like that again," to the band member who screams, "I touched him!" we are awash in Tebow admiration (ESPN 2011).

The admiration is, in some fairly obvious ways, curious. Though Tebow was a wildly successful college football player, the transferability of his skills to the professional game was dubious, as *Everything in Between* makes clear. The consensus of most football experts at the time was that Tebow's basic throwing mechanics had serious flaws, which would be exposed at the professional level. As a result, many expected that he would be selected in the middle rounds of the NFL draft and would almost certainly occupy a backup quarterback role for any team that signed him. The intense fan interest surrounding Tebow—to which the existence of the film testifies—was certainly much greater than what one would expect for a likely benchwarmer.

Despite his limitations, Tebow attracted a fan base that idolized him. The loyalty Tebow inspired—particularly in white evangelical Christian circles, where he became a larger-than-life hero—was at its height in 2010 and 2011. This devotion is on conspicuous display in the film. Fans carry signs and display shirts reading "Tebow: God's Gift to Football Fans" and "The Chosen One." In a scene at the 2010 National Prayer Breakfast in Washington, he is referred to as "a role model for the youth of America." We later meet a man who has painted his personal racecar with Tebow's jersey number and the University of Florida's colors, who explains, "He's my hero, so I wanted to carry his number, and let everybody know when they see my racecar that I'm a Tebow fan." At an autograph signing in his hometown of Jacksonville, Florida, we meet a young woman in line for an autograph wearing a wedding dress and veil who half-jokingly suggests that she is hoping to marry Tebow "if he asks." The climax of all of this adulation occurs as Tebow stands between a man and a woman who are evidently a couple, when the man drops to his knees to ask his girlfriend, in all seriousness, "With Tim Tebow as our witness . . . will you marry me?"

This last interaction is particularly striking: the setting of the proposal is symbolically evocative of a marriage ceremony, as the couple is arranged around an officiant and before an assembled crowd; the rhetorical substitution of Tebow for "God" as the solemnizing witness is clearly no accident. Yet the positioning of Tebow as the setting for the engagement—as a particularly special sort of background scenery—paradoxically illustrates his objectification and makes salient some key features of hero worship in cases of star athletes like Tebow. First, it makes clear that Tebow is functioning in this moment as a lusory object. He is not simply Tim Tebow the person but a fantasy, a symbolic image of the values, virtues, and aesthetics these fans conceive as worthy of emulation and with which they want to identify; that identification is made all the stronger for its linkage with the ritual context of marriage. Second, however, this act of fan identification, with the others on display in

Everything in Between, makes clear that hero worship occurs when the object of its focus is conceived as a *representative* of the values and virtues of a particular community that explicitly exceeds the sporting context. That is, fans engaging in hero worship do so not only because their hero is an athletic superstar or a symbol of athletic prowess; they do so because they conceive their hero, as a person, to represent something worthy of identification—to represent, in short, the idealized version of themselves.

That Tebow was compelling to his fan base because he appeared as a kind of Platonic ideal of themselves—to be, in short, just like them, but better—speaks to an important feature of hero worship first discussed by William James. Though not as involved in athletics as many of his contemporaries, James vociferously defended hero worship in two essays extolling the importance of individual geniuses in advancing history.[3] Marveling over the mystery of how such heroic individuals chance to come about and change the world, he writes, "An unlearned carpenter of my acquaintance once said in my hearing: 'There is very little difference between one man and another; but what little there is, is very important.' . . . [The sociologists Grant] Allen and [Herbert] Spencer, in inveighing against hero worship, are thinking exclusively of the size of the inch; I, as a hero-worshipper, attend to its seat and function" (1992b, 648). In celebrating these small differences between individuals that make some people capable of true greatness, James underlines the distinguishing feature of hero worship: the hero worshipper must be able to see just how much "like us" these great men are and to identify with their heroes by imagining themselves in their position. This identification is crucial for James, as it is the basis, he claims, for the moral value of hero worship: "in picking out from history our heroes, and communing with their kindred spirits—in imagining as strongly as possible what differences their individualities brought about in this world . . .—each one of us may best fortify and inspire what creative energy may lie in his own soul" (651). James's description of the inspirational value of hero worship makes clear that heroes are at once relatable and mythic: we should learn the details of their lives, he argues, to contemplate the wonders of individual efforts in lives just like ours. Whether or not people actually use hero worship to inspire moral greatness in themselves, it is clear that fan identification with heroes is dependent upon their recognizing—or believing themselves to recognize—something of themselves in those they idolize. When people engage in hero worship, in other words, they conceive their object as "ours" in the sense of representing their best, or their greatest possibilities.

Because heroes are not merely the players of a role on the field but representative of an ideal or ideals, identification with them involves not merely identification with a single person but with an idealized "we." The athletic competition thus becomes a venue to vicariously play out the symbolic victory of their own values. With this in mind, it is illuminating to reconsider James's suggestion that hero worship enables us to contemplate what greatness we might be capable of. In the sporting context, hero worship invites such contemplation not merely in the sense that James seems to have intended—that is, to inspire individuals to imagine a future in which they, too, accomplish greatness. Rather, hero worship enables individuals to think of themselves, their community, and their values as great and as embodied in the exploits of their heroes on the field. Importantly, this symbolic identification is possible precisely because the athletes who are taken up as heroes are taken to be individuals who represent something more than the role they play in the sporting context.

As a paradigm of hero worship, Tebow is idolized as a representative of the good character of evangelical Christians and small-town (white) America. Fan adoration and sports media attention is as likely to be explicitly focused on Tebow's evangelical Christianity, his support for pro-life political organizations, his "character," or his good looks as it is on his performance on the football field. In 2012, thirty thousand fans came to Georgetown, Texas, to see him preach a sermon on Easter Sunday, and his personal memoir, *Through My Eyes*, was the best-selling sports book of 2011 (Orenstein 2014). His association with conservative Christianity and "family values" made him both a household name and an object of lighthearted ridicule—as "Tebowing"[4] became a popular Internet meme, and *Saturday Night Live* produced a skit in which Jesus visits Tebow in the Denver Broncos locker room to tell him to "take it down a notch." Ironically, this ridicule seemed primarily to increase Tebow's popularity in evangelical Christian circles, where he was portrayed as persecuted and undervalued by sports media for his religious beliefs. Christian fans of opposing teams began rooting for him after he was broadcasted singing the praise song "Awesome God" before a game, and fans consistently proclaimed a passion for Tebow rooted in the fact that "he stands up for what he believes in" (Lake 2013). Despite the trend of Tebow mockery, fans and sports media who praised him spoke repeatedly and effusively of his faith, his leadership, the strength of his convictions, his work ethic, his respectfulness—in short, his character.

The repetition of the discourse of character, honor, respectability, and family values around Tebow is consistent with a pattern of discourse documented by James Rhodes in his study (2011) of media and film representations of white, working-class boxing heroes. Whether in fictional films like *Rocky*, *The Fighter*, *Cinderella Man*, and *The Boxer* or in media coverage of actual white working-class boxers, Rhodes argues, "It is [the] idea of 're-spectability' . . . on which the heroic status of the White, male boxer rests" (352). Respectability, as Rhodes describes it, is coded in key patterns of de-scription and representation of these heroes: they are routinely described as disciplined and tough—emphasizing their masculine virtues—in addition to being down-home, boy-next-door types. In contrast to some of boxing's more flashy, big-talking stars, boxer Ricky Hatton is described as being "one of those homespun heroes who takes his washing home to his mum . . . and prefers a game of darts down at his local [pub] and prefers crispy duck to caviar." These heroes are "just like us, if we had a smidge more athletic tal-ent" (367). They also remember—and value—their roots, even if those roots lead boxing's establishment to underestimate their talents. These heroes are appealing, then, not merely for their performance in the context of the sport but for their embodiment of a certain set of values, or a certain aesthetic, that sets them apart from their competitors or teammates. Often, Rhodes points out, this distinguishing feature is described in more or less explicitly nostal-gic terms. The boxers Rhodes examines are all described at various points as having "heart" and as being "throwbacks" (356)—fighters who remind boxing enthusiasts of the classic heroes of a bygone era. The nostalgia of this hero worship is evident not only in the repetition of the explicit contrasts between these heroes and boxing's contemporary, more ostentatious stars; it is also re-flected in the fact that so "much is made, for instance, of [their] old-fashioned training methods that involve swinging sledgehammers, flipping tires, and pushing cars" (365).

As if following a script, *Everything in Between* represents Tebow using nearly all of the tropes Rhodes identifies in the case of white working-class boxing heroes. After the opening montage of Tebow praise, we see Tebow alone in a parking lot, patiently trying again and again to start his modest se-dan that has clearly seen better days. We follow him as he exercises in a train-ing facility, flipping monster-truck tires, and again on his family farm, where he swings sledgehammers into trees and pushes a sport utility vehicle down a country road. We see him hug his mother before watching the NFL draft in his family's living room. We watch Tebow croon a country song, "Where I'm From," by Jason Michael Carroll, with his friend on the way back home to Jacksonville—somewhat incongruously, aboard a private jet—that nostalgi-cally declares,

> . . . [T]ake me home to my family and my friends
> Where the quarterback dates the homecoming queen
> The truck's a Ford and the tractor's green

And "Amazing Grace" is what we sing.
Where there's a county fair every fall,
Your friends are there no matter when you call.
It may not sound like much, but it's where I'm from.

(CARROLL 2009)

By the end of the film, Tebow is not so much a football star as an ideal. He is disciplined, he is respectful, he is goodness, humility, small-town family values, and masculine strength rolled into one. The film ends abruptly, cutting off the moment before the climax of Tebow's draft by the Denver Broncos, congealing an image of nostalgic hero worship that is made possible precisely because it is not focused on his on-field performance—which turned out to be lackluster—but on his image as the idealized embodiment of a simpler time.

It is not difficult to make the case that the fan nostalgia these images appeal to is at least implicitly a nostalgia for "an era of White [sporting] domination" (Rhodes 2011, 360), given the comparatively recent development of racial integration in sport. We might also point to the centrality of imagery strongly associated with whiteness in this nostalgic rhetoric—as in the case of the rural or small-town imagery associated with Tebow, the discourse of "family values," or the "working class" label associated with white boxers (a label not typically used for people of color, even those of comparable socioeconomic status). It is also worth noting the differences in the rhetoric used to discuss white athletes: whereas athletes of color are regularly described as being machinelike in their efficiency and "flashy" in their attitudes, white athletes are described with rhetorical devices associated with days gone by: "heart," "grit," and "character." As Daniel Grano notes in his study of popular sports rhetoric (2010), "character" discourse is so consistently racialized that it is almost never used positively when athletes of color are the subject of discussion; in those cases, rather, there are usually "character issues" or concerns to be dealt with. White athletes' character, in contrast, is brought up by fans and commentators in contexts that explicitly connect them with virtue, leadership, and the nostalgic image of the conquering hero.

Perhaps even more telling is the coupling of hero worship with specifically white evangelical Christianity. Although one might argue that Tebow's following developed because he was taken to be representative of a particular faith, not a particular race, this is less persuasive when we consider just how widespread Christianity is in American athletics, particularly football. Explicitly religious performance is, as sociologists point out, a regular feature of American sport—including the "expression of thanks to God—pointing to the sky, thanking Jesus in interviews . . . the conflation of athletic and religious identity in college football, especially in the South" (Butterworth and Senkbeil 2015, 2). Football in particular is so overwhelmingly Christian that Houston Texans star Arian Foster made waves by "coming out" as an atheist in 2015 (Keown 2015). A great number of the Christians in football are, of course, black, though none has inspired the same obsessive evangelical fan following associated with Tim Tebow—not even Russell Wilson, who, like Tebow, is a star quarterback with a squeaky-clean image who talks openly about saving sex for marriage. The discrepancy between the outsized fan obsession with Tebow and the comparatively tame response to Christian athletes of color suggests that Tebow (and perhaps other white evangelical heroes before him, like Kurt Warner) is a touchstone for fans anxious about the perceived cultural threats to normative white masculinity. As one sports-writer put it, "Tebow is the 'WASPiest WASP in this great big WASP nest we call America'" (Butterworth 2013, 19).

Indeed, no one athlete of the past decade has been able to embody the idealized norms of white evangelical Christian masculinity quite so effectively as Tim Tebow. In addition to a life embodying white working-class values, Tebow is held up as a poster child for the pro-life/antiabortion movement, having starred in a commercial with his mother about her decision to reject medical advice to have an abortion, and as the ideal of heterosexual masculine desirability. An evangelical scholar describes his appeal thus: evangelical "mothers want their sons to be like him and their daughters to marry him" (quoted in Orenstein 2014, 71). There are indications that some white evangelical women took this desire seriously, attending games with signs professing their love for Tebow and even, during his college days, attempting to meet him "by waiting for him outside his apartment" (Lake 2013). Fans' responses to Tebow were decidedly not limited to his performance on the field. In fact, the opposite is closer to the truth: fans identified with Tebow's instantiation of idealized masculinity, character, and white evangelicalism—and *this* is what motivated them to view him as their representative on the football field, which became the setting for the symbolic replaying of the American culture wars, in the hope that, in this case, old-fashioned family values would win out.

The hero worship that characterizes fan relations to Tebow is a familiar one in the history of American football and—not coincidentally—in the perpetuation of masculine domination and white supremacy. The adulation of this form of hero—the rugged individual who is "one of us," but for his outsized accomplishments, who understands the value of family, faith, and the simple things in life—arose near the end of the nineteenth century in the

United States, as the industrial revolution fueled anxieties about the end of masculinity. It was in this context, in fact, that football first developed, its violence heralded as a means to preserve manhood in colleges populated by young men who had never physically labored. This was particularly true at elite schools like Harvard and Yale, where, despite the objections of the faculty, President Roosevelt (then on Harvard's Board of Overseers) suggested that because "I emphatically disbelieve in seeing Harvard, or any other college, turn out mollycoddles instead of vigorous men . . . I do not in the least object to a sport because it is rough" (quoted in Townsend 1996, 110). The importance of using dangerous sports, particularly football, to teach manliness at Harvard, was celebrated by many of the most prominent figures at the university at the time. These athletics enthusiasts included Oliver Wendell Holmes Jr., who claimed to "rejoice at every dangerous sport which I see pursued," which provided a substitute and preparation for heroism in war (quoted in Townsend 1996, 103). The advent of this form of rugged yet honorable masculine hero was explicitly celebrated in Francis Walker's 1893 Phi Beta Kappa address on college athletics at Harvard:

> Walker proceeded to contrast an image of the college hero in the days before the Civil War with a postwar model. The earlier specimen was "a young man of towering forehead, from which the hair was carefully brushed backwards. . . . His cheeks were pale; his digestion pretty certain to be bad." And inevitably it followed that "he was self-conscious, introspective, and indulged in moods." . . . But this young man, with his literary and debating societies . . . had been superseded by men of action, and by muscular Christians, who knew that "it is a glorious thing to have a giant's strength." . . . The honorable man of the present age would be strong, firm, resolute, active. (98)

The values of "muscular Christianity" were not only espoused by Walker. As Donald Hall points out in his analysis of Victorian values and anxiety about masculinity, this reactionary attitude to the sweeping social and technological changes of the time produced a widespread movement that "was an attempt to assert control over a world that had seemingly gone mad: 'In such a mood, not of cynicism but of bitter exasperation, the objective correlative is the destructive force of a *conquering hero*'" (2006, 9; emphasis mine). The hero worship of the Victorian era—which is, in many ways, the hero worship of today—reiterates the importance of faith in white masculine individualism's ability to overcome all, even in the face of a changing world.

    With this in mind, there is little mystery or paradox to Tebow's appeal. It is simply not the case that, as Rebecca Watts (2014) claims, there are funda-

mental "incongruities" in the values Tebow embodies. Although on the surface we might be perplexed to find the Christian values of humility, love, and
service in the same person who is the most visible star of a hypermasculine,
violent game, the logic of this coupling becomes clearer when we recognize
the discursive associations of white evangelical Christianity with conservative American politics. As Butterworth and Senkbeil put it, certain discursive
tropes—like "character," certainly, but also the others already mentioned—
"become discursive shorthand to promote athletes who embody the attributes" of "Protestantism, Whiteness, masculinity, and militarism" (2015, 4).
In a cultural context where open celebration of whiteness and heroes who
defend it is increasingly frowned upon, the metonymic substitution for associated discourses offers a means to engage in the same celebration in more
covert ways.

Such racialized sports rhetoric is of a piece with a long tradition of more
explicitly racist, nostalgic sports rhetoric that became popular during the
era of football's development. Oliver Wendell Holmes's celebration of the
violence of football explicitly connects the importance of masculine forti-
tude with the "breeding of a race fit for hardship and command" (quoted in
S. Watts 2003, 51) and other rhetoric around sports heroes at the time made
use of similarly eugenicist justifications for their importance.[5] Well into the
twentieth century, southern whites explicitly celebrated their football victories as symbolic reiterations of the dominance of white masculinity and as
sites for the preservation of racial purity and the symbolic overcoming of the
white South (Borucki 2003). Although contemporary mainstream fan rhetoric is less overt in its valorization of white masculinity, it is replete with the
same nostalgia, the same symbols, and the same hero worship as its previous
instantiations.

In identifying with and valorizing Tebow, the white evangelical fans who
seemed to worship him valorized and positioned *themselves* as part of a particular "we." That "we" is concerned with "character," conceived as normatively masculine, and nostalgic for an image of America as Christian, non-
elite, and distinctly white. Importantly, that "we" is imagined not merely as
symbolized by Tebow but as *represented* by him—one of the "men of God . . .
who are willing to stand up and act like *men*, rather than *wimping out* when
it gets a little controversial . . . to stand for the truth" (Lake 2013; emphasis in
original). Tebow may function as a lusory object for the "we" of such fans, but
he is at the same time unambiguously a member of the community thereby
represented.

Mascotting

Although the word "mascot" often carries affectionate connotations, the centrality of instrumentalization to the mascot role is evident in even in the lexical definition of the term and its etymology. The *OED* says that a mascot is "a person or thing that is supposed to bring good luck; (now) *esp.* something carried or displayed for this purpose" (2015b). Worth noting here is that the mascot's role is defined by its usefulness for others; groups who adopt mascots do so precisely because of what such entities can *give* them. Tellingly, the word itself is thought to have originated in the nineteenth-century French operetta *La Mascotte*, whose plot centered on "a farm girl [who] is supposed to bring good luck to whomever is fortunate enough to possess her, although she must remain a virgin or her powers are lost" (Traubner 2003, 86). Captured in this plot is the clear sense that a mascot is distinguished by being treated as an object in someone else's drama: the *mascotte*'s usefulness precludes her from acting as a desiring subject. She is, moreover, a commodity to be sought and traded for the benefit she will bring her possessors. Mascots, in early twentieth century usage, might be *simply* objects—as in, for example, a good luck charm carried by a card player (*OED* Online 2015b)—but even when they are animate, they exist in objectifying and instrumentalizing relation.

In the second chapter of his *Autobiography*, "Mascot," Malcolm X describes his childhood experience as the only black boy in his class in rural Michigan in terms that echo the original *mascotte*'s usage as a kept object or pet. The young Malcolm Little had been sent to live with a white family, the Swerlins, after his father was killed and his mother declared unfit by the state. Although Malcolm's stay with the Swerlins was originally supposed to have been temporary—their "detention home" was a way station for troubled boys on their way to a "reform school"—he stayed with them longer than originally intended and enrolled at the local school. This was, at least initially, cause for happiness. The Swerlins, Malcolm recalled,

> all liked my attitude, and it was out of their liking for me that I soon became accepted by them—as a mascot, I know now. They would talk about anything and everything with me standing right there hearing them, the same way people would talk freely in front of a pet canary. They would even talk about me, or about "niggers," as though I wasn't there, as if I wouldn't understand what the word meant. (X and Haley 1964, 27)

The Swerlins' simultaneous affection and disregard for Malcolm makes the deeply ambivalent nature of the mascot relation salient. The Swerlins evidently care for Malcolm—they take him into their home, allow him to eat with them and to become (from their perspective) a member of the family; they are evidently distraught when Malcolm, as a result of his increasing consciousness of racial injustice, withdraws and ultimately moves away. Despite their affection for him, they think nothing of using racial slurs to refer to black people or of making sweeping claims about black people's supposedly poor judgment; neither do they flinch at doing these things openly in his presence. Though they were entirely well meaning, Malcolm X suggests, "it just never dawned upon them that I could understand, that I wasn't a pet, but a human being. They didn't give me credit for having the same sensitivity, intellect, and understanding that they would have been ready and willing to recognize in a white boy in my position" (28). Their open willingness to disparage black persons while evidently liking him suggests to Malcolm X that the Swerlins—and white people in general—are comfortable with blackness only to the extent that it remains constrained, nonthreatening, and in a firmly subservient position.

This view is further reinforced by the young Malcolm's experiences at school, where, again, he appears to be well liked and popular. As the only black person in his class, Malcolm says, "I was kind of a novelty," (X and Haley 1964, 29) and by seventh grade, "I was elected class president. It surprised me even more than other people. But I can see now why the class might have done it. My grades were among the highest in the school. I was unique in my class, like a pink poodle" (32). Although one might think that his election as class president was evidence of his classmates' acceptance, Malcolm notes that outward appearances here, as in the case of the Swerlins, are deceiving. Consistently, his peers and teachers express affection for or identification with him, which paradoxically comes alongside the more or less explicit expression of the importance of his staying "in his place." In the case of his peers, though he was accepted and celebrated on the basketball team, it became clear that there were certain things he simply should not do—notably, dancing with white girls at the regular postgame dances (31). Malcolm X recounts a particularly painful interaction with his favorite teacher at the time, Mr. Ostrowski, which marked a significant turning point in his racial consciousness. When a young Malcolm told his teacher that he hoped to be a lawyer someday, the forthcoming response was startling:

> Mr. Ostrowski looked surprised, I remember, and leaned back in his chair and clasped his hands behind his head. He kind of half-smiled and said, "Malcolm, one of life's first needs is for us to be realistic. Don't misunderstand me, now. We all here like you, you know that. But you've got to be realistic about being a

nigger. A lawyer—that's no realistic goal for a nigger. You need to think about something you can be. You're good with your hands—making things. Everybody admires your carpentry shop work. Why don't you plan on carpentry? People like you as a person—you'd get all kinds of work." (38)

Given the restriction of his choices, Ostrowski's assertion that people liked Malcolm Little "as a person" is arguably false. The claim itself is belied as much by the clear indication that Malcolm does not and cannot inhabit the same world as his peers as it is by his celebration as a kind of novelty, who is admired just insofar as he conforms to others' expectations of him.

Malcolm X does not offer a theoretical explanation of what it means to be loved "as a mascot," but his first-person account offers a striking set of examples whose analysis is fruitful for understanding the concept. First, to be treated as a mascot is to be treated as something less than a full person. From the Swerlins, who openly insult him without thinking, to his classmates, who appreciate his performance on the basketball court but expect him to be restricted from the full range of social activities, and his teacher, who balks at his expression of aspirations that move outside of his expected social role, Malcolm is treated as less than fully human and less than fully free. Certain possibilities are, quite simply, *not* possibilities for him; he is expected to play his given role. Second, and relatedly, to be a mascot for a certain group of persons is to exist for the comfort and amusement of that group—to be, as Jean-Paul Sartre might put it, *for others*, rather than to be for oneself. For young black men like Malcolm Little, this means to be subordinate, to be deferential, to be, above all, nonthreatening. As in the case of the mascotting of Native Americans, in order to serve as an adequate mascot, one must not constitute a real threat to the community doing the mascotting. It is telling, for example, that once Malcolm begins to be conscious of the injustice of racial oppression and to express the slightest hint of resistance to it, he is sent away to live with another family. Though he continued to answer when called upon, Malcolm X recounts, "Where 'nigger' had slipped off my back before, wherever I heard it now, I stopped and looked at whoever said it. And they looked surprised that I did. . . . [N]obody, including the teachers, could decide what had come over me. I knew I was being discussed" (X and Haley 1964, 38–39). Shortly thereafter, having refused to give comfort or explanation to those who insulted him, Malcolm went to live with the only other black family in town. Being a mascot requires that one—like the pet "pink poodle" to which Malcolm compares himself—give no indication of existing for or desiring purposes beyond those that serve the instrumentalizing community. A mascot who exists for himself is no mascot at all.

The form of mascotting that Malcolm X describes here is of the first type I mentioned: the treatment of persons as nonthreatening "pets" who are "ours" not as representatives but as objects or commodities. Although persons subject to this form of mascotting may be the object of significant affection by the white community mascotting them, they are not full members of the community they thus serve. A particularly vivid example of this version of mascotting is that of James Ivy, a black man known for years on Ole Miss's campus as "Blind Jim." The story of James Ivy is cited, somewhat ironically, by defenders of Ole Miss's "Colonel Reb" mascot, a cartoonish white man dressed in the style of an antebellum plantation owner, who, critics suggest, constitutes an impolitic nostalgia for the state's slave-owning past. In response to the growing movement to change the mascot, in 2004 the Colonel Reb Foundation began circulating an alternative explanation for the origins of "Colonel Reb," purporting to show that the mascot did not glorify slave-owning Confederates but rather, a black man who had been "an integral part of the University of Mississippi" (quoted in Newman 2007, 322). According to the Colonel Reb Foundation, the man known around Ole Miss as "Blind Jim"

> was blinded in his early teens when coal tar paint got into his eyes while painting the Tallahatchie River Bridge. Ivy became a peanut vendor in Oxford and was considered the university's mascot for many years. Ivy attended most Ole Miss athletic events and was fond of saying, "I've never seen Ole Miss lose." . . . According to [Ole Miss faculty member] David Sansing, "If you look at the photo of Blind Jim in the three-piece suit, with the hat, there's a striking resemblance. The original Colonel Reb emblem is a spitting image of Blind Jim Ivy, except for white skin." (Newman 2007, 322)

The "three-piece suit" Sansing refers to was one given to Ivy by the students of Ole Miss. He was, apparently, photographed in a new suit while surrounded by the members of the freshman class each year, having been nicknamed the "Dean of the Freshman Class." Ivy had come to this notoriety by accident; the legend circulated among Ole Miss fans is that during a particularly difficult game, while in the stands selling peanuts, Ivy began cheering for Ole Miss with his "big booming voice," which rallied the fans and inspired a surge of scoring by the Ole Miss team (King and Springwood 2001, 133). It was after this unlikely victory that Ivy grew to have a central role in the ritual of Ole Miss athletics—though not, of course, in any official university capacity, as the university remained segregated until 1963. Ivy remained a fixture at Ole Miss games, and in the freshman class photo, until his death in 1955, at which point students collected funds for a Blind Jim scholarship for a black student.

Notably, this scholarship was not good for attendance at the University of Mississippi but at one of the black colleges in the area (134).

Regardless of whether the "Colonel Reb" mascot bore any historical relation to Ivy, the Colonel Reb Foundation's characterization of Ivy as a "mascot" is apt. His initial acceptance into the Ole Miss fold was based on his status as a good luck charm—his "booming voice" supposedly bringing victory to an Ole Miss baseball team that was in danger of losing (King and Springwood 2001, 132). His continued relationship with the university only expanded with this mascot status: he was a kind of landmark in the stands at each game, often literally wearing a sign around his neck reading "Blind Jim"[6]—or, sometimes, a musical score, when he could be positioned so it was visible to the audience (133). Ivy is celebrated not as a full human being but as a token in the history of Ole Miss. His status is made clear not only in his treatment as an object in the stands but also in his "Dean of the Freshman Class" moniker—a tongue-in-cheek joke about freshmen at Ivy's expense—and in the repetition of Ivy's catchphrase in the stories about "Blind Jim" circulated by the Ole Miss faithful: "I've never seen Ole Miss lose." The double-entendre of the phrase depends upon Ivy making a joke about his own disability, but more than this, it figures him as the happy, subservient black man who literally sees no evil. Given Ole Miss football's role in the maintenance and reproduction of white southern aristocracy, Ivy's position as mascot serves as a ritualized reenactment of white supremacy, portraying a "good" negro whose entire purpose is the entertainment of the white community. His treatment is, in fact, exactly the sort to which the young Malcolm Little objected: the surface-level appearance of acceptance that has as its price the expectation that one smile, be deferential, and above all, stay in one's place.

To treat an athlete as a mascot is to relate to him or her as an instrument for one's own benefit as a sports fan and thus as an object existing primarily to serve the ends of the constitution and reproduction of one's own social identity. In the cases of James Ivy and the young Malcolm Little, we see certain key features of the mascotting relation: mascots are viewed and treated as one-dimensional entities, not full persons with desires, goals, or aspirations beyond those that are part of their given role; they are, moreover, required to be nonthreatening and to exist for the benefit or amusement of the mascotting person or group—to be, in other words, like a pet.

Beyond treatment as a "pet," in the sporting context, there is a second form of mascotting: the instrumentalization of athletes of color as a vehicle for the vicarious experience of aggression, sexuality, or violence. This form of mascotting is understandable as a subset of BIRGing and is intimately connected with the performance of masculinity so often central to the practice of sports fandom. To make sense of this form of mascotting, it is useful to recall the classes of mascot types that I discussed in the previous chapter. Although some team mascots, I argued, are idealized images of the community itself, others, like Native American mascots, are better understood as simply fantastical images of power, force, or superhuman ability, bearing no clear descriptive relation to the community they represent. The mascotting of individual athletes often involves a similar practice of fan engagement with a fantasy of power, dominance, or aggression—and, I argue, a similar exclusion of the mascotted athlete from full membership in the mascotting person's community. In this form of mascotting, in other words, fans identify with and cheer for players not as individual human persons but as symbols of power and fierceness. Fans are thus able to vicariously experience the fantasy of being dominant, great, and hypermasculine by identifying with players on the field or court with whom they would not associate in a nonsporting context. Specifically, this form of mascotting enables white fans to vicariously experience a fantasy of black masculinity within safely circumscribed limits.

The paradox of mascotting is thus that fans can, within the lusory attitude of the sporting context, identify with persons they might otherwise find undesirable or dangerous. Malcolm X captures this paradoxical relation in contrasting his experiences as a star on the basketball court and an uncomfortable presence at the school dance. Though it was clear, he says, that he ought not dance with the girls in his class, privately, several of his male classmates pressed him to sneak off with one of these white girls (sometimes even their sisters)—presumably for some kind of illicit tryst. Malcolm X suggests that these encouragements were motivated by a desire to be able to blackmail the girls with the knowledge of their violation of the social-sexual taboo against interracial relations, but one can imagine that their motivations might be more complex than this. Given their identification with Malcolm on the court and the associations with masculinity and domination that often accompany sports fandom, it is not difficult to imagine that the boys encouraging Malcolm to get sexually involved with his female peers at the same time relate to him as a symbol of hypermasculinity, or even as a vehicle through which they might vicariously inhabit a fantasy of masculine sexuality—if only in a closely circumscribed context that could be easily disavowed.

Here too, fans are engaged in a rather different kind of identification than they are in hero worship. Their identification is localized within the specific context of the athletic competition. Though both hero worship and mascotting involve engagement with a fantasy, in hero worship, fans valorize features of the athlete that they embody or value outside of the athletic context, whereas the one-dimensionality of mascotting need not have anything to do with life outside the sporting context and typically involves vicarious indulgence in affects or behaviors that would not be socially acceptable in those same fans' daily lives. Such temporary identifications are thrilling or salacious because they are impossible in "real life." Because dominance, physical aggression, and hypermasculinity are not available or plausible for most fans, the mascotting relation provides a useful means of experiencing, even vicariously, these phenomena.

We can see evidence of the importance of this kind of fantasy of domination, violence, or masculinity in the language fans frequently use when discussing certain players or features of the game. "Sportspeak," as Jeffrey Segrave (1997) has pointed out, is full of violent—and often sexual—language. Fans and commentators (who serve as mouthpieces of and mass-media interlocutors with fans) gush over a batter *crushing* a ball with a big hit, *destroying*, *killing*, or *ripping* an opposing team. Fans and sports enthusiasts have used metaphors like *beating* to describe victory so long that they no longer appear to have violent connotations. Football, in particular, is surrounded by images of violence, masculinity, and sexuality, featuring fans who cheer for increasingly violent hits. Moreover, as Alan Dundes (2002) points out in his psychoanalytic account of football, the agents of this violence are men wearing uniforms that exaggerate the masculine body—including oversized shoulder pads and skin-tight pants over a codpiece-like athletic support—and commentators who regularly extemporize on the "penetration" of the defense.

It is common, moreover, to find fans discussing individual players (particularly players of color) who excel at dominating on the field in either animalistic or mechanistic terms—as in the cases of, for example, Marshawn Lynch, the Seattle running back who is said to be in "Beast Mode" when he knocks down potential defenders; Tyrann Mathieu, who has been unable to shake the fan-conferred nickname "Honey Badger" for his quick defensive play;[7] Pedro Martínez, who, at the height of his stardom as a pitcher for the Boston Red Sox, was referred to as "a horse" for his stamina; basketball stars LaMarcus Aldridge, Artis Gilmore, and Lionel Hollins, who were known during their careers, respectively, as "L Train," "A Train" and "L Train"; or Aroldis Chapman, a pitcher who, having emigrated from Cuba, regularly throws at over one hundred miles per hour and is referred to enthusiastically by fans as "the Cuban Missile." Fans' engagement with these star players of color, particularly when fixated on such symbolism, seems to be more than simple BIRGing in the sense of feeling part of a collective victory. Rather, their identification is with feelings of domination, power, hypermasculinity, violence, or animality that are otherwise inaccessible.

In this respect, mascotting bears significant resemblance to the nineteenth-century practice of blackface minstrelsy, through which white audiences were able to indulge temporarily in the licentiousness they associated with blackness. The minstrel show, which featured white performers in blackface acting out grotesque stereotypes, parodied musical performances, and salacious jokes, became popular during an era of explicit racial segregation and hierarchy—even before the official end of slavery in the United States. In his classic analysis, Eric Lott argues that minstrelsy "arose from a white obsession with black (male) bodies that underlies racial dread to our own day, [yet] it ruthlessly disavowed its fleshly investments through ridicule and racist lampoon" (1992, 23). The minstrel show allowed its white audiences and performers alike to indulge in a transgressive interaction with blackness and with the prohibited desires, actions, and affects that they associated with it. As in the case of mascotting, "'Black' figures were there *to be looked at*, shaped to the demands of desire; they were screens on which audience fantasy could rest" (28). The specifics of that fantasy become clear when we analyze the content of these shows:

> "blackness" provided the inspiration as well as the occasion for preposterously violent, sexual, or otherwise prohibited theatrical material that evinced how unsettling was the black power white performers intended to subjugate. One notes in particular the relentless transformation of black characters [in minstrel show songs] into things, as though to clinch the property relations these songs fear are too fluid. (28–29)

Similarly, the discursive habit of referring to black athletes in animalistic or mechanistic terms—suggesting that such athletes have innate physical endowments that make them somehow other than or more than human—reveals a concomitant anxiety about and fascination with black masculinity. Fans who engage in mascotting, like fans of minstrelsy, are able to revel in a temporary identification with those extrahuman and prohibited emotions they imagine characterize blackness. Whereas minstrelsy's disavowal of its obsession with black masculinity is evinced through the medium of grotesque comedic ridicule, mascotting's ambivalence is expressed more subtly—by valorizing those features of its subjects that support a stereotypical view of black masculinity as physically powerful, uncontrollable, and so on, and by restricting that valorization to the safely contained lusory context of the sporting arena. Both minstrelsy and mascotting figure black and brown male bodies as objects of spectacle and as the occasion for white audiences to engage in a fantasy of themselves as inhabiting transgressive affects, bodies, and behaviors.

Mascotting, then, is not the valorization of particular individuals that it appears to be. Though hero worship, too, is concerned with the celebration of something other than or beyond the individual who is its object, the hero is celebrated as an individual who is also a representative of some identity valued beyond the sporting context. Mascotting, in contrast, allows fans to vicariously experience affects, behaviors, or on-field successes by reducing the mascotted athlete to his (or her) role in the fan's lusory engagement—often by imagining that athlete not as a full human person but as power, domination, violence, or masculinity personified. This analysis gives good reason to question the assumption that to cheer for a player is to affirm his value as a human being and, by extension, Tamburrini's argument that the diversification of sports fandom's objects has been an obvious good for people of color. If athletes of color are regularly subject to mascotting by white fans it is by no means clear that the current state of affairs is a boon to the goal of racial justice. Rather, it would seem, on the contrary, to reinforce the values and persistence of white supremacy.

Dominican *Peloteros* as Heroes and Mascots

The difference between hero worship and mascotting is more vivid when we consider contrasting fan responses to the same players. That contrast is particularly vivid in the cases of two (former) star Major League Baseball players from the Dominican Republic, Manny Ramírez and Pedro Martínez. To adequately situate the rise of Dominican players—or, as they are known in their home country, *peloteros*—in MLB, some background is in order. Because of its long history in the United States, baseball carries strong cultural associations with nostalgic images of Americanness, proudly celebrating its nickname, "America's pastime." In keeping with other instances of American nostalgia, baseball has a reputation of being the whitest of the three major revenue sports.[8] Despite Jackie Robinson's much-celebrated breaking of the color line in 1946, baseball's reputation as a "white" sport is not without basis. In 2015, nearly 59 percent of MLB players were white, whereas white players accounted for approximately 29 percent of NFL rosters and 23 percent of NBA rosters (Lapchick and Nelson 2015). Likewise, fan bases for baseball are significantly whiter than those of other leagues: fans at the Red Sox's Fenway Park in the mid-1980s could be up to 99 percent white (Klein 2000), and black fans accounted for fewer than 5 percent of MLB game attendance in 2014 (Brown and Bennett 2014).

Despite its white fan base, baseball has undergone significant changes in recent years, primarily due to a major influx of players from Latin America and the Caribbean—particularly from the Dominican Republic and Venezuela.[9] This influx resulted largely from the league's efforts to find cheaper labor pools (Rudolph 2010, 63), an effort that has involved the creation of large-scale recruiting operations in the Dominican Republic, the country from which fully 20 percent of MLB players now come[10] (Makuhari Media 2011). The racial and ethnic diversification of baseball has meant that MLB now more closely resembles the demographic mix of the United States in general, with a sizable and growing Latino population. Yet this shift toward "Latinization" (Klein 2000) has resulted in significant ambivalence and tension in baseball's white fan base, whose nostalgic view of the quintessential "Americanness" of baseball is thereby threatened. White fans have embraced Latino players to the extent that they help their teams win, but it is far from clear that the same fans treat these players as representatives of their community or as anything other than mascots.

Considering the discourse and fan practices that Latinx fans—and Dominican fans in particular—use to root for Ramírez and Martínez provides an instructive point of contrast. Both players attracted sizable Dominican fan bases to the usually white ballparks on the days they played; these fans were conspicuous to other fans and to media by virtue of their display of Dominican flags, cheering for Ramírez and Martínez, and singing Dominican songs. Consistently, Dominican fans treated the play of Ramírez and Martínez as a point of nationalist pride and an opportunity to encourage one of their own to achieve greatness. By attending games primarily on days that Ramírez or Martínez were playing, these fans did treat their play as "a venue to perform Dominican pride" (Rudolph 2010, 69)—but more than this, such fans were concerned with supporting men they took to be their compatriots. In a study of Dominican fans who came to Fenway Park on days that Martínez pitched for the Boston Red Sox, fans repeatedly expressed concern for Martínez's well-being and thought of themselves as providing important support to a member of their community: "We [come] to support him, to let him know he's got people from home here"; "In Montreal he felt there weren't enough Dominicans around so we're here to show him support"; "I've been a Red Sox fan for 15 years, but most Dominicans were not. Now they come when Pedro pitches to give him support, and he feels better" (quoted in Klein 2000, 416). This concern for Martínez and Ramírez as individual persons, not merely as team commodities, suggests that these fans view them not only as full human beings in need of emotional care but also as members of their communities.

That community membership is underscored by fan discourse indicating a clear relation of community belonging. In the stadium, fans said of Martínez, "It's good to *have* Pedro"; "With Pedro *we got* a Cy Young winner and we get more respect"; "He's paid more than any one and *he's one of us*" (quoted in Klein 2010, 416; emphasis mine). Even beyond the stadium, casual Latinx baseball followers expressed this form of community relation: "We're all proud that a Latino is making it," and "he puts a nice face on our community" (411). In the case of Ramírez, this discourse of community membership even withstood his involvement in a steroid scandal. In Washington Heights, New York, to which Ramírez immigrated as a teenager, neither the passage of time nor Ramírez's missteps have been enough to result in fan abandonment. "The overwhelming consensus is that Manny is still a vital member of the Washington Heights community, even in absentia" (Rudolph 2010, 71). Describing the roots of her unwavering support, one Dominican fan put it thusly: "I like Manny because he's Dominican. And we support our own. He made an error. But it's a forgivable error. This is his community. He lived here. He ate here" (quoted in Rudolph 2010, 71). Ramírez is described as inextricably bound to the Dominican community in Washington Heights and as connected to fans as members of a tightly knit community—even when they themselves do not know him.

These Dominican (and more broadly Latinx) fans identify with Martínez and Ramírez in clear instances of hero worship. Though the vast majority of them do not know these players personally, through the lusory attitude, they project themselves into Martínez's and Ramírez's stories and understand their actions on the field to be meaningful in ways that exceed the physical space of the baseball game. Yet in this projection they treat Martínez and Ramírez as persons who are "ours," not in the sense of commodity ownership, but in the sense of community belonging. Martínez and Ramírez are treated as "one of us," as important representatives of the community. Thus, although fans feel themselves and their community enlarged by their successes, they do so with pride in the success of one of their own. This hero worship is qualitatively different from the hero worship of Tim Tebow, insofar as it does not valorize the "character" of white Christian masculinity but, instead, Dominicanness as such. As in the case of Tebow, however, fans who engage in hero worship do so precisely by recognizing something of themselves in that hero and imaginatively identifying with him or her both on and off the field.

It is by no means clear that white fans do the same with Martínez or Ramírez, despite being fans of their teams. Although many white Boston fans clearly embraced Martínez as a pitcher, the language they used to describe their identification with him was rather different. One such fan enthusiastically remarked, "This guy's an ace and a horse, just what we need. And, I hear he's not an asshole like the others" (quoted in Klein 2000, 413). The operative "we" here is clearly the Red Sox, and perhaps the city of Boston more broadly. Importantly, the fan identifies with Martínez insofar as he brings

dominating—even animalistic—athletic talent to the team, thereby constituting a valuable addition for "us." We are left to wonder which "others" the fan
thinks of as "assholes," but given other similar fan remarks claiming that Martínez has "class" and gives back to the community, it is reasonable to infer that
he has in mind other athletes (probably other athletes of color) who are self-
aggrandizing. In the case of Ramírez, Boston fans were happy to identify with
his power hitting but grew impatient with what they perceived as his lack of
professionalism—typified in his (supposedly) lazy defensive play (Rudolph
2010), and his preference for a baggy uniform and either an Afro or dread-
locks. Of the latter, one Asian American fan remarked, "He looks like if he
weren't a baseball player, he'd be stealing my hub caps" (76). Though Ramírez
seemed to redeem himself in the eyes of some Boston fans by becoming a
naturalized American citizen in 2004, on the whole, non-Latinx fans strictly
limited their identification with him to his abilities as a power hitter. In limiting their identification in this way—and in particular, by discursively distanc-
ing themselves from Ramírez the person by describing him as lazy, childlike,
and even criminal—mainstream (mostly white) fans of the Red Sox tacitly
excluded him from the community he purportedly symbolized.

That Ramírez and Martínez were the subjects of mascotting by white fans
is made more salient when we consider the concomitant reception of Dominican *fans* by the same white fans who cheered these players. Whereas
white fan response to Martínez at Fenway Park was overwhelmingly positive,
the same fans had a much more tepid response to the Dominican fans who
came to cheer him, often verging on explicit hostility (Klein 2000). Though
some white fans welcomed this new Dominican subset of Red Sox fans, many
others expressed disgust, particularly at the Dominican fans' display of Dominican flags ("We don't go for that shit. This is America." "What's the world
coming to?" [414]). Other white fans appeared to insult Dominicans in clearly
racist terms, likening them to "banshees," expressing irritation at "the fuckers
darting around the aisles with their flags," and implying that they were criminals who might scale the walls of the ballpark "after the game with ladders
and poles" (415). Finally, as if to ensure the coverage of both racist and sexist
responses, one white fan suggested that "having Dominicans around was fine
'as long as the Mamasitas come along'"[11] (414). As Klein suggests, it is hardly
obvious that white fans' valorization of Martínez (or Ramírez) constitutes le-
gitimately antiracist or color-blind fandom. Rather, "The same fans who view
Latinos in a less-than-positive light are willing to suspend such views *when
a particular Latino can provide them with a championship*" (417; emphasis
mine). Significantly, as I have argued, this "suspension" of negative views is
not total. Rather, in mascotting Martínez and Ramírez, white fans instrumen-

talize them while tacitly excluding them from the realm of full community membership. Though they may be granted provisional or partial acceptance insofar as they are useful to the white community—as elite athletes, as "good" immigrants who assimilate, as men with "class" who conform to expected norms, or even as vehicles for sexually desirable women—they are decidedly not included in the "we" of the Boston community they represent.

Hero or Mascot? Michael Jordan

I want to close this chapter by looking at a limit case: an example of a larger-than-life black star who, during his playing career and beyond, was beloved by white fans and celebrated as a paragon of sporting virtue—even as the greatest athlete ever to play his game. Michael Jordan was arguably the most iconic athlete of the twentieth century. Jordan was (and is) not only a man but a brand and so appealing to such a wide fan base that he became the face of Nike shoes, Gatorade, Hanes, Wheaties, McDonald's, and a host of other companies (Crawford and Niendorf 1999). He was, during his career, repeatedly held up as a role model—so much so that a Gatorade ad campaign featured him playing with a multiethnic group of children alongside the catchy, kid-recited jingle "I want to be like Mike!" It would appear, in other words, that Jordan, if anyone, was the subject of hero worship, and that his wide ranging appeal marked just the sort of racial boundary breaking celebrated by Tamburrini. However, I will argue in the remainder of this chapter that even fans' love for Jordan is, for the most part, understandable as mascotting rather than hero worship and thus that there is good reason to suspect that contemporary sports fandom is not the setting for racial equalization.

There is at least a prima facie reason to believe that fan obsession with Jordan constituted hero worship. Fans the world over identified with him, not only cheering for him on the court, but also wearing his brand-name clothes in an effort to physically embody that identification. Fans came from locales as diverse as Arizona and Taiwan to visit the site of Jordan's final game in Chicago in 2003, where, despite no longer playing for the home-team Bulls, he was greeted with a standing ovation of over three minutes. In 1999—just after Jordan's *second* "retirement" from basketball—one writer mused that Jordan "is even more than a celebrity. He is something much rarer: a hero. Jordan is almost universally adored, not just as a great player but as a man of honorable character. In a recent survey of Chinese students Jordan tied with [the first premier of the People's Republic of China] Zhou Enlai as 'the world's greatest man.' . . . Jordan is the ultimate role model" (Crowley 1999, 41). After the announcement of his *first* retirement (in 1993), Chicago fans reacted as though faced with the sudden death of a loved one: many called in sick to work, were plagued by insomnia, and wondered, in their mourning, whether they could ever be happy again (Mitchard 1993).

Yet we need to think more carefully about the content of fan admiration for Jordan. What, precisely, did this worldwide following of fans identify with? On those occasions in which his "character" is invoked, with what sorts of descriptors is it associated? It is too simple to accept the claim that Jordan was admired as a good person in the full sense of the term, or as a representative of some community, for fan descriptions of him—consistent with his public image—are almost universally hollow, apart from their descriptions of his on-court role. Kids wanted to "be like Mike" on the court, as the Gatorade commercial made clear through its montage of playground footage of young people copying Jordan's iconic tongue-out, leg-pumping jump style. Off-court emulation was limited to the collection of Air Jordan apparel, through which children and adults alike could, if not dunk like His Airness, at least dress like he did while doing it. The linkage of Jordan's appeal with marketing is no accident. From even before his arrival in the NBA, Jordan had become a brand (the Nike contract for the eponymous Air Jordans having been signed in 1985, prior to his league debut)—and that brand was of a piece with the representation of Jordan as nothing other than a basketball star. He was marketed relentlessly neutrally. As one commentator put it, Jordan has "always been incredibly careful not to say anything that might interfere with the massive marketing apparatus that he built or could in any way give the perception that the entire totality of his being wasn't focused on destroying any and all opponents in his path on the court" (Silverman 2014). Jordan was the embodiment of pure success—if not athletic, then capitalist. When his character was explicitly described, it was either in athletic terms (as a competitor or hard worker) or in celebration of all that he was *not*. He did not care too much about sports (Mitchard 1993), he was not like the "spoilsports and malcontents" in the rest of the NBA (Leland 1995), he was "not a social disgrace" (Andrews 1996, 136), and, importantly, according to the owner of the Chicago Bulls, was not "black" as such—rather, "Michael has no color" (125).

It is difficult, in short, to make the case that Michael Jordan was the object of hero worship in the full sense. Fans did not seem to know much about him at all, beyond his on-court exploits. He embodied greatness but did not consistently stand for any particular set of values beyond athletic discipline. We might say, along with sociologist David Andrews, that Jordan was "articulated as the living, breathing, and dunking vindication of the mythological American meritocracy" (1996, 138). One might argue that this constitutes a form of hero worship, insofar as it involves the celebration of a particular set of values. Yet this hero worship would be quite thin, since the glorification of winners *always* involves this tacit celebration of meritocracy. Moreover, the negative theology surrounding Jordan—he is not prideful, he does not boast, he is not flashily self-seeking, he is not "too black"—strongly suggests that he is being treated like Malcolm X's "pink poodle": nonthreatening, docile, not too uppity.

Despite the fact that Jordan obviously benefited from fan obsession, it is demonstrable that he was subject to mascotting in the same way that James Ivy and other black men were. He occupied a kind of ambivalent position for many white fans: he was approachable and nonthreatening, while simultaneously instantiating a fantastical image of power and athletic force. By identifying with him, white fans could inhabit a fantasy of themselves—as "good [non-racist] people—we love Michael Jordan" (Andrews 1996, 139), as vicariously embodying a fantasy of the power of the black masculine body within safely circumscribed limits, and as winners in every sense of the word. The commercials and commentary during Jordan's career reflect the various elements of his mascotting.

The first commercial for Air Jordan shoes, aired during his 1985 rookie season, depicts Jordan flying toward the basketball goal in slow motion to complete a dunk, over the sound of a jet accelerating, then taking off. Jordan hangs in the air for what seems an impossible stretch, as the sound of wind rushing over the wings of a plane continues; when the ball finally goes through the rim and Jordan himself disappears from the frame, leaving only the sky, the ball, and the goal, we hear his voice: "Who says man was not meant to fly?" Jordan is thus figured, at once, as superhuman and as a machine: he is the power of a jet engine, astounding, yet thoroughly reliable in his mechanistic execution of the seemingly impossible. In the end, moreover, he delivers the viewer to the heavens—we find ourselves among the clouds with him, imagining that we, too, can defy gravity, at least as long as he will take us there. The audience is thus able to temporarily inhabit a fantasy of black masculinity as preternaturally physically gifted, machinelike in its efficiency, and existing for the viewer's own personal enrichment. The "I Want to Be like Mike" Gatorade commercial offers a similarly mascotting experience to its audience, though its focus is less on the power of black masculinity and more on emphasizing a domesticated, Disney-fied[12] version of it. The accompanying jingle, inspired by the song "I Wanna Be like You" from Disney's *The Jungle Book* (Rovell 2016), is set to peppy, vaguely African-inspired music, featuring steel drums, a whistle, and a backing gospel choir. Its earworm-inducing chorus is sung by a group of children, echoing the montage of children in urban playgrounds who "want to be like Mike" flashing across the screen—interrupted only by shots of Jordan heartily laughing while drinking Gatorade. Like its *Jungle Book* inspiration, the commercial draws its audience into a safe, cartoonlike experience of blackness. White audiences are able to fantasize about occupying a space they would not likely inhabit in real life—an inner-city basketball court with a black man who can leap several feet at a standstill—from the safety of their racially homogenous suburban living rooms.

That Jordan was viewed as offering a domesticated, safe form of blackness in which white viewers could temporarily indulge is even more striking when we contrast fan and commentator discourse on the NBA once Jordan left. Young black stars like Charles Barkley, Derrick Coleman, Dennis Rodman, and Latrell Sprewell were outspoken, known for trash-talking and for having flashier public personas than Jordan. In the months after Jordan's retirement, fans and commentators bemoaned the state of the NBA, suggested that its players' high salaries made them uncontrollable and disrespectful, and in one case, claimed that "the animals control the zoo" (quoted in Andrews 1996, 150). In contrast to Jordan, whom fans loved for his "class," his winning ways, and his neutral public presence, the players of the new NBA were too self-aggrandizing, too "trashy," and "to put it plainly, 'too black'" (139).

The fact that fans cheer for, and even identify with, players of diverse racial and ethnic backgrounds is simply not enough to offer assurance that contemporary sports fandom is a site of racial progress in this country. As I have argued, not all fan practices are alike, and not all identifications are created equal. White fans, in at least some instances, indulge in hero worship that glorifies heterosexual white masculinity and revels in nostalgia for the simpler times of white supremacy and conservative "family values." At the same time, white fans often identify with players of color by mascotting those players, which allows for their treatment as harmless (though not fully human) pets and the vicarious indulgence in a thrilling stereotype of black masculinity within safely circumscribed parameters. Like the mascotting of Native Americans, the mascotting of individual black and brown players treats these persons as instruments for social benefit, who are simultaneously excluded from full membership in the communities they serve. Mascotting and hero worship, where they exist, can and do function to reinforce standard patterns of white supremacist social organization. Sports fandom's racial integration does not necessarily imply overcoming of racial hierarchization; it may actually be a key site of its perpetuation.

"Honey Badger Takes What He Wants": Southern Collegiate Athletics and the Mascotting of Black Masculinity

In 2011, Tyrann Mathieu was one of the most famous athletes in the United States. An exemplary season of defensive play at the cornerback position for the LSU football team led to his selection as an All-American and, ultimately, a finalist for the Heisman Trophy. Beyond being known for his stellar play, though, Mathieu had become a cultural icon, known across the country by his nickname: the Honey Badger. The Honey Badger name was a quirk of the digital age—popularized by a fan who created a video on YouTube that overlaid in-game footage of Mathieu catching interceptions and recovering fumbles with the audio from a viral nature video in which a narrator cattily remarks that the "nasty honey badger," which survives by stealing bee larvae from the hive while being stung and killing and eating king cobra snakes, "takes what he wants."[1] The video spread quickly, and soon, the Honey Badger name was inseparable from Mathieu. The association was so close, in fact, that Honey Badger T-shirts appeared all over Louisiana at unlicensed vendors—which, as LSU warned in cease-and-desist letters, could mean loss of eligibility for NCAA competition for Mathieu, since the governing body's strict amateurism rules meant that even the whiff of possibility that he profited from the sale of his own image, even an image of a cartoon badger wearing his number 7 jersey, could render him ineligible to play. This ominous warning by LSU's legal team crystallized the paradox of Mathieu's existence that year: he was a national celebrity yet forbidden the profits of celebrity status; he was an elite athlete yet reduced to the status of a cartoon animal on a knock-off T-shirt. Mathieu, in short, had become a mascot.

Mathieu's predicament offers a particularly striking window onto the world of collegiate athletics in the United States and the intense, fraught relationship that fans of collegiate athletics have with the athletes on whose performance the institution depends. Despite its humble beginnings as a feature of student life and physical education, intercollegiate athletics is big business in the United States, particularly in the American South. Collegiate teams, especially basketball and football teams, attract fan followings that rival, and sometimes eclipse, the followings of professional teams—if not in quantity, then at least in the vociferous quality of their devotion. College games are broadcast nationally, drawing millions of viewers in addition to the thousands in attendance at the arena or stadium. Yet, intercollegiate competition is, at least by rule, not a business at all, but an amateur league populated by "student-athletes." The NCAA, the governing body of intercollegiate athletics, ensures this amateur status through rules against the compensation of college players: student-athletes may not be paid a wage by their institution, nor may they earn money by endorsement deals or accept gifts. Many players do earn partial or full scholarships to attend their institution, though this attendance occurs with varying levels of consistency and success. NFL and NBA rules require potential professional athletes to be at least one year removed from their high school experience to be eligible for selection in their respective drafts, which means that many athletes enroll in college merely because they want to play professionally, and intercollegiate competition is the best way to prepare to do so. What results is the attachment of what amounts to an unpaid minor league system to a series of institutions of higher education—an arrangement that is, as many have pointed out, as apparently nonsensical as it is morally dubious.[2]

Beyond consideration of institutional structure, however, I want to argue that attending to fan identity and engagement will show that the moral problems of collegiate sports fandom run far deeper. Collegiate sports fandom in its current state is—particularly in the American South—a central mechanism in the reproduction of whiteness as a hierarchizing racial category. This is not to say that individual sports fans have racist beliefs (though many do); rather, it is to claim that the structure of collegiate athletics and the mascotting of black athletes in the American South contribute to the constitution of regional and community identities that are racialized as white and to the maintenance of a white supremacist social order. Moreover, I will argue, because the mascotting of black male athletes is based on the racist association of blackness with hypermasculinity, it is instrumental in reinforcing heterosexism, homophobia, and misogyny. Black masculinity is positioned as at once desirable, disposable, and potentially dangerous—as both an object of fantasy and a convenient scapegoat for the social ills to which the current organization of collegiate athletics gives rise.

My argument will proceed by first examining the development of collegiate athletics in the United States, including its position vis-à-vis community identities and the ways in which that position changed after the racial integration of NCAA competition. Next, I will analyze three different examples of black male athletes who were mascotted during their collegiate careers (Tyrann Mathieu, Kevin Ware, and Kenyan Drake). I will argue, drawing on Billy Hawkins's analysis of race in college athletics in *The New Plantation* and Shannon Sullivan's critical analysis of the habits of whiteness, that the mascotting and exploitation of these athletes has the effect of reproducing whiteness as dominant, reasonable, respectable, and cultured, in contrast with black masculinity as violent, out of control, and in need of correction. Finally, by looking more closely at the specific language and imagery used by fans in these mascotting relations, I will suggest that the efficacy of mascotting is dependent upon the ridicule and repudiation of homosexuality and (perceived) feminine masculinity.

Playing for Manly Respectability

College football (the first institutionalized intercollegiate sport) was born in an era fraught with anxiety about the end of masculinity, toughness, heroism, and respectability. Its proponents championed it as a means of making boys into men and of preserving the ideals of good breeding. Though some at the time expressed concerns about what good intercollegiate football actually did[3]—notably philosopher Josiah Royce, who argued in 1908 that even if football benefitted its players, it did virtually nothing for its spectators— these voices were drowned out by the overwhelming majority of fans who were already deeply devoted to the game. Though football's inception was in the elite universities of the northeastern United States, it quickly moved southward, as southern institutions mimicked those universities they aspired to emulate. As football moved beyond the Ivy League and into wider American society, concerns grew about the effects of this democratization. Many voiced suspicion that some schools now in competition were fielding players who were not students at all and worried about what this might mean for the respectability of the game itself. The first amateurism rules grew out of this explicitly elitist outlook; as games increasingly drew crowds, teams were incentivized to recruit beyond the halls of their institutions, and the need to keep the rabble out became a matter of acute importance (Buford 2010). If intercollegiate competition were not purely a contest between gentlemen, it might lose its efficacy as a means to cultivate socially legitimate manly respectability.[4] Southern universities soon followed suit, finding ways to restrict participation in football, and creating leagues to enforce those restrictions.

The most prominent of the rules to restrict participation was the "one year rule," which restricted eligibility to those players who had completed at least one year of academics in good standing at their university, ostensibly to prevent athletes from enrolling at an institution just long enough to play and quitting school by season's end (Swanson 2015). Such rules supposedly existed to ensure that sanctioned competitions really were instances of gentlemanly engagement—there were no such things as athletic scholarships in those days—but beyond this class restriction, there were others. For example, because the "one year rule" prohibited colleges from playing significant numbers of its students, it left specific types of schools at a distinct competitive disadvantage—namely, smaller schools with more limited student populations. The schools most disadvantaged by this restriction were, perhaps unsurprisingly, those in more rural locales and those for black students. Black "normal" schools—the majority of institutions for black students at the time—which offered two-year programs focusing primarily on trade education, stood to lose the most, as their size and scope made fielding teams comprised entirely of sophomores virtually impossible (184). The formation of conferences, and the concomitant enforcement of eligibility restrictions, thus had the unstated effect of precluding competition across racial and class groups.

Intercollegiate football, then, functioned as a site for elite southern schools, like their northern counterparts, to claim and reproduce cultural legitimacy. This might seem odd, given football's oppositional, violent nature. Though it is easy to see how restrictions on participation in more collaborative or congenial interactions might be used to shore up privilege—as in the case of prohibitions on intergroup marriages, for example—it is less obvious, at least initially, why restrictions on an activity defined by opposition and the pursuit of dominance might be similarly useful. One might try to explain this by appealing to the social consequences that could attend defeat of a wealthy white school by a poor black one. If the fortunes of one's football team were taken to be metonymically representative of the fortunes of one's social group (as was sometimes explicitly the case in the white South), then the possibility of defeat by a subordinated social group might be too much to bear, symbolically. Though this sort of self-interested consideration offers a plausible psychological explanation, it is difficult to support with clear evidence. It becomes even more dubious when we consider that, in addition to the black "normal" schools, smaller elite white southern schools—notably Vanderbilt—were effectively excluded from competition by the "one year rule" (Swanson 2015, 180). The production of cultural legitimacy through the exclusion of some competitors from sport could not be *simply* a matter of the fear of defeat at the hands of a socially subordinated group.

To understand the rationale for exclusive competition, a statement from the University of Iowa's athletic director in 1908 is particularly instructive: "In order that a man shall benefit by a contests, it must be a real contests [*sic*], between men whose strength is comparable. . . . If contests are held with institutions of equal rank, they will be carried out on a broader basis and with a manlier spirit" (quoted in Swanson 2015, 180). This explanation is of a piece with the suggestion, often encountered in the philosophy of sport, that the best competitions are between rivals that are evenly matched, whose outcome remains in doubt as long as possible.[5] The hollowness of victory over an outmatched opponent gives rise to an extensive network of segregated competitions, which restrict competition between disparate age ranges and levels of talent and segregate athletics along gender lines.[6] In order for competition to be meaningful—to have the desired effect of producing an enhanced sense of self—we must compete against equals. Thus, however counterintuitive it might be, athletic competition *needs* its rivals to respect and admire one another, even as they seek to dominate. Total domination may sound appealing, but if the loser poses no real challenge, domination quickly loses its appeal. The paradox of competition is that rivalry is built upon cooperation, insofar as it is dependent upon the need for our rivals to do well enough for our victories over them to be meaningful. We can genuinely compete, in other words, to the extent that we recognize in one another worthy competition.

In the case of the early eligibility restrictions on competition, there are at least two forms of nonrecognition at work. On the one hand, as in the case of Vanderbilt, some are excluded as a form of collateral damage in the pursuit of the goal of "the purification of college athletics through the South" (Swanson 2015, 172). Though Vanderbilt itself was a respectable institution full of young men from "good 'Southern stock'" (180), its exclusion was required in order to maintain the integrity of the "one year rule," which would ensure that intercollegiate football remained a gentlemen's competition (tellingly, Vanderbilt eventually joined one of the leagues requiring adherence to the one year rule). On the other hand—as in the cases of historically black schools like Southern University, Howard University, and Prairie View A&M—some are excluded directly, as the very entities whose presence constitutes a threat to the efficacy of the competition as intended. The centrality of rules sharply delimiting the sphere of legitimate participation in the institution of intercollegiate football make clear that the preservation of a specific (white, masculine, respectable) identity is a central feature of the practice itself. The language institutions used at the time to describe their willingness (or unwillingness) to compete with other institutions illustrates the gravity of such a decision for the identity of the institution. Universities regularly chose to resume or break off "athletic relations" with other institutions—sometimes on the basis of their adherence to norms like the "one year rule," and other times because of perceived slights on the field (179). The decision to suspend "athletic relations" with another institution was a serious one, and "denoted something deeper than a simple refusal to play a game versus another school" (178). In Hegelian terms, we might say that the denial of athletic relations constituted a refusal to recognize that institution, or the persons it represented, as worthy of opposition. The fact that the institutional structure of white intercollegiate athletics precluded *any* athletic relations with teams from black institutions is thus indicative of both deep contempt for and serious anxiety about the importance of such structures to produce the recognition of respectable white masculinity.

With this in mind, it is not surprising that racial integration of athletic competition came so late in the American South. Collegiate football was taken to constitute an assertion of southern legitimacy, and fans held up victories over colleges from the northern and western United States as moments that redeemed the South from its previous Civil War defeat and denigration by northern elites (*Sporting News* 2009, 32; Borucki 2003). Yet the racialized restriction of competition not only offered a reinforcement of the values of the Confederacy; it was also required by the exclusionary logic of intercollegiate athletics as a whole, which had as its organizing principal the preservation of prestige and the concomitant restriction on participation. That Louisiana passed a law in 1956 against interracial athletic competition, that the University of Kentucky did not start its first black football player until 1967 (Greenlee 2015), and that the University of Alabama did not do so until the 1970s are surely indicative of the climate of the Jim Crow South and the fallout of the *Brown v. Board of Education* decision. But in addition to this, these failures to racially integrate suggest an extension of college football's central logic, which has functioned to preserve community identity by seeking recognition from and offering it to a select few—who are acceptably masculine, white, and wealthy. Fan participation in this racially exclusionary regime thus indicated not only an unwillingness to identify with individual players on the field but an unwillingness to relinquish a practice that had served to confer cultural legitimacy by its very (exclusive) nature.[7]

The racial integration of collegiate athletics, particularly in the South, thus seems initially to undermine collegiate athletics' usefulness as a mechanism for the preservation of exclusivist cultural legitimacy and white supremacy in particular. However, as I will argue, the mascotting of black athletes[8] allows

white fan bases to continue to participate in the prestige economy of collegiate athletics by replacing pure exclusion with instrumentalization. This
instrumentalization, particularly when found within the exploitative framework of contemporary intercollegiate athletics, ensures that NCAA competition remains a mechanism for the reproduction of social hierarchy. This
hierarchy, I will argue in the final section of this chapter, is not only racialized;
it perpetuates both masculine and heterosexual normativity.

Mascotting Black Masculinity

HONEY BADGER DON'T GIVE A SHIT

Tyrann Mathieu looks back on his time as the "Honey Badger" less than enthusiastically. Months after becoming a national celebrity and nearly winning the Heisman Trophy, Mathieu was in trouble—dismissed from the LSU
football team for failing blood tests for marijuana and in jail for marijuana
possession. His fans had abandoned him, he was widely referred to as an idiot
and a thug, and ESPN published a piece that disappointedly suggested that
he was following in the footsteps of his father, who spent his adult years in
prison for murder. Though Mathieu would eventually be drafted by the Arizona Cardinals to play professionally (albeit at a lower draft position and sal-
ary than he would likely have commanded had he stayed out of legal trouble),
he recalls the period of his fame at LSU with regret. In a recent interview,
Mathieu expressed discomfort with the nickname, telling his interviewer that
he wished that people would stop referring to him as "the Honey Badger" and
use his name instead. The nickname reminded him of this dark time, he said,
and in particular, of his stint in jail (Weinfuss 2015).

There were good reasons for Mathieu to be uncomfortable with his fame as
the "Honey Badger" even before his dismissal from the team. Though he was,
in some ways, in an enviable position (both locally and nationally famous),
this came at the cost of being reduced to a caricature—to the image of a grin-
ning cartoon rodent stealing footballs on ten-dollar T-shirts. His popularity
was built upon fan consumption of his image as the embodiment of powerful,
vicious hypermasculinity. That image was neatly encapsulated in the (con-
trolled) lawlessness of the fan-created viral video that showed him stealing
passes and forcing fumbles on a repeated loop, in tandem with a narration
that was at once titillating and condescending: "Nothing can stop the honey
badger when it's hungry. . . . Oh, what a crazy fuck, look, honey badger don't
care. Honey badger don't give a shit, it just takes what it wants. . . . 'Thanks for
the treat, stupid!'" The audio, taken from a viral video that paired this sassy

narration with images of an actual honey badger stealing food from other animals, was repurposed to narrate Mathieu's on-field defensive highlights, figuring him as the object of a particularly cheeky nature documentary. Fans identified not with Mathieu the person but with the fantasy of the Honey Badger; in the confined, safe space of the football field, through the Honey Badger image, fans could indulge in a fantasy of domination and animalistic freedom from prevailing social norms.

This fantasy draws on and contributes to the long-standing racist stereotype of black masculinity as animallike and out of control. Footage of Mathieu forcing a fumble, which is pursued and recovered by a group of three of his LSU teammates, all of whom are black, is narrated thusly: "The honey badger does all the work while these other animals just pick up the scraps." Later, the audience is invited to gaze at still images of Mathieu's athletic body, as the narrator turns to content more typical of a nature documentary: "The honey badgers have a fairly long body but . . . distinctly thickset, broad shoulders." The documentary format presents Mathieu—and to a lesser extent, his black teammates—as a dangerous but fascinating exotic animal, whose habits have been captured for display to a curious audience. The audience is positioned as omniscient, unseen observer, able to indulge in the voyeuristic pleasure of football-cum-nature film. Black masculinity is thus rendered safe for the consumption of white audiences who would not dare venture into its "natural habitat."

Fan consumption of "the Honey Badger" was certainly enthusiastic, at least for a time. Fans bought Honey Badger T-shirts in droves and made signs celebrating the Honey Badger that were regularly featured on ESPN and broadcasts of LSU's football games. This support came to an abrupt halt, however, on Mathieu's dismissal for marijuana use. Fans who had celebrated him as an icon one day disgustedly left him behind the next. This rejection, importantly, was not based on a dis-identification with violent actions or (as in fan rejection of steroid users) with cheating. It was, rather, a rejection based almost entirely on the fact that Mathieu was no longer eligible to play—and thus no longer a possible object of mascotting. Without his on-field antics in an LSU Tiger uniform, Mathieu had become useless to his fans; outside of the context of the football field, his lawlessness was a liability and a reminder of the specter of criminality that haunts black masculinity in the world of white supremacy.

WARE'S THE TROPHY

Clad in red, white, and black, thousands of supporters of the University of Louisville basketball team leapt to their feet—cheering as time expired, marking a victory for the Cardinals over the Wichita State Shockers in the 2013 NCAA men's basketball tournament semifinal game. The crowd of Louisville fans, which included men, women, and children of all ages, broke into euphoric, frenzied celebration: screaming, jumping, embracing one another, waving signs and arms, and shaking pom-poms in the team's cardinal red. Many fans wore shirts or carried signs with the number "5" or the name "Ware." Others held aloft cardstock cutouts of a photo of the head of Kevin Ware, the backup sophomore guard to whom the signs and shirts paid tribute. Below the waving, disembodied images of his head and punning references to his name or number—such as "Ware's the Trophy" and "Ri5e to the Occasion"—crowding the arena, the real Kevin Ware got to his feet with the aid of crutches and made his way from the end of the Louisville bench to the edge of the court, where he met his father. The two embraced, the elder Ware holding his son silently in the midst of the euphoric fans around them.

Six days earlier, Ware had suffered a grotesque injury before another shrieking crowd, breaking his right tibia so badly during a hard fall on the basketball court that the bone protruded six inches from his skin. In the intervening period, as Ware had surgery to repair his injured leg, fans across the country rallied around his image. By the time he returned to sit with his team during the Cardinals' game against the Shockers, Ware was a national celebrity: Adidas and the University of Louisville had marketed a special-edition T-shirt featuring his number 5, millions of people had watched and rewatched the gruesome replay footage of his injury and his subsequent *Late Show with David Letterman* appearance, and ESPN reported that a retired professional basketball player had donated the funds to give Louisville fans a thousand of the Ware "Big Head" cutouts to wave in the stands during the game. The resulting scene was uncanny: thousands of Ware heads waving around the arena as the real Ware looked on, unable to play or to stand without crutches—and, of course, unable to gain anything from the sudden popularity of his image. Through the remainder of the Cardinals' championship season, Ware was a symbol, his image sold and exchanged by fans and authorized retailers alike. By the end of the next season, he would leave Louisville, largely forgotten, transferring back home to Georgia State.

An article profiling Ware the year after his transfer describes a young man deeply uneasy with his short-lived celebrity status and relieved to have returned to a more normal life. During his stint as Louisville's unofficial mascot, he recalls, he went to dinner with his mother while trying to hide his face from the restaurant full of fans. His mother had suggested that he was embarrassed to be seen with her—but he clarified that, in fact, he did not want to be seen by anyone (Lake 2015). Ware's discomfort with his sudden celebrity came sooner than Mathieu's, which is understandable, given an important qualitative difference in their treatment: Ware became a mascot not as a result of his on-court dominance but as a result of his sudden, intense vulnerability. Whereas the "Honey Badger" was glorified and idolized as a symbol of uncontainable will, Ware was reduced, as the result of his gruesome injury, to an object to be waved in the stands like a pom-pom, to a collectible (even if desirable) *thing*, as the "Ware's the Trophy" pun suggests. Although fans' celebration of Ware could be read as supporting a fallen comrade, its reliance on the transformation of Ware to a symbol to coalesce fan spirit in advance of Louisville's championship victory makes that celebration appear much less interested in Ware himself and thus much more like mascotting than legitimate support. Ware was, in effect, left to deal with the consequences of a traumatic injury at the same time that he was being instrumentalized in the service of team spirit. It is no wonder that he did not want to be seen.

Though fans left both Ware and Mathieu behind when they were no longer useful as mascots, the difference in the quality of their usefulness illuminates the different ways in which mascotting can occur. Ware's mascotting was not so much dependent upon his representation as hypermasculine or powerful as it was on his status as a nonthreatening symbol, or pet. As a result of his injury, Ware became not just another black man on the basketball court but the image of human vulnerability. Although black masculinity is typically cast as preternaturally physically gifted, and at once super- and subhuman in athletic skill, Ware's broken leg transformed him into a black male body in need of care. That Ware was not a fan favorite prior to the literal breaking of his body suggests that this brokenness was a constitutive feature of his appeal. The voyeuristic and repeated replaying of his injury by fan (and nonfan) communities online revealed an audience fascinated—and perhaps titillated—by the spectacle of his violent injury.[9] In subsequent games, his literal immobilization on the sideline was the very thing that made him available to fans as a symbol to be bought, traded, and carried on wooden sticks (the latter creating a fan of Ware's face, with which fans could, ironically, cool themselves by fanning). Ware's mascotting, in other words, was predicated on the limitation of his physical agency; his status as an inspirational symbol for Louisville fans was built upon the foundation of his broken body. Ware became a mascot, then, in precisely the sense that James Ivy did—the image of black masculinity as domesticated and "kept" for the benefit of the community for whom he serves as a heartwarming symbol. Like Ivy's blindness, Ware's physical limitation was a necessary condition for his celebration by that community: just as "Blind Jim" became and remained an icon for never having "seen" Ole Miss lose, Ware was a mascot to the extent that he remained physically sidelined, his fame waning as he regained his mobility. Also like Ivy, Ware's body was explicitly instrumentalized: where Ivy served as a music stand for band members or as a landmark in photographs, Ware's head became a prop through which fans declared their allegiance to the Louisville team and created connections with one another. In the cases of both Ivy and Ware, black masculinity is mascotted not by providing a vicarious experience of power or aggression but by being reduced to a symbol of the community: a good story, a heartwarming image, a trinket emblematic of something larger than itself. This symbolic reduction is facilitated, moreover, by black masculinity's literal reduction—the acquisition of physical limitation that renders the black man at its center possessable rather than threatening.

USING FOOTBALL PLAYERS TO RECRUIT SORORITY SISTERS

In the fall of 2014, Kenyan Drake was a star running back for the University of Alabama's football team. During a game in October of that year, he sustained a horrific injury while being tackled, breaking his leg and dislocating his ankle, which visibly stuck out from his body at a nauseating angle. Drake's season was over, and he underwent surgery to repair the injury—but unlike Kevin Ware, his sidelining did not result in a marked rise in Drake's public profile. In truth, Drake was already a celebrity on his campus and throughout the Southeastern Conference, where he was a significant competitor and (prior to his injury) a potential prospect for the NFL draft. After his injury, his public presence, if anything, diminished, as fans focused on players still competing. As he recovered from surgery and rehabilitation, Drake's profile was fairly low outside of the state of Alabama—though fans within the state continually asked after his health, annoying his coach, Nick Saban, with repeated inquiries about whether he would be ready to return to play at the start of the 2015 season.

During the summer prior to Drake's return, he was again, suddenly, in the national news—but for a somewhat unexpected reason. Drake appeared in a glossy, big-budget recruiting video[10] produced by the University of Alabama's chapter of the Alpha Phi sorority, which had gone viral on the Internet for reasons unrelated to his appearance. The video, composed almost entirely of slow-motion shots of the Alpha Phi sisters smiling, dancing, and being almost uniformly blonde and beautiful in various settings, was criticized for its shallow, sexualized, and homogenous portrayal of college women, first in local Alabama news sources, and ultimately on *Good Morning America* (ABC News 2015). The purpose of the video was to attract new women to rush (that is, apply for admission to) the Alabama chapter of the sorority, primarily by portraying the Alpha Phi sisters and their lifestyle on campus as desirable and elite. Set to electropop dance music, the video features the Alpha Phi women as its centerpiece, displaying their bodies, clothes, smiles, hair, and affection for one another against a variety of backdrops associated with high-status college parties. These settings include the meticulously decorated Alpha Phi house, a lakeside retreat, a lush open field, and at the musical climax, Bryant-Denny Stadium, the home field of Alabama's football team. Notably, until the scene at the stadium, no men and no people of color appear in the video. Once the Alpha Phi sisters enter the stadium, however—clad in oversized jerseys that mostly conceal their tiny cutoff jean shorts—Drake appears, alongside "Big Al," Alabama's plush elephant mascot. It was this appearance, months before his return to play following the previous season's devastating injury, that thrust Drake back into the national consciousness. Interestingly, in this moment of reappearance, he was decidedly not the video's "star."

Drake appears for less than a minute in the video, and in many of his shots, he is nearly interchangeable with "Big Al" as a signifier of Alabama football. He poses and walks with the Alpha Phi sisters but occupies a central spot in only one shot. In the shots of the group dancing in the stadium, "Big Al" is the focus—twerking at the center of a circle formed by the sisters—with Drake on the periphery of most of the shots. In the remainder of the stadium scene, Drake visibly interacts with only two of the Alpha Phi sisters: one beats him in a race—perhaps a nod to his injury—while the other somewhat suggestively bends over several yards in front of him to complete a long snap of the football. Although both of these interactions seem choreographed to sexualize the women who are the focus of the shots, using angles and poses that emphasize their rear ends, the sexual subject for whom they are performed is the viewer, not Drake, who is positioned either at a distance from the women in question or so that he is not privy to the sexualized body part. For most of the video's duration at Bryant-Denny Stadium, in fact, Drake is part of the scenery. He, along with the stadium and "Big Al," form a visual backdrop of the University of Alabama's traditions, against which the Alpha Phi sisters perform an almost caricatured version of desirable southern white femininity.

Given the recruiting purpose of the Alpha Phi video, it is unsurprising that the video functions to position the women in it as explicitly southern and socially elite, reiterating their sexual and social desirability. What is interesting, however, is the way in which sports fandom—and specifically, the mascotting of Kenyan Drake—is leveraged to accomplish this goal. The women's appearance on the field of Bryant-Denny Stadium, a space that is typically reserved for the hypermasculine elite of the University of Alabama, makes their petite stature, perfect makeup, and (mostly) platinum blonde hair extremely striking; the effect is enhanced by their wearing of oversized football jerseys, which presumably have been borrowed from men, if not actual Alabama players. The images position the Alpha Phi women as the embodiment of idealized white femininity: small, fair, and, as Sandra Bartky has put it in another context, "subject to the evaluating eye of a male connoisseur" (1990, 28). Though the rest of the video makes the importance of an "evaluating eye" obvious, fixated as it is on slow-motion images of the women's bodies, the backdrop of the masculine space of the stadium, football, jerseys, Big Al, and Drake focuses that evaluation to convey sexual desirability by men specifically. Importantly, this heterosexual desirability is conveyed by the specific content of the women's performative connection to Alabama sports fandom: though they inhabit the restricted space of the stadium, the women are not watching a game; their dancing on the field suggests a connection to Alabama sports that is more concerned with the social events surrounding the games than the game itself; their interactions with Drake and the football he carries are either playfully humorous (falling down while laughing without catching the ball) or choreographed to appear sexually appealing. Their performances of sports fandom convey, in short, that they value Alabama football but not to an extent that would be threatening to masculine fans.

Their performance's visual connection to Alabama football specifically reiterates the significance of fan practices around the Crimson Tide to the constitution of regional identity. The presence of the symbols and iconography of Alabama football, including Drake, tacitly cite the tradition and rituals of Alabama football fandom and position the Alpha Phi women as elite members of the social order that it is used to reproduce. The fact that typical students and fans of the University of Alabama football team would not have access to the field of Bryant-Denny Stadium, Big Al, or star players under any circumstances—much less for a private dance party—figures the Alpha Phi women not only as part of the tradition of Alabama football but as members of the upper echelons of the southern aristocracy. That this figuration occupies such a central place in Alpha Phi's recruiting video illustrates the significance of access to Alabama football—and the bodies of the players that make it up—as a means of displaying, reproducing, and transmitting social capital.

This usage of college football is not new, as I showed in the first section of the chapter. What is striking about the Alpha Phi video, however, is its demonstration of a shift in *how* elite social status, particularly for the white southern aristocracy, is reproduced and transmitted following the racial integration and (apparent) democratization of college football. Whereas college football previously created hierarchy primarily by restricting access to the game itself, postintegration football fandom can remain a bastion of white southern aristocracy by transforming the relationship between fans and players to one of mascotting. Drake's mascotting is evident in the video insofar as he is simultaneously instrumentalized and socially excluded: he is instrumentalized as a symbol of Alabama football—and by extension, as a unifying symbol of the region represented by it—and also as a means of reinforcing the Alpha Phi women's sexual desirability. The latter is accomplished in part by his positioning as the lone masculine figure in the video and as a reminder of the masculine gaze that operates in the background. Though the video is ostensibly aimed at women and features women onscreen almost exclusively, the hypermasculinity of the space of the football field, the wearing of men's football jerseys, and the repetition of the image of dancing women, evoke the image of fraternity house parties, and positions the Alpha Phi women as the objects of (desired) sexual conquest therein. Just as importantly, however, Drake's instrumentalization as a status marker for the Alpha Phi women functions to make them sexually desirable specifically as members of the southern white elite. The social status conferred by his appearance occurs specifically within the Greek system, which functions largely to facilitate heterosexual coupling among persons of elite social status—and so to transmit that status to future generations. The fact that all seventy-five of the Alpha Phi women are white, and that Drake is the only person of color to appear in the video, is not, in other words, a mere coincidence. The video, rather, offers a vivid illustration of the transformation of white supremacist (and, as I will explain, heterosexist) sports fan practice in the face of social reform: as Patricia Hill Collins puts it in a slightly different context, "black athletes, and their varying degrees of acceptance and rejection . . . become important visual stages for playing out the new racism" (2004, 153–154).

In light of this analysis, a Fox Sports report on the Alpha Phi video is especially revealing. Clay Travis's blog post on the "Hot Alabama Sorority" video puts the matter thus: "Credit to Alpha Phi for flipping the hot girl script, instead of being used to recruit football players, they're using a football player to recruit new sorority sisters. . . . SEC! SEC!" (2015). Travis's use of the "SEC!" chant—used by fans of teams in the Southeastern Conference to signal pride in the conference as a whole, and southernness more generally—makes clear how college athletics is used to foster social status and southern pride through the instrumentalizing exclusion of young black men. Drake's social exclusion may not be quite as obvious as his instrumentalization—but it becomes clearer in light of the video's visual racialization and its navigation of the issue of miscegenation and black sexuality. Though the video hints at

Drake's sexuality by featuring him as the sole masculine presence amid a sea of dancing white women, it studiously avoids positioning him as the sexual subject of their movements. That he had recently experienced a serious injury likewise symbolically limits his power and thus undermines his potential status as a sexual "threat" in the white imaginary, which envisions black masculinity as sexually insatiable and aggressive. Moreover, the conspicuous visual absence of black women (or any other women of color) in Alpha Phi reiterates the sorority's position in the economy of sexual exchange between white social elites. The video thus forecloses the possibility of miscegenation—and, it seems, the possibility of general social interaction among persons of different races—even as it holds Drake up as a visual instantiation of the practices of sports fandom that constitute southern white identity. He is, as Travis puts it, used to re-create and sell the significance of membership in an institution for the transmission of elite social status.[11] Drake does not, for all that use, enjoy full membership in the social elite that he helps serve to constitute. In that sense, Drake forms an ideal case of the mascotting of black masculinity in southern collegiate athletics. As I will argue in what follows, this mascotting is significant not only for its portrayal and exploitation of black masculinity but also for its effects on the meaning and function of southern whiteness.

Mascotting, Exploitation, and the Reproduction of White Supremacy

In his essay for *ESPN: The Magazine*, "How They Do in Oxford," Kiese Laymon describes the surreal experience of attending an Ole Miss football game for the first time—ironically, on "white out" day, when the masses of mostly white fans came to the stadium dressed all in white. Though he grew up in Jackson, Mississippi, Laymon's childhood experience of football fandom was located squarely within the Southwestern Athletic Conference—a conference populated entirely by historically black colleges and universities (HBCUs) —so Ole Miss football and its traditions were entirely unfamiliar to him until he took a fellowship at the university as a writer in residence. Because of the racial politics of the state of Mississippi, Laymon's family was wary of his accepting a position at the symbolic center of the white southern aristocracy—a wariness that he himself seemed to feel as the sea of whiteness grew on that first day. "I'm wondering who, and what, pays the price for ritualized Southern comfort and uniformity," he writes. "I can't take my eyes off the backs of the student-athletes who play for the football program at Mississippi. Their uniforms are a bright bloodred. Twenty of the 22 starters look black like me" (2015). The blackness of the players on the field—and, it seems, Laymon's own blackness, in the crowd of white—becomes hypervisible in the space of the stadium; yet it is a hypervisibility that nevertheless countenances a kind of annexing identification, as that sea of white fans cheers and boasts of the accomplishments that "we" make on the field. Taking in the scene Laymon describes, it is difficult not to recognize the appropriateness of his grand-mother's declaration: "These white folks ate good off of our work."

The fact that whites "eat good" on the athletic labor of black masculinity remains true in a variety of ways. Mascotting black masculinity, I will sug-gest, has concrete effects for white sports fans and white communities more broadly that can be categorized both as obviously material (i.e., having to do with economic well-being) and as subjective (i.e., having to do with one's habits of conscious interaction with the world as a human subject). These effects accrue as a result of at least three overlapping phenomena, which are, to greater and lesser extents, features of the examples of mascotting I have examined thus far: the economic exploitation, symbolic annexation, and ritu-alized instrumentalization of black masculinity as a stage for the performance of whiteness. Significantly, these practices help to reproduce whiteness as a hierarchizing and normalizing category, *not* by foregrounding whiteness, but by making it invisible as a mode of racialization. Through mascotting, white-ness is reiterated not only as culturally normative but as empowered, in con-trol, autonomous, and (in Shannon Sullivan's words) ontologically expansive. Ironically, however, as the mascotting relation makes clear, these features of whiteness are dependent upon the subordination, exploitation, and instru-mentalization of racial others.

ECONOMIC EXPLOITATION

In recent years, the economics of intercollegiate athletics has been a hot topic in the American national news, the primary focus of which has been the in-justice of NCAA regulations on eligibility barring athletes both from receiv-ing direct pay or gifts as compensation for playing and from profiting from their likenesses (e.g., by selling autographs). This conversation has been fu-eled in part by some college athletes' attempts to unionize (CAPA 2014) and in part by *O'Bannon v. NCAA*, in which a federal court found for the plaintiff, a former college athlete who filed an antitrust class action lawsuit against the NCAA for permitting video game maker EA Sports to use his likeness—and that of other college athletes—without compensation. Ed O'Bannon, a former basketball star at UCLA, successfully argued that the NCAA violated US anti-trust law by restricting even those players who had graduated from profiting from their own images. This case, like the cases of Ware and Mathieu, offers a stark example of the potential implications of the NCAA's rules: collegiate athletics generates significant revenue, which is shared by private corporations, the NCAA itself, and (to a lesser extent) the sponsoring institutions. Yet the persons at the center of that revenue-generating activity—the athletes themselves—receive no financial compensation and are barred from profiting from it, even indirectly.

Those opposing compensation for athletes usually do so on the grounds that athletes *are* compensated via tuition scholarships—some going so far as to argue that these confer upon the athletes an obligation to remain on the college team rather than "going pro for the dough" (Corlett 2013, 297). Yet, as proponents of what philosopher J. Angelo Corlett calls the "Risk of Injury Argument" (301) point out, the risks associated with continuing to play college ball are significant: the longer an athlete plays at the college level, the greater the risk that he (or she) will be injured and thus undermine his (or her) future earning potential. Rationally self-interested athletes who could do so would quite reasonably choose to forgo their remaining years of college in order to be compensated as soon as possible, given the inevitable decline of physical capabilities with age. Moreover, it is by no means clear that athletes at elite NCAA institutions even receive the alleged benefit of their play. Cheating scandals, fake courses, and the extraordinarily demanding schedules of college athletes make it difficult, in many cases, to believe that the "student-athletes" cited so widely by the NCAA receive anything resembling a true college education. Beyond those cases in which coaches recruit star athletes explicitly to play for one year only prior to going pro,[12] there are reports of athletes being routinely pushed to majors or courses of study in which they have no interest, with the idea that these majors will be the ones most likely to ensure grades that maintain athletes' eligibility. In other cases, athletes received credits for classes they never attended, and athletes were recruited to institutions while being functionally illiterate and without regard for their ability to do college-level work.[13] Compounding the problem, some athletes reported that because of their limited financial resources, they often went to bed hungry. All the while, the television broadcasts of these athletes' play result in millions (often billions) of dollars in earnings. Whatever compensation is derived via athletic scholarship, in sum, is not likely to be proportionate to the funds that athletes generate by their work on behalf of the university.

From a Marxist perspective, there are obvious reasons to be dubious of the ethical status of the NCAA's prohibition of compensation—the arrangement, in this view, is built upon the refusal to pay athletic workers the value of their labor, which is as unjust here as in any other capitalist transaction. Beyond this, though, I argue that the economic exploitation of college athletes, particularly in cases of black athletes at predominately white institutions, has hierarchizing effects that reinforce white supremacy. These result not only from the extraction of surplus value from the labor of black athletes but also from the overwhelming whiteness of the authorities that regulate, administer, and coach the teams and institutions involved, the denigration of those athletes who resist the current arrangement, and the impoverishment of HBCUs to which the current system of NCAA athletics contributes. Importantly, these hierarchizing effects result not in any explicit celebration of whiteness but in the tacit normalization of whiteness through its repetition as "an invisible datum, an unmarked given" (Roelofs 2005, 96) of contemporary American culture.

College athletics as it is currently practiced figures the young black men involved, not as full agents but as commodities to be managed and children in need of paternal discipline. Coaches, NCAA officials, and university administrators and staff are overwhelmingly white (Hawkins 2010, 143), regulating the lives, earnings, bodies, and play of the black men whose labor drives the economy of college athletics. Athletes at elite programs are subject to extraordinarily detailed regulatory mechanisms—with nearly every hour of the day managed for them, from hours spent in study hall to the hours spent at meals and hours spent in the weight room—producing exemplary versions of what Foucault would call "docile bodies," (1995, 135) from which it is possible to extract maximal athletic performance. The fact that this regulation is not, however, limited to the regulation of bodily capacities treats the athletes in question as less than fully autonomous adults. The management of tutoring programs and study halls, the widely reported designation of majors without athletes' consent, the refusal to allow for profit on the grounds of "protecting" athletes from predatory businesses, and the most recent solution of allowing athletes to have some minimal profits deposited in a "trust" only accessible upon completion of the college career all suggest that these athletes—who are disproportionately black—cannot make the same kinds of choices that nonathlete students regularly make for themselves. That this paternalistic management happens in tandem with economic exploitation is no accident, as Billy Hawkins points out in his analysis of collegiate athletics, *The New Plantation* (2010). The two are, as Hawkins argues, complementary features of the same colonial outlook.

Both the reconsolidation of wealth under white control and the paternalistic constraint on black athletes' autonomy are justified by—and contribute to—a conceptualization of black masculinity as childlike and in need of direction. What results is, as Patricia Hill Collins has pointed out, a repeated rehearsal of a symbolic "family drama" (2004, 156), with white male coaches (and less visibly, white-controlled institutions) playing the role of the "father figure" that troubled young black men are presumed to lack, correcting their behavior and training them for their role in mainstream (white) society. When players resist their role in this narrative—by, for example, attempting to unionize, speaking out about the injustice of their lack of compensation, or resisting authority—they are castigated by fans and sports media in the language one might expect to be used to describe a child: spoiled or ungrateful.[14]

It is important to note, however, that the subjectivizing implications of these practices and patterns of discourse are not limited to the representation or constitution of black masculinity; rather, they have too-often unmarked effects on the reproduction of racial whiteness. By "whiteness," I mean not the biological facts of phenotype, like skin color or hair texture, nor a natural fact about one's genetics,[15] but rather a set of social meanings that accrue to those phenotypic features and that result in certain patterns of interaction. In adopting this meaning of whiteness, I am following George Yancy and other philosophers of race in recognizing racial designations as characterized and constituted by their concrete social and political consequences, which are thoroughly hierarchical. Although whiteness as a category of classification is, on the surface, used to refer to people having certain physical characteristics, (real or imagined) geographical origins, and familial lineages, it is also characterized by "a multitude of individual, collective, intentional, isolated, systemic actions that synergistically work to sustain and constantly regenerate relationships of unequal power between whites and nonwhites" (Yancy 2004, 14–15). Those unequal relations of power need not take the form of slavery or segregation; rather, as Yancy points out, everyday features of contemporary white lives are marked by unequal power relations, even when they are explicitly antiracist. "After all," Yancy points out, "after a day of theorizing, the white theorist rides back to the suburbs, escapes being profiled, walks up and down the streets of all-white neighborhoods without fear of being harassed or labeled 'a problem,' and finds it easy to hail a cab if necessary" (16–17). Significantly, these social effects are rendered hierarchizing precisely because nonwhite *others* are figured as a problem or threat—as when, for example, white homeowners' property values increase when they move away from the "bad neighborhoods" inhabited by nonwhites and into suburban enclaves. The dependence of this hierarchy on the hypervisibility and overdetermined meaning of nonwhiteness (and particularly, of blackness) has the ironic effect, today, of rendering whiteness invisible to whites, who tend to think of race as "something others possess," whereas "whites are just 'normal'" (Jones 2004, 70). White privilege depends upon the maintenance of black subordination, even when it is not explicitly attended to.

The current structure of intercollegiate athletics fits this pattern. It is crucial to note, for example, that the current NCAA structure does not simply exploit athletes, many of whom are black; this exploitation ensures that the wealth produced by means of these athletes' labor is recirculated into white communities—both through the NCAA and media corporations that profit from it and through the outsized salaries that are made possible for head coaches, university presidents, and so on. As public funding for higher education dwindles in the United States, the extraction of value from the labor of these athletes becomes increasingly important.[16] Concomitantly, as Hawkins points out, HBCUs are increasingly impoverished: lucrative programs at predominately white institutions (PWIs) have the financial resources to recruit the best players in black communities away from HBCUs, which in turn reinforces their athletic dominance and thus their financial clout and recruiting influence. Unable to compete with such top-tier programs, athletic departments at HBCUs have diminished capacity to generate funding to help support themselves or their institutions (2010, 28–31). PWIs are, accordingly, positioned as the only institutions that really matter, athletically or otherwise. The enrichment of PWIs, then, alongside the enrichment of actual white persons, reinforces the equivocation of white civilization with civilization as such. As a result, it is not surprising to find white fans with the sense of entitlement that is required to view those who would resist their own exploitation as "spoiled": the belief that black college athletes "owe" whites their athletic labor is supported by the assumption that access to white institutions is extraordinarily valuable, according to which such athletes are "lucky" to have been admitted.

ANNEXATION

The form of mascotting most akin to blackface minstrelsy—the identification with black masculinity as a sensational experience of violence, sexuality, or animality—likewise has implications for the meaning and reproduction of whiteness. First, just as the paternalistic treatment of black men as unruly children tacitly figures whiteness as civilizing, the figuring of black masculinity as exotic, extrahuman, and titillating tacitly reinforces the normalization of whiteness. White fans' willingness to identify with black men temporarily, in the exceptional social context of the sporting venue and for the apparent purpose of indulging in forbidden affects, treats the black masculine body like a vacation destination—"a nice place to visit, but you wouldn't want to live there." This treatment has two related effects. The first, more obvious effect is the tacit presumption of white society as neutral and respectable. The treatment of black men and black culture as "a momentary aesthetic thrill" or worse is, as Monique Roelofs (2005, 96) puts it, the corollary of whiteness's normalization. The second effect, related to the first, is the production of whiteness as paradigmatically free from restraint—or, as Shannon Sullivan puts it, as "ontologically expansive." She writes: "White people tend to act and think as if all spaces—whether geographical, psychical, linguistic, economic, spiritual, bodily, or otherwise—are or should be available to them to move in and out of as they wish" (2006, 10). The fact that whiteness is coded as racially neutral means that individual white people tend not be viewed as a threat when they enter unfamiliar spaces and tend to have the means to move where they wish. This absence of constraint in movement (they are not targeted by police while driving or by security guards when trying to enter university buildings) gives rise to a subjectivity that presumes its own unencumbrance and freedom to "travel"—whether that traveling be to an "ethnic" neighborhood to experience the pleasure of "authentic" cuisine or a temporary dabbling in exoticized black masculinity.

To understand why this form of mascotting would have significant effects on white subjectivity, it is useful to consider Sullivan's suggestion that ontological expansiveness is a "habit" in the thick, pragmatist sense of the term. Habits, for Deweyan and Jamesian pragmatists, are not merely personal preferences, nor are they obviously objects of conscious will that could be easily altered like a change of clothing. They are, rather, both (1) "transactional"— that is, occurring across and through the interaction of an organism and its environment, including other organisms therein—and (2) productive of significant physiological and psychological effects, which become deeply entrenched over time, and which can be altered only by replacement with a different habit. To speak one language rather than another, for example, affects my environment and that of those around me, while at the same time producing in me both cognitive effects (particular ways of conceptualizing the world) and physiological effects (e.g., the ability to move my mouth and tongue in some ways but not others, wrinkles around different parts of my mouth than those of French-speakers). Importantly, these effects enable me to do some things and make others more difficult. There is no way to eliminate habits entirely, nor would we want to; it is through habits that humans come to know and interact with our worlds.

Yet, as Sullivan demonstrates, some habits are racialized, and some have the effect of reproducing white privilege. The habit of moving into and out of whatever spaces one wishes results in a white comportment to the world that tends not to impose limits on itself and that treats felt limitations as a kind of injustice or "violation of the 'natural' order of things" (2006, 149)—

as when, for example, white people are distressed by feeling uncomfortable in a black neighborhood or indignant that they are not "allowed" to say "the N word." Unrecognized in this discomfort is the fact that nonwhites tend not to be so ontologically expansive, having a clear sense of what sorts of spaces they are likely not to inhabit without difficulty and what sorts of language, movements, or dress they must adopt in order to avoid appearing threatening. White habits of ontological expansiveness enable whites to move freely and unthinkingly in the world, but they also constrain white people from recognizing when they are imposing (even unintentionally) upon the freedom or personal space of others, particularly nonwhite others. In white gentrification, for example, well-meaning young white people may move into nonwhite neighborhoods and start frequenting restaurants and places of worship founded by and for nonwhites in an effort to expand their cultural outlook without recognizing the importance of such locales as refuges for marginalized groups or the potential of their presence to displace the very residents who make them what they are. In such cases, the habit of ontological expansiveness reinforces white privilege while subordinating nonwhites, even if unintentionally.

Mascotting is a type of ontological expansiveness. When white fans mascot players of color by imaginatively identifying with (a lusory version of) them, cheering for them, imitating their movements or speech, or wearing the clothing or jerseys of those players, they treat those players as space to which they have obvious access. In cases where fans limit their identification with black players to those moments of athletic power or hypermasculinity and discard them when they no longer serve the purpose of granting vicarious access to those feelings, fans both tacitly reinforce the exoticization of black masculinity and contribute to the habit of viewing and treating black bodies as things that should be available to them when useful and hidden when they are not—like toys that get in the way when one is not playing with them.

RITUAL STAGING

When mascotting functions to reproduce whiteness, the role of black players is more complex than it initially appears. In the image of the twenty black Ole Miss players whose athletic performance occupied the spatial center of the ritual Kiese Laymon witnessed, for example, it is not entirely correct to say that they constitute its exclusive focus. The fans involved are concerned with the players primarily to the extent that their presence or performance constitutes a venue for whites' own ritual performance. The "white out" that

Laymon describes is but one example of this phenomenon of self-referential ritual performance. The effect of the white out is meaningful to no one but the fans who engage in it—it does not, for example, intimidate the opposing team to see a stadium full of people in the same color. Its purpose, rather, is to encourage "team spirit"—which is to say, to make salient one's membership in a collective identity by reflecting mirrored performances of that identity back to oneself. As I have suggested, such ritual practices of identification offer a significant means of cultivating and reinforcing racial and regional identity; in this section, my concern is with the extent to which individual black bodies are used by fans, as Collins has put it, as symbolic "stages" (2004, 154) for the performance and cultivation of those identities.

As we have seen, racial integration in collegiate athletics has not posed a serious threat to white supremacy, which has been able to adapt to the presence of black athletes. The use of black athletes as a stage or background against which rituals of community identification are performed is one such adaptation, as in the case of Kenyan Drake. But even fan rituals less obviously staged than the Alpha Phi recruiting video make use of this treatment, particularly in the cases of mostly black teams at PWIs. Media scholar Pamela Wonsek, in her analysis of the visual representation of the 1992 "March Madness" basketball tournament, shows that the televised ritual of the game is characterized by extensive focus on the images of mostly white ritual surrounding the court itself, which is populated disproportionately by black players. She writes, "Not only does this place the black players in a secondary and entertainment role, but it may also serve to reassure the white majority that its dominance is not really being threatened" (1992, 454). By cloaking the players in the images and iconography of the team and fans they are supposed to represent— and by concerning themselves with those players only within the space of the arena, where they function as fungible symbolic representatives—fans are able to use the sporting contest and the athletes who populate it as a space for the ritual staging of the performance of their own communal identities. The centrality of (mostly white) fan ritual to athletic contests is dramatically visualized, as Wonsek points out, by the repetition of camera cuts to the faces and reactions of white fans, white cheerleaders, white dancers, white band members, white commentators, and white coaches. This effect is exacerbated in the case of football, in which players' helmets (sometimes with the addition of visors) obscure their faces, rendering them anonymous in contrast with the individual white faces that populate the screen and arena. The physical and symbolic features of the sporting event allow white subjects to participate in the various practices of sports fandom without thinking about the humanity of the athletes at its center.

That white fans are able to engage in cultural practices of such significance without recognizing their dependence upon the labor, bodies, and
discipline of young black men speaks to another feature of whiteness as it
is constituted in relation to nonwhiteness. Whiteness—again, not merely as
a phenotype, but as "a set of power relations" (Mills 1997, 127) that accompany it—is radically dependent upon others, despite consistently misrecog-
nizing itself as prototypically autonomous and civilized. In the case of collegiate sports fandom, particularly in the American South, white community
self-identification and reproduction is dependent upon the labor of young
black men, even as fan practice and discourse foreground "tradition," imagery, and a "we" that is more often than not exclusively white. White fan self-
recognition thus functions similarly to Lacan's "mirror stage" in the production of self-consciousness in infants. The infant who is first able to catch sight
of his or her reflection in the mirror does not realize that this is only possible
because he or she is supported by something or someone and is thus able to
develop "the illusion of autonomy," the sense that he or she is a sovereign self.
This moment of narcissistic gazing is, for Lacan, both a founding moment of
individual consciousness and indicative of the "constitutive misrecognition"
(1999, 80) of the human ego. The formation of the "I" is characterized by the
ability to break oneself off from the rest of the world—to negate it by recognizing it as "not me"—yet, ironically, this negation is fundamentally illusory,
as the self, like the supported infant in front of the mirror, is dependent upon
others for its continued existence. The practices by which fans recognize
themselves as subjects of a certain sort—an "I" that bears a clear relation to
a (white, regional) "we"—are similarly narcissistic and similarly dependent
upon the failure to see their dependence upon others, whose physical labor
functions as an unacknowledged foundation.

The identity formed through white sports fan practices is, of course, distinct from the identity formation Lacan describes by virtue of its collectiv-
ity. But this *collective* failure to recognize the role of others' subordination or
service in one's own social position has been documented by many thinkers
as a persistent feature of whiteness and colonialism. In *Discourse on Colonialism*, for example, Aimé Césaire argues that although European colonizers believed themselves to bring civilization and prosperity to the colonized,
that civilization was invariably dependent upon "a few thousand subordinate
functionaries, 'boys,' artisans, office clerks, and interpreters necessary for the
smooth operation of business" (2001, 42). Because the continued functioning
of European society depends upon—while studiously ignoring—the exploitation and subordination of non-Europeans, Césaire writes, "colonization =
'thingification.'" He continues: "They [colonizers] talk to me about progress,

about 'achievements,' diseases cured, improved standards of living. *I* am talking about societies drained of their essence, cultures trampled underfoot, institutions undermined, lands confiscated, religions smashed, magnificent artistic creations destroyed, extraordinary *possibilities* wiped out" (42–43). Importantly, Césaire does not claim that the white Europeans who depend upon the subordination, destruction, or divestment of colonized peoples actively hate the colonized; rather, they are so narcissistically focused on the "achievements" and identity of white civilization that they simply fail to recognize their exploitation as a necessary condition for its continued existence. Similarly, contemporary philosophers describe the failure of whites to recognize the effects of white privilege in opening up possibilities for them at the expense of others as "the epistemology of ignorance"—a pattern of epistemic lack that is a constitutive feature of white subjectivity.

Although white fans do, of course, literally *see* and cheer for the physical labor and heroics of the black athletes they treat as mascots, mascotting prevents fans from recognizing those persons as fully human and as exceeding their symbolic role. Moreover, mascotting prevents white fans from recognizing the extent to which the fan rituals and practices most dear to them depend upon the instrumentalization of young black men. Rather, like Césaire's white colonizers, white fans are disposed to recognize in the labor, physical sacrifices, and athletic excellence of "their" black players evidence of the achievements and greatness of the white institution or community they symbolize. White fan rituals performed against the backdrop of the physical sacrifice of black male bodies, particularly in the American South, offer a particularly vivid example of the continuation of colonial subjectivity. Here, community pride is played out on a ritual stage whose foundation is the very persons least likely to benefit from it. Mascotting, in short, poses no threat to white supremacy; mascotting is, rather, instrumental in the reproduction of whiteness.

Mascotting as Misogyny

Revenue sports are, to state the obvious, overwhelmingly masculine. The fact that so much cultural significance is attached to a rigidly gender-segregated activity in which men function as the primary (and often, only) agents makes clear that the celebration of normative masculinity is a central feature of contemporary sports fandom. According to dominant racist discourses, which are operative everywhere from fixations on the size of the mythic black penis to the suggestion, persistent since slavery, that black women are naturally unfeminine and that blackness just *is* naturally more physically powerful and therefore more masculine. Given the racist association of blackness with hypermasculinity, it is unsurprising that black male athletes become the principal objects of mascotting. In the context of a practice grounded in the preservation of manly respectability, the assembly and ostentatious display of hypermasculine greatness in the form of young black men functions to position the fans and institutions with which that display is identified as elite and powerful. However, the celebration of black masculinity as the embodiment of hypermasculinity and hypersexuality also functions to tacitly reinforce both misogyny and heterosexism—a fact that has significant implications for the collegiate setting, in addition to the broader cultural context.

HYPERMASCULINE AGENCY

The celebration of masculine agency is discursively reiterated throughout the sporting arena, including in fan practices associated with intercollegiate athletics. During the weekly broadcast of ESPN's program *College Gameday*, fans traditionally make clever signs that can be held up behind the broadcasters to be seen in the background of the anchor shot. Often, those signs involve "humorous" insults of players or coaches on the opposing team. Frequently, such insults involve the association of a player or coach with femininity or allusions to homosexuality. In one such sign, for example, a fan declared that "Les Miles likes being the little spoon"; another altered an image of pop star Miley Cyrus riding a wrecking ball to use Michigan coach Jim Harbaugh's head— giving the appearance that he had a female body positioned in a sexually suggestive manner; another proclaimed that "[quarterback Zach] METTEN-BERGER SHAVES HIS LEGS," while a Clemson fan taunted the entire Notre Dame football team by suggesting that "ND Players Drink Pumpkin Spice Lattes." Each of these signs imply their target's feminization, whether through the implied sexual passivity of "being the little spoon," the explicit association with female bodies and feminine grooming practices or the suggestion of feminized aesthetic/gastronomic choices. In other cases, signs insult opposing institutions by suggesting that the women who attend that institution are sexually promiscuous. Despite higher education's (perhaps undeserved) reputation for political progressivism and feminism, fans of intercollegiate athletics remain entirely comfortable with sexist or homophobic humor that presumes and reiterates the celebration of masculinity through the denigration of femininity.

This denigration is a key feature of the culture of sport as it is currently practiced. No insult is quite so ubiquitous or cutting as the suggestion that an athlete "throws like a girl." Misogynist abuse is such a regular feature of "sportspeak" that it often goes unnoticed. This is true even in women's sports, where it is still common to hear coaches to tell players to "man up"—that is, to push through difficulty or play through pain. In men's sports, coaches and players commonly use feminine language as an insult designed to motivate players, which ranges from the comparatively tame hurry-up call *"Today, Ladies!"* to the more colorful uses of "cunt," "bitch," or "pussy" to indicate an athlete's inadequate effort. A notable example of the normalization of this language is the case of Mike Rice, former Rutgers University's men's head basketball coach, who was fired after a video of him surfaced using these slurs, in addition to calling players "faggots" and "fairies" while pushing, kicking, or throwing basketballs at them (Zirin 2013). It is noteworthy that the Rutgers athletic department knew about Rice's behavior for months (Eder 2013) but chose only to suspend him for three games until ESPN aired the video, precipitating outrage from several quarters, including New Jersey governor Chris Christie. Moreover, the media coverage of the firing—in particular by ESPN, which first broke the story—focused almost entirely on Rice's physical violence toward the players and his use of the slur "faggot." Completely unremarked in most of the coverage was Rice's repetition of feminine terminology as graphic insult. The media's collective failure to attend to the misogyny of Rice's language suggests that it is simply a taken-for-granted feature of sports culture.

Misogynist fan discourse mimics and reproduces the misogynist and homophobic discourse of sports culture. In addition to alluding to homosexuality through taunting images of sexual passivity, fans regularly insult players they view as the unworthy beneficiaries of outsized media attention with explicit sexual references—suggesting that the media will "GET ON THEIR KNEES" for a player or sarcastically asking whether they can "ride his nuts any harder."[17] The imagery of male players being fellated or otherwise sexually gratified by members of the (typically) male sports media is used to disparage both the player in question and anyone who would identify with or praise him. The insult "works," to the extent that it does, precisely because it is homophobic and heterosexist: suggesting that such athletes receive oral sex from women would not constitute an insult to the players in question (though it might, ironically, still function to denigrate the women involved). It is by raising the specter of homosexuality—which is equivocated with feminization—that fans who resent a particular player's status are able to symbolically take him down a peg. To link a player with homosexuality is to call into doubt his hypermasculinity—and thus his potential to be either a hero or a mascot.

The reinforcement of heterosexism and the tacit disparagement of homosexuality is on display, additionally, in the Honey Badger video of Tyrann Mathieu. The narrator of the video uses an almost caricatured—high-pitched, lisping—"gay-sounding" voice; this voice was, arguably, the principal reason for the video's appeal. The narrator, Randall, is himself the joke in the video. This is not only because his word choice is over the top and apparently inappropriate for a nature video ("the honey badger is really pretty badass"); it is also because those words are spoken in an exaggerated lisp. Mathieu's masculinity—and supposed animality—are put into relief and amplified by the playful, feminized narrative framing; this juxtaposition is a primary feature of the video's humor. Additionally, Randall's narration in the video facilitates the negotiation of white fans' ambivalent fascination with black masculinity, which is characterized at once by desire, awe, and fear: the viewer is invited to gawk at and fantasize about Mathieu's animallike masculinity, while disavowing the potentially sexual content of their gaze by projecting that sexuality onto the video's sassy narrator or disavowing it entirely through laughter. Finally, it is important to remember that Mathieu simply would not have had the high profile and fan following that he did were it not for the spread of the Honey Badger video and nickname. Mathieu's mascotting is quite literally made possible by the lighthearted ridicule of homosexuality.

The disavowal of homosexuality is, as several theorists have noted, a central feature of the reinforcement of hypermasculinity[18]—particularly in the arena of sport. One of the ways this disavowal is enacted is, ironically, through the nearly ubiquitous practice of patting or slapping one's teammates on the rear end to congratulate them on a good play. This form of touching between men—along with the practice of showering together in open rooms—"would be disapproved of in any other context" but is accepted in the sports context "without a second thought" (Arens 1975, 79). The openness with which typical norms of masculine bodily contact are violated in the homosocial sporting arena functions, counterintuitively, as an explicit repudiation of homosexual desire. By performing such acts openly and repeatedly, male athletes can demonstrate that they mean nothing—that is, that they are explicitly drained of any sexual significance. In such a context, ironically, to admit discomfort with having one's bottom patted by a teammate is to open oneself to the charge of being gay. Football requires a particularly high volume of homosexual disavowal through the performance of potentially sexualized acts—including, as Alan Dundes points out, the repeated adoption of the bent-over "three point stance" (2002, 244) and the placement of the quarterback's hands between the legs of the center while in this position[19]—which is, perhaps, one explanation for football's reputation for hypermasculinity.

Because the hypermasculinity of sport requires the disavowal of homosexuality, mascotting seems to fail in the few cases of players who are openly gay. Michael Sam, for example, the first NCAA football player to come out as gay, might have been a prime target for mascotting. A young, attractive, talented black athlete at the University of Missouri, in 2013 Sam earned the title of defensive player of the year and was a potential NFL draft prospect. After coming out, though he was the subject of extensive ESPN coverage, Sam did not retain much of a fan following, and his draft prospects fell significantly. Initially predicted to be selected in the early rounds, Sam was ultimately drafted by the St. Louis Rams in the seventh round—lower even than Tyrann Mathieu, who had been arrested for marijuana and sat out his final college season—and was cut by the team before ever starting in an NFL game. Given that the "dominant discourse pertaining to black and gay male athletes holds them to be culturally incompatible categories" (Anderson and McCormack 2010, 145–146), Sam quickly became unthinkable as an NFL player, much less as a mascot. Though this fact kept him from being instrumentalized by fans, it also resulted in the end of his football career.

The glorification of hypermasculinity that mascotting requires functions by more or less explicitly repudiating or denigrating femininity and queer masculinity. The glorification of the masculine agent is evident, moreover, in the identification choices that fans *do* make. Concomitant with the racism of mascotting, in other words, is the valorization of explicitly masculine agents and the fantasy of vicariously inhabiting a thoroughly dominant masculinity through identification with black male athletes in the safe space of the sport. Mascotting, then, is motivated not only by an antiblack racism but also by a deep-seated misogyny or fear of (perceived) femininity.

OBJECTIFICATION OF WOMEN

Images of black masculinity as hypermasculine and hypersexual are so pervasive in the cultural imaginary that, as Angela Y. Davis points out, the "myth of the black rapist" (1981, 172) has been a nearly ubiquitous feature of white American society since the time of slavery. The myth of the black rapist envisions black men as (hetero)sexually insatiable and thus as potential sexual predators from whom "our women" (that is, white women) must be protected. This myth provided justification for the terrorism of lynching; it has also been used to prop up contemporary trends of mass incarceration.[20] White anxiety about black masculine heterosexuality and miscegenation also fueled the fight against integration of colleges and—by extension—of intercollegiate athletics. The transformation of that anxiety into mascotting since integration poses a new sort of problem. White fans who mascot black players may enjoy the idea of temporarily identifying with the power, animality, and sexuality they associate with black masculinity, but they are wary of the possibility of that masculinity exceeding its bounds. If the nostalgic trope of "the quarterback [who] dates the homecoming queen"[21] is to remain safe for the white supremacist imaginary, what happens when the quarterback is a black man? If black masculinity is purported to be hyper-heterosexual, and if white supremacy can neither countenance miscegenation nor give up its mascots, it must find a way to direct these athletes' supposed sexual appetites toward more "appropriate" objects.

The "objects" toward which black masculine sexuality can be acceptably redirected turn out to be, unsurprisingly, black women. The corollary of the myth of the black rapist, Davis argues, is the myth of the promiscuous black woman, who is sexually available and therefore unrapeable (1981, 182). The figuration of black women as naturally promiscuous has justified white men's rape and sexual exploitation of them since the time of slavery. As collegiate athletics is racially integrated, this racist and sexist image is used to justify the sexual instrumentalization of black women as a recruiting tool—and not only in the distant past.

> Howie Evans, a one-time black assistant coach at Fordham University, once told sports-studies scholar Richard Lapchick that during his years of work at a black community center in New York in the 1990s, recruiters from white Southern schools would arrive seeking to sign black women to attend their schools. The reasoning, according to Evans, was that these women would be able to provide the black athletes at these Southern schools with *appropriate* female companionship. (King and Springwood 2001, 118)

The recruiter is disinterested in these potential black women recruits as students—he is unconcerned with whether they will benefit from attending a PWI in the South or with the large-scale recruiting of black women—or as agents of their own sexuality, who may or may not desire a romantic or sexual relationship with the athletes at his institution. The women in question are treated simply as toys with which to satiate his mascotted athletes. It is assumed that they will be sexually available and that this sexual availability can be used as a means to keep the black men to whom they are offered working for the team in question, while keeping their hyper-heterosexuality from outstripping its bounds.

The objectification of women, especially black women, as tokens of sexual exchange continues to function as a recruiting tool at predominately white institutions. In 2015, reports emerged that an assistant at the University of Louisville hosted parties in a campus dorm for recruits to and members of the men's basketball team using sex workers, who both stripped and had sex for money. Although head coach Rick Pitino denied any knowledge of these activities, Katina Powell, who claims to have provided sex workers for the parties, told reporters that she was paid by one of the graduate assistants on the Louisville staff (Barr 2015). In her interview with ESPN, Powell explicitly links her role in the sexual transactions, almost all of which involved black women, to the project of recruiting athletes to come to Louisville. Asked if she thought of herself as part of the recruiting team, Powell answered, "Yes . . . I did everything to make those guys sign. When you offer what you offer, then of course 'hey, I'll sign on the line, if this is what they're giving, they're providing, sure.'" (Barr and Goodman 2015) Though the report that sex workers were a regular feature of recruiting at Louisville produced a major scandal, many fans were nonchalant about the accusations. The most common theme among commenters on the ESPN website was the suggestion that this sort of practice happens everywhere and that anyone surprised by the allegations is hopelessly naïve. In support of their view, some fans cited the Spike Lee film *He Got Game* (1998), whose plot revolves around the recruiting of a promising black athlete to play basketball at a predominately white institution; a key feature of his recruiting is the provision of women—in this case, two white women—for sex. Although this scene and the Louisville case differ in their racialization and negotiation (the women in the *He Got Game* scene were not paid sex workers), they both suggest that there are good reasons to believe that "high school recruits being provided women for sex on campus is standard operating procedure" (Wilbon 1998).

This is not to say that the women who have sex with mascotted athletes have no sexual agency. In the Louisville case, sex workers reported being able to name their price, and in the fictionalized *He Got Game* case, we have good reason to believe that the women having sex with recruits or players want to—perhaps because they, too, have internalized an image of these athletes as hyper-heterosexual, exciting sexual partners. Despite the agency of these individual women, the practice of providing women for sex as a recruiting tool treats women as fungible objects of exchange and contributes to the expectation that their bodies will be available for use when desired. Moreover, when this type of relationship between male athletes and their sexual partners is normalized, the prevalence of intimate partner violence is hardly surprising. If the women in these settings are imagined to exist primarily to serve as sexual satiation for uncontrollably masculine athletes, their harm is no great cause for concern. In those locales where miscegenation is a serious social taboo, the sexual expectations—and concomitant disregard for their experiences of violence—will be all the greater for black women.

When considering the effects of mascotting on women, particularly black women, it is telling what sorts of violations by athletes mascotting can sustain. When, in other words, does athletes' behavior result in fans' total dis-identification with them, and when do fans continue to identify with their hypermasculinity and hyper-heterosexuality from a "safe" distance? I will return to the question of fan dis-identification in the following chapter; for the present, it is enough to note that violence against women—including sexual violence against women—appears to pose no threat to fans' identification with mascotted players. We can observe this fact in a few different ways. First, the hypermasculinity of the athletic context appears to make collegiate athletes more likely to commit acts of sexual violence against women than the general college population—but *less* likely to face punitive action. Multiple studies suggest that male athletes at NCAA institutions are disproportionately likely to be reported for sexual violence,[22] to accept sexual aggression and violence, and to accept common (victim-blaming) rape myths (Boeringer 1999; McMahon 2007). Fan concerns about the arrests of high-profile players for violence against women is typically limited to whether the athlete in question will be available to play for his team as usual and, if he is suspended, how quickly he can be reinstated. Even in the most high-profile recent case of a player being dismissed for assaulting a woman, involving Ray Rice of the NFL, the suspension came only after video of the assault was publicized, creating a media problem for the league.[23] Fans seem to have little trouble continuing to cheer for athletes who assault women.

Fan involvement in the licensing of violence against women can be direct or indirect. A *New York Times* investigation of the Tallahassee Police Department documents some particularly egregious cases of direct involvement. Consistently, according to the *Times*, officers failed to follow standard protocol in investigating cases involving Florida State football players—often noting in their reports that they had contacted a supervisor to help handle the situation because it concerned an FSU player. The police department, like the city of Tallahassee, is full of FSU fans; in one case, an officer declined to arrest a player because he did not want his name on the arrest record of a member of the FSU football team. In two of the most troubling cases, star players Jameis Winston—a Heisman trophy winner—and Karlos Williams were accused of rape and domestic violence, respectively. Charges were never brought in either case. In the case of Winston, FSU (in an apparent agreement between the athletic department and the police) did not conduct its own investigation of his accuser's charges until months later, after the football team's national championship victory. In the case of Williams, the officer responding to a 911 call about a man punching a woman holding a baby did not turn the report over to a local domestic violence crisis center, as protocol requires, and did not seek access to videotapes that would have captured the altercation on film (McIntire and Bogdanich 2014).

Even when fans do not have the power to police or prosecute violence against women, their fandom can contribute indirectly to its normalization. This is particularly true in mascotting, which enacts a sharp break between identification with the player as athlete and as off-the-field individual. Insofar as fans depend upon mascotted athletes to facilitate a fantasy of their own power, masculinity, or communal identity, they *need* such players to (minimally) remain active members of the team and to be the sorts of persons whose individuality does not get in the way of their instrumentalization. In this context, law enforcement and the larger social milieu are disincentivized from treating such players as equal under the law. For institutions of higher education, this disincentive has significant financial implications, as fan spending on "their" teams is increasingly important, particularly for underfunded public institutions. Moreover, because the mascotting already involves imagining such players as hypermasculine and hyper-heterosexual, fans have good reason to respond to sexual and other violence against women by their favorite mascots with relative nonchalance—shaking their heads at these young men who "go overboard," but ready to jump back into cheering for them as soon as they are cleared to play.

Mascotting is certainly not the only phenomenon to contribute to the objectification of women and the pathologizing of homosexuality. Yet its prevalence in the context of intercollegiate athletics is a major cause of concern. This is so not only because so many tangible and intangible goods (from money to school spirit) are bought at the price of exploitation but also because this dubious transaction appears to be working at cross-purposes with contemporary efforts by American colleges and universities to foster more inclusive learning environments and to address the pervasive culture of sexual violence on American campuses. The normalization of heterosexism and the objectification of women (especially black women) that comes alongside mascotting is antithetical to the mission of higher education and counterproductive of the aims of Title IX compliance.

Mascotting as Hierarchizing Mechanism

Collegiate athletics has changed substantially since its inception. What has not changed, however, is the extent to which it functions to reinforce entrenched social hierarchy in the face of perceived threats to it. Whereas intercollegiate competition began in an era in which the privilege of white American masculinity seemed precarious, it continues in a time when the preservation of social hierarchy is as pervasive as it is unspoken. The phenomenon of mascotting allows white fans to continue to participate in rituals to reproduce gratifying experiences of whiteness—especially southern whiteness—while disclaiming explicit white supremacy. Likewise, mascotting reinforces subordinating and exploitative relations to blackness and tacitly contributes to the sexual objectification of women and the disavowal of queer persons. The fact that few of these effects are explicitly sought by fans of collegiate athletics does not mitigate their effectiveness. Changes to the racial makeup of intercollegiate competition have not succeeded in purging these practices of their discriminatory and oppressive roots. Mascotting has redirected those effects in more palatable and seductive directions—but these are all the more insidious for being hidden beneath the glorification of local power and team spirit. Those effects are laid bare when the mascotting relation breaks down, as we will see in the following chapter.

6

From Mascot to Danger

This shocking act of disloyalty from our homegrown "chosen one" sends the exact opposite lesson of what we would want our children to learn. And "who" we would want them to grow up to become.

OPEN LETTER FROM DAN GILBERT, Cleveland Cavaliers owner, 2010

Richard Sherman: What a model for today's Taliban youth.

JOHN PODHORETZ, *New York Post* columnist, on Twitter, January 20, 2014

Sports fans love to hate. While fandom is often thought of as a practice of support, identification, and admiration, fans engage just as vociferously in ill will, dis-identification, and hatred. This negative fandom may take a variety of forms, from team-based rivalries to antipathy for individual players. In this chapter, I examine fan practices of dis-identification and argue that these further expose the racialized and racializing character of sports fandom in the contemporary United States. In particular, analyses of cases in which fans dis-identify with or reject players for extra-athletic violations (that is, for violations of norms that do not have clear relations to the game itself) reveal that fans are not only—or even primarily—expressing moral judgments about players' behavior. Rather, fan loathing of and ill will toward individual players function to reiterate a particular notion of communal identity. In fact, I will argue, the most prominent cases of fan dis-identification expose the tenuous relationship between white fans and black players and reveal a deep-seated anxiety about black masculinity. In these cases, I will argue, athletes of color who had been previously used as mascots come to be figured as dangerous threats to the community. When black men behave in ways that obviate white fans' efforts to deploy their imagined power for their own ends—when they refuse to be mascots—they risk being portrayed as selfish thugs whose very existence constitutes a danger to the healthy body of society.

In 2010, LeBron James, who was widely acknowledged to be the best player in the NBA—and perhaps one of the best basketball players ever—announced that he would leave the Cleveland Cavaliers to sign with the Miami Heat. Although he had grown up in northeast Ohio and had spent the first seven years of his career with the Cavaliers, James explained on a nationally televised program that he wanted an opportunity to win championships and that "taking [his] talents to South Beach" (Abbott 2010) would afford him that opportunity. His choice was, to put it mildly, controversial. James was the subject of a scathing open letter by Dan Gilbert, the Cavaliers' owner (for which Gilbert was eventually fined by the league commissioner); he was widely reviled in sports media, and fans throughout Cleveland staged public burnings of his jersey. Disgust at James was, moreover, not limited to Cleveland fans: multiple polling services found that James, previously one of the most admired sports figures in the country, became one of the most hated athletes in the United States overnight, joining the ranks of Michael Vick and Tiger Woods.[1] Echoing the remarks of Dan Gilbert, many repeated the accusation that James was selfish, narcissistic, disloyal, and a blight on the game of basketball who had set a dangerous example for the many children who no doubt emulated him.

A similar media firestorm erupted in 2014 around Richard Sherman, cornerback for the Seattle Seahawks. Sherman, widely considered the best cornerback in the NFL at the time, defended a pass in the end zone with only seconds left in the NFC championship game, preventing a come-from-behind win by divisional rivals the San Francisco 49ers and securing the Seahawks a trip to the Super Bowl. Following his successful defensive play, Sherman taunted 49ers players and gave an emotionally charged interview to reporter Erin Andrews. In the brief interview, Sherman, clearly still caught up in the excitement of the victory, declared himself the best corner in the league and shouted aggressively into the camera, "Don't you ever talk about me!" (Fox Sports 2014). When pressed, Sherman clarified that he was aiming his remarks at Michael Crabtree, the 49ers receiver for whom the final pass was intended. Subsequently, Sherman's interview with Andrews was the subject of intense media scrutiny and impassioned debate. Some reporters and analysts suggested that Andrews looked rightfully frightened during the exchange, while others claimed that Sherman acted like a "thug"—or, in the case of a New York Post columnist, a "model for . . . Taliban youth" (quoted in Coates 2014). Although Sherman did not initially appear to suffer the same extent of fan hostility as James, many fans mirrored the disgusted and hostile attitudes of these analysts and declared that they would root against the Seahawks in the Super Bowl simply out of dislike for Sherman.

In 2007, Michael Vick, star quarterback of the Atlanta Falcons, was arrested for violating federal prohibitions on dogfighting. Though Vick's guilty plea to financing the dogfighting ring was accompanied by a not-guilty plea on charges of animal cruelty (which were later dropped), horrific news reports of dogs subjected to starvation, electrocution, and hanging were linked to the operation, after which many reporters and fans began to call disgustedly for his imprisonment and expulsion from the NFL. Vick was indeed imprisoned for nearly two years but was later reinstated by the league's commissioner. His return to play in 2010 prompted a wave of discourse, particularly from white fans, about the difficulty of rooting for a player who would be involved in such grotesque crimes. Although there was some public support for Vick's reinstatement—most notably from people of color, including President Obama, Princeton professor Melissa Harris-Perry, and former NFL coach Tony Dungy (Bacon 2010; Harris-Perry 2010; Maske 2009)—news outlets from NPR to the *New York Times* and NBC ran stories about fans' predicament in having to choose between supporting "their" teams and refusing to cheer for a man who "makes [them] sick" (Miller 2009). Meanwhile, pundit Tucker Carlson suggested that Vick should have been executed for his crimes (*Hannity* 2010), the website SackVick.com organized anti-Vick protests at Philadelphia Eagles games, and talk-radio callers expressed sentiments like that voiced by seventeen-year-old *Talk of the Nation* (NPR) listener Natasha: "I am appalled that anybody could forgive Michael Vick. He did horrible, horrible things to dogs. And the fact that this guy can say that he would forgive a murderer—that person took someone's life. They took someone's life. . . . And I was a Michael Vick fan—not anymore. And I won't ever forgive him" (National Public Radio 2010).

In each of these three cases, athletes who had previously been wildly popular with fans became the objects of intense loathing, both on the field or court and off. But what does it mean to root *against* an athlete, to hate an athlete, or to dis-identify with an athlete? If fans' identifications with athletes—whether as heroes or mascots—are indicative of those fans' own senses of identity, self-perception, and communities, how can we understand their loathing, rejection, or refusal of goodwill? How, in particular, can we make sense of fans' dis-identification with players *as players* on the basis of some decision, action, or personality trait that—at least in theory—has nothing to do with their play?

Some philosophers have suggested that sports fans tend to expect our most famous and celebrated athletes to function as general moral exemplars or, in the common parlance, as *role models*. Because we are accustomed to thinking of and identifying with them as excellent athletes, this account suggests, fans inevitably slide into thinking of and identifying with these athletes as excellent per se (Feezell 2013). When we are presented with evidence to the contrary, it might be understandable that the rejection of or disgust with an athlete as a person translates into a similar rejection or disgust in the context of the game. But this explanation is complicated when we consider cases like those of James and Sherman, who arguably committed no moral transgressions, and when we consider that, in certain cases, moral failings on the part of athletes—even, in some cases, violent ones—do *not* result in substantial fan repulsion. Indeed, mainstream fan reaction to Vick, James, and Sherman is striking not only in its quality but also in its divergence from a great many other fan reactions to players involved in off-the-field controversies. Not all famous athletes who disappoint fans inspire hatred, and very few players become the target of long-standing loathing on the basis of actions that have no bearing on their team's performance.[2]

In what follows, I argue that, often, this particular form of fan loathing—in which a player moves from being a fan favorite to a subject of widespread dis-identification as a result of an extra-athletic action—is racialized and occurs when and because the mascotting relationship breaks down. Although such rejections are purportedly moral, analyses of specific cases show that the values at stake in these rejections are less those of moral character than of a particular perception of communal identity. If mascotting occurs primarily when fans are able to deploy the imagined power of black masculinity for their own purposes within a closely delimited sporting context, then this form of fan rejection is characterized by fear of the failure to contain black masculinity within the acceptable limits of white supremacist norms. When prominent athletes who are black men refuse or fail to play by the unwritten rules for mascots—when they choose to leave the community that "claimed" them, when they demonstrate self-interest that does not defer immediately to the team or the community, or when they exhibit characteristics or values that are "too black" for white fans to identify with—they often become objects of hatred and fear. The discourse around hated athletes in these cases figures them as threats to the social body, a contagion that must be contained, if not excised. No longer mascots, these athletes are portrayed as dangers to the communities they might otherwise have symbolized. Thus, when fans like NPR listener Natasha express unwillingness to root for players like Vick, Sherman, and James, they are expressing not merely an abstract ethical judgment. They are, rather, reproducing a sense of their own identity, and of their community: *I am not like you; you are not one of us.* Though the borders of communal identity become blurred in the case of mascotting, they become quite clear when white fans and reporters grow uneasy with black masculinity that resists mascotting. Whether in mascotting or rejecting athletes who are black men, however, white fans' relations to these athletes reinforce the normalization of whiteness.

In order to support my claim that the rejection or hatred of athletes is racialized, and that its effect is to reinforce a white supremacist view of the community represented by a particular team or sport, I will defend four major claims about the cases of James, Sherman, and Vick. First, I will establish that communal identity is at stake in these cases of fan rejection; they are not merely instances of moral judgments or the expression of individual preferences. I will support this claim in part by analyzing the frequent repetition of the rhetorical trope of concern for children in player rejections. I will argue, second, that this oft-repeated "think of the children" discourse expresses a thinly veiled anxiety about the status of black masculinity in the community, not merely—or even primarily—individual children. Third, I will argue that the communal-identity discourse that so frequently accompanies player rejection functions to reiterate the stability of the social norms of a white supremacist public, precisely when they begin to appear tenuous. Finally, I will conclude by arguing that player rejection itself, particularly when it is framed in terms of a danger to the community, is a form of racial normalization that functions like a Foucaultian "mechanism of security" (2007), in which white fans often participate, and whose effects are not limited to the sporting arena.

"Haterade": Fan Antipathy and Communal Identity

Fans often develop animosity for rivals, which tends to result in their wishing such teams and persons ill, if not failure. Red Sox fans are, for example, known to declare that their second-favorite team is "whoever is playing the Yankees." Rivalries offer an especially salient display of the importance of exclusion or negativity to the reproduction of identity: knowing who we *are* is quite frequently a matter of knowing who we *are not*. This is not only because a team's, or a community's, history is a long story about interactions with, victories against, and defeats at the hands of some collection of others but also because the ability to clearly reject some of those others for inclusion in "our" space is a fairly reliable way to increase the perceived value of inclusion in it. Anyone who doubts the effectiveness of hatred for rivals for increasing a community's morale has only to visit Fenway Park and observe the marked boost in spirits produced in Boston fans when someone begins the "Yankees Suck" cheer—regardless of the opponent on the field—or note the frequency with which the famed Ohio State marching band incorporates the symbolic destruction of a University of Michigan flag in its halftime performances at football games. Being a fan is often as much about loathing, identifying against, and hoping for the failure of Team Y as it is loving, identifying with, and hoping for the success of Team X, and the two are, as many fans will confirm, two sides of the same coin.

But rivalries are only part of the story when it comes to fan negativity. Fans also have antipathy for individual players—a phenomenon that is as widespread as it is inadequately named. Because such antipathy is typically directed at prominent celebrated players (rare indeed is the second-string middle linebacker who is the object of strong fan dislike), we might be inclined to class this form of antipathy as a form of Nietzschean *ressentiment*. Ressentiment, though it purports to be born of indignation at injustice, is actually born of envy and low self-esteem and the frustrated desire to exact revenge (Nietzsche 1989). Insofar as fan antipathy often involves the desire for the failure of specific star athletes and actively rooting against them, it certainly resembles ressentiment. Yet, attention to both philosophy of emotion and philosophy of sport suggests that ressentiment is inadequate to describe what fans *do* in rooting against individuals: fans' antipathy for individual players is not merely experienced as a negative, seething affect, as ressentiment is; it also often contains clear elements of glee—the bitter pleasure of hoping for the object of one's antipathy to be taken down a peg. When such hope is fulfilled, fans experience *schadenfreude*—which is certainly connected to envy and ressentiment but is not always reducible to it (Portmann 2000, McNamee 2003). Even schadenfreude, however, does not adequately describe fan antipathy, for while that antipathy may be pleasurable to a certain extent (and sometimes gives rise to schadenfreude, when things turn out as fans hope that they do), this pleasure does not always find its desired fulfillment in schadenfreude—the delight we experience at the suffering of certain others.

Writing in a rather different context, Aaron Ben-Ze'ev (1993) offers a helpful analysis of the roots of the pleasure that is felt at others' misfortune, arguing that schadenfreude may grow out of either anger or hatred, which are distinct moral emotions. Although both anger and hate contain elements of delight—which is here derived both from the release of negative sentiments and from the concomitant hope for or expectation of revenge—they are distinguished by their motivating focus. In anger, Ben-Ze'ev argues, the angry person's emotion is action-directed; that is, it is focused on a particular perceived wrong done by someone. As a result, it is a short-term emotional state. Hate, in contrast, while still directed at an individual person, is focused in its concern on that person's "character" (1993, 92). Because hate is focused on a supposedly intractable feature of someone's character, it is a longer-term, dispositional affect—and, importantly, more likely to dehumanize its object as a result. Thus, "we love to hate someone," as Ben-Ze'ev puts it (98).

Fan antipathy toward individual players typically has much more in common with hate than anger, insofar as fans do not know players as individual persons and thus cannot typically conceive themselves as having been harmed by a particular action of theirs (though there might be exceptions, as I will argue, in cases where athletes cheat). Yet even "hate," strictly speaking, seems to pose a problem as an adequate classification of fan antipathy, insofar as fans also lack access to reliable information about athletes' "characters," despite the fact that they engage in a global dislike of what they imagine to be their object's person—often apparently motivated by envy of the perceived injustice of that athlete's successes. In the case of most fan antipathy, in other words, we see a unique affective response that contains elements of both ressentiment and hate. Contemporary sports media often refer to this disposition, characterized by the combined vilification of and ill will for particular players, as "haterade," a mash-up word that combines the idea "drinking the Kool-Aid" or "Gatorade" with an apparent reference to the hip-hop adage "haters gonna hate."[3] Those who indulge in or "drink" "haterade" seem to thrive on their antipathy for others, meaning that they display the delight motivated by the expectation or hope for revenge that Ben-Ze'ev suggests characterizes "hate." Importantly, however, "haterade" is not merely a deep-seated and delighted dislike but is characterized by the "hater's" desire to see the object of hatred fail, to be taken down a peg, or to be proven undeserving of the adoration that he or she receives. It thus also contains clear elements of envious, seething ressentiment. Because neither "hate" nor "ressentiment" (nor schadenfreude) is adequate on its own to describe this fan emotion, for ease of reference, I will continue to refer to the combination of loathing and gleeful rooting against as "haterade."

We can distinguish two forms of haterade: rivalry-motivated haterade and individually directed haterade. The first form is best understood as a species of rivalry, in which the identity of the individual subject of hate is less important than—or is significantly altered by—his membership on a particularly hated team. Derek Jeter, longtime Yankees shortstop, is a prime example of an object of rivalry-motivated haterade: although Jeter is beloved by Yankees fans, he is widely disliked by fans of other teams, many of whom view him as the beneficiary of the perennially overblown media attention bestowed upon his team, which is more the result of financial resources and power than true greatness. Were he not a Yankee, Jeter would likely be largely unknown, "haters" point out (Magary 2014)—meaning that were he not a Yankee, he would also likely not be the object of their haterade. Jeter hate is not primarily motivated by anything about Jeter per se but about Jeter qua Yankees captain.

Individually directed haterade, in contrast, is not primarily motivated by the player in question's team, nor is it limited to fans of rival teams. While fans of opposing teams may be more intense in their loathing of individual players, the fact that this style of haterade has its primary object in an individual rather than a team means that such haterade can come from fans who have no preexisting feelings about that player's team at all or even from fans of their own teams. In the latter case—of which Michael Vick is a prime example—fans express deep feelings of ambivalence: they identify with the success of "their" teams but feel discomfort with extending that identification to the individual object of "hate." Often, individually directed hate or anger is explicitly motivated or justified by individuals' violations of the rules or norms of the sport: athletes like Ryan Braun and Barry Bonds, for example, are widely reviled for their alleged usage of performance-enhancing drugs; Claude Lemieux was similarly hated by hockey fans for being a "dirty" player; Terrell Owens fell from fan grace for gaining a reputation for pouting when the ball was not thrown to him often enough and for generally failing to be a "team player." In another class of cases, however, a player becomes hated for actions or perceived character flaws that are unrelated to his or her in-game performance and that arguably have no direct sports-related effects. Extra-sporting actions or characteristics inspiring anger or hate are often moral or legal violations but may also be less serious—and more difficult to pinpoint— violations of some social norm.

Because individually directed haterade typically happens as the result of the violation of a sporting, moral, legal, or social norm, it is tempting to understand it as simply an expression of disapproval or disapprobation—or, in Ben-Ze'ev's terms, anger. This is a mistake, however. First, it is important to note that fans can and do express disapproval of or anger at players' actions without engaging in haterade. Perhaps tellingly, fans seem more than willing to express moral disapproval of or anger at acts of violence against women committed by their favorite athletes and return to rooting for them shortly thereafter[4] (Benedict 1999, Crouse 2014). Second, even if we accept the premise that moral or social disapproval always accompanies individually directed haterade (a premise that is, I think, contestable), it is unclear why we ought to view the rooting-against or wishing-negative-fortune-upon elements of haterade—or the easy transferability of these elements to entire teams associated with such players—as reducible to judgments of disapproval. Although disapproval may be accompanied by the actions associated with haterade in some cases, they are not *themselves* judgments or expressions of disapproval, and mere disapproval is easily detached from them.

If individually directed haterade itself is not disapproval as such, then what is it? Although rivalry-motivated haterade is more obviously of a piece with the other practices of fandom that reinforce a particular sense of communal identity, individually directed haterade is less saliently so, in part because it is capable of overriding or operating independently of team allegiance. It is important to remember, however, that the identity features at stake in sports fandom are not limited to those associated with a particular team or local community. The disciplinary practices of sports fandom—including interest in teams, sports knowledge, and player identification—are instrumental in, for example, the performance of heterosexual masculinity in the contemporary United States. Individually directed haterade, I argue, can also function as a means to reinforce particular features of group identity, *even if* the identity in question is not that of a specific team or local community.

In order to see why this is plausible, it is useful to consider again Feezell's analysis of sports heroes—that is, athletes who are the objects of the opposite of haterade: admiration, identification, and goodwill. Although fans think of themselves as loving and rooting for the success of such persons, individual sports heroes are, according to Feezell, best understood as "lusory objects" (Feezell 2013, 149). In other words, sports heroes are, for fans, not *people* at all, but objects whose meanings are dependent upon their roles in the game—itself a certain kind of make-believe in which fans are imaginatively complicit. Like the continuous teams of which they are a part, individual sports heroes are constituted, qua heroes, by the attention and imagination of fans, who "are projected into their [the heroes'] stories," and who make those stories their own (150). Michael Jordan, the athlete beloved by fans, is, according to Feezell, no more Michael Jordan, the person, than a fictional character. Thus, the general admiration of athletes and the question of their status as moral exemplars off the field is motivated by a fundamental confusion: fans believe themselves to be admiring *people* when they are doing no such thing. Rather, fans' deeply felt attachments to the fates and achievements of people they do not know and have never met are attachments to something like the heroes of an epic narrative. Just as Odysseus's power to compel admiration in the Greeks is dependent more upon the identification with and reiteration of Homer's narrative than on the historical facts of a person called "Odysseus," the admiration of sports heroes, in this account, tells us more about the audience than it does the person that audience is supposed to admire. Specifically, it tells us what sorts of traits they find admirable and with what sorts of characters they prefer to identify—and imagine themselves to be like.

Individually directed haterade is a fan practice nearly identical with the admiration of sports heroes except for its diametrically opposed sentiment: instead of deeply felt love for a stranger, there is deeply felt loathing; in place of identification, rejection; in place of a hope for success, a wish for failure. Yet, just like fans' admiration of sports heroes, the objects of individually directed haterade can be conceived as lusory objects: Pete Rose the person, no matter how reprehensible, does not inspire the same type of dis-identification as Pete Rose the great ballplayer who sullied the game by betting on baseball. The concomitant disgust and dis-identification of haterade relies upon fans' abilities to imagine their object as fitting into a particular narrative or persona that must be rejected. Fans relate to the objects of their individually directed haterade not so much as people as symbols, as is evident in the language used in the examples associated with James, Sherman, and Vick with which this chapter began. Fans refer to the "lessons" offered by the example of a particular player or to the "model" he or she instantiates; they speak of the values or ethos with which that model is imbued (disloyalty, thuggery, criminality), not only of disappointment in a particular individual. Fan rejection, or haterade, is not mere dislike of an individual or mere disapproval of particular behaviors. The rhetoric fans use to express and justify their haterade indicates that their antipathy for and rooting against individual players is a practice whose ends are much larger than the individual who is their ostensible object. Extending Feezell's insights about sports heroes in the opposite direction, it would seem that individually directed haterade tells us more about the fans engaging in it than the persons who are the objects of fans' ire. Perhaps, indeed, the ends of haterade are precisely those of fan identity. To get clearer on the specific content of those ends, however—that is, on the particular function of haterade in the cases above—we will have to examine the rhetoric surrounding them in greater detail.

Think of the Children!

In his 1998 article "Is Our Admiration for Sports Heroes Fascistoid?" Torbjörn Tännsjö answers his titular question in the affirmative, arguing that sports fans' admiration for individual players always involves a celebration of strength and concomitant contempt for weakness. This contempt, Tännsjö writes, may or may not be motivated or supplemented by nationalism but is, nevertheless, fascistoid (1998, 26). Although I find Tännsjö's reasoning unpersuasive (since, among other things, admiring strength does not necessarily involve contempt for weakness), I agree that there is an element of fascistoid or racist sentiment involved in both hero worship and mascotting. This element is more salient, however, in cases of fans' rejection of or explicit dis-identification with athletes, particularly when attending to the rhetorical tropes of community—and especially, of concern for the community's *children*—that so frequently characterize that rejection. Although it is certainly not the case that concern for children is necessarily fascistoid or racist, the appeal to children as a rhetorical strategy to enforce communal norms and exclude those who violate them has clear resonances with the "us versus them" sentiment that Tännsjö (I think) rightly characterizes as fascistoid. Significantly, as I will argue, such appeals to children in the contemporary American context of sports fan rejection often express a covert racism—specifically, a nostalgia for idealized (white) American heroes and a discomfort with uncontained black masculinity.

It is astonishing how frequently fan discourse refers to children—or, perhaps better, it *would* be astonishing, were American sports discourse not so consistently full of such language. It is often suggested that professional athletes are men who are paid to play children's games, which is just one in the litany of nostalgic misrememberings that characterize sports fandom in this country. Football developed in college competition, and professional baseball competition sprang up almost as soon as the game itself. And while games in general are more associated with children than adults, *sports*, as games of physical skill, are more frequently played by adults than other types of games (and probably played more by adults, or at least adolescents, than children). The demographics of sports fans no doubt include a wider age range than the demographics of athletes, but it is hardly the case that sports fandom is overwhelmingly the province of children. Yet concerns about social, legal, or game-related violations by athletes are routinely expressed as concerns for the children of the fan community. Most frequently, these concerns include some variation on the rhetoric offered by Dan Gilbert in the epigraph to this chapter: this person sets a dangerous example for our children. Given the significant adult presence in sports and sports fandom, however, it is worth asking why appeals to the welfare of children, and to the examples they might observe as sports fans, are so prominent in negative fan discourse—and especially why they crop up so frequently in association with individually directed haterade.

To answer this question, it is useful to consider what kinds of concerns are expressed in "think of the children"–style appeals. First, such appeals are *not* frequently made in reference to specific children. Although some sports writers report that they experience anxiety about the welfare of their own individual children when athletes commit some violation or other, these individual appeals are hardly the majority. In most cases, instead, the "think of the children" appeal refers to some nebulous, idealized collection of youngsters who need protection. The status of that need for protection is, however, ambiguous. The concern with "examples" and "role models" that dominates this rhetoric suggests that the interest of the speaker is not so much in the protection of children for their own sake (that is, for the direct harm or disappointment they might incur as fans) as it is in the protection of children for the sake of *others*: who do "*we . . .* want them to grow up to become?" Because children are ironically, as Kelly Oliver has pointed out, both innocent and violent (2007, 116–117), malleable and uncontrollable, they function as an extremely salient metonym of the future of society itself. Because of their youth and impressionability, children, as philosophers from Plato to Aristotle and John Dewey have suggested, offer a particularly efficient point of entry to affect the shape of the social world to come. With this efficient malleability, however, there is a concomitant danger to which Gilbert alludes. The "think of the children" refrain, like the "kids these days" grumble, reflects an anxiety at the precariousness of the social order as *we* know it: if we are not careful, our future will be imperiled.

The precise nature of that threat is, however, often only alluded to, without being stated outright. Generally speaking, the concern appears to be with the potential proliferation of some form of vice or other. But the specification of that vice is quite difficult, for two main reasons. First, the context in which the transmission of vice is supposed to be threatened is that of sports fandom: in order for this threat to be a serious one, identification with an athlete on the field (that is, as a lusory object) must be likely to produce identification with or emulation of extra-athletic behaviors. But there is no necessary correlation between these two forms of identification, as is evident both from many fans' general ignorance of athletes' lives beyond the field (the better to project themselves imaginatively into such athletes' exploits) and from the ease with which fans manage to distinguish between these two forms of identification in a great many cases. Of course, concerns about children's inability to make such distinctions, or to reliably choose the "right" behaviors to imitate, are long-standing and well founded.[5] But it is difficult to see why this would entail a danger specific to sports fandom and athletes (as distinct from the mere existence of other vicious behaviors in view of children) unless we believe that athletes constitute more powerful influences than other highly visible persons in children's lives. This might be true, but it is not obviously so— which raises questions about the frequency with which "think of the children" rhetoric is repeated in conjunction with athletes.

Making matters more complicated is that, second, it is hardly the case that the specific "vices" cited in cases of "think of the children" discourse *always* occasion such discourse—nor, in some cases, that they are obviously vices. LeBron James, for example, was castigated as a dangerous influence for displaying the vices of "disloyalty" and "selfish[ness]." Setting aside for a moment the fact that James's supposed violation was leaving his previous employer for a more desirable job, it is worth noting that James's decision is one repeated almost daily by professional athletes, which almost never occasions the tenor of anxiety or anger shared in the case of James. Although fans of the teams left behind by star players in such cases are typically embittered—as was the case, for example, when Johnny Damon left the Red Sox for the Yankees in

2005 and when Brett Favre came out of retirement for a second time to join the Minnesota Vikings, archrivals of his former Packers team, in 2009—this animosity was not nearly as widespread as that directed at James. Nor did it occasion "think of the children" rhetoric. Similarly, although Richard Sherman's boasting, trash-talking outburst at the end of the NFC championship was perhaps not aligned with the mainstream of American sports fans' taste for humility and a team-first attitude, his posturing was received quite differently than similar behavior by other athletes. Larry Bird, for example, was widely known for his trash talk during his basketball career (and conveyed in at least one instance a sentiment similar to Sherman's indignation at being "tried" by a supposedly inferior player),[6] which even escalated into an on-court scuffle and ejection in 1984. This behavior of Bird's did not widely tarnish his reputation, and it certainly did not result in the suggestion that he was a thug, a role model for terrorists, or frightening. When contrasted with Bird in the abstract, in fact, Sherman's offense looks relatively benign: he did not use profanity in his interview with Andrews, there was no violence threatened or carried out, and although the league fined Sherman for taunting during the game, it declined to find official fault with the interview itself. What vice, then, was Sherman supposed to have displayed, and what was the specific threat that he—and by extension, the specter of "Taliban youth"—supposedly posed?

It is useful here to contrast the rhetorical "our children" invoked by Gilbert and others with the "Taliban youth" mentioned by Podhoretz. To begin, it is clear that the contrast between the two groups is mutually exclusive: the former are objects of concern and protection, while the latter are rhetorically denied true childhood, figured as potential menaces to continued existence of "our" American children. The "children" to which "think of the children" rhetoric refers are thus a specific subset of children, not just any youth. This tacit limitation of one's concern for "children" to a very specific group of children is consistent with a long and rich history of similarly exclusive rhetorical appeals to children and family in the United States. As Ladelle McWhorter persuasively argues in *Racism and Sexual Oppression in Anglo-America*, the valorization of the nuclear family and the importance of raising good (i.e., middle-class, white, heterosexual) children came to stand in for explicitly eugenicist arguments in the 1940s, 50s, and 60s, once phrases like "human betterment" and "eugenics" became too closely associated with Hitler. "In the postwar years," McWhorter writes, "*family* would become the semantic substitute for *race*" (2009, 250). Even when not deliberately eugenicist, rhetorical appeal to "family values" has, in the United States, been racially and sexually coded: there is a clear contrast drawn between this "family" and its children and the "Welfare Queen" and her "brood" (263); while pundits publicly fret about upper-middle-class women delaying pregnancy for career and education, black women are subject to health care policies encouraging the surveillance and curtailing of their fertility (Roberts 1997); the same politicians who invoke "family values" in their election campaigns think nothing of supporting policies that criminalize the misbehavior of schoolchildren at an increasingly young age, resulting in what has been called the "school-to-prison pipeline" for black children, whose behavior tends to be seen "as inherently more disruptive and therefore more deserving of punishment" (M. Smith 2014). As Dorothy Roberts puts it, "The powerful Western image of childhood innocence does not seem to benefit Black children. Black children are born guilty. The new bio-underclass constitutes nothing but a menace to society—criminals, crackheads, and welfare cheats waiting to happen" (1997, 21). Just as appeals to "family values" constitute the valorization of a very specific image of the American ideal, rhetorical invocation of "the children" as an object of concern constitutes a veiled expression of anxiety about the future of *one image* of American society—an image from which men like Richard Sherman are decidedly excluded.

By aligning him with "Taliban youth," Podhoretz rhetorically removes Sherman from "our" community. Though neither Muslim nor ethnically Arabic, Sherman is classified, instead, with other nonwhite threats to American society. His figuration as a dangerous "other" was further exaggerated by speculation that the reporter interviewing him, Erin Andrews—a young white woman—"looked petrified" (quoted in Howard 2014). Though Andrews herself rejected the idea that she was afraid of Sherman, his thirty-second interview with her resulted in his being castigated in the media as a man whose behavior and whose person put him beyond the pale: as, simply, a "thug."[7] That thirty seconds of speech containing no profanity or threats could be understood by so many as threatening, fearful, or thuggish suggests that the fan and pundit reactions to Sherman had less to do with moral disapproval than with discomfort with the idea of an out-of-control black man being in such close proximity to an apparently helpless white woman. The absence of an actual threat to Andrews was, for such logic, irrelevant. Here, as in the logic of lynching, the need to "defend their [white] women" functions, as Angela Y. Davis has pointed out, as an excuse to justify both fear of—and violent attempts to contain and control—young black men (1981, 189).

Like Emmett Till's supposed crime of whistling at a white woman, the cases of James and Sherman involved social violations that amounted to failures to do what was expected of them *and*, importantly, the choice to flout those expectations in ostentatious and self-aggrandizing ways. James not only gave up allegiance to his former team, he did so on a nationally televised ESPN special dedicated to his decision; Sherman not only talked trash, he did so in the presence of a reporter and directly into the camera. That these behaviors were *self*-aggrandizing violations is important, for the mere violation of typical social norms is, as I have suggested, a central component of team sports—and the enjoyment of such "violations" an important component of sports fandom. In fact, mascotting, as I have argued, involves a kind of vicarious reveling in the imagined exploits of great athletes, particularly in their power, ferocity, or violence. In the mascotting relationship, however, fans are able to use these athletes as tools for their own fantasies of greatness and domination *precisely because* they are treated as not quite humans that begin and end on the field or court—as objects for "our" betterment. When violations of the typical social order happen on the field or court—for example, by physically dominating opponents within the constraints of a violent game—this relationship is facilitated. Yet when such violations exceed these boundaries, and particularly when they are committed unapologetically, and by young black men, the mascotting relationship breaks down, and the athletes involved begin to be perceived as threatening, dangerous, and potentially damaging to the future of the social order.

Mascots and Scapegoats

Mascotting, I have argued, depends upon a kind of ambivalence toward the athletes who are its objects. On the one hand, fans who treat athletes as mascots often admire their abilities, exploits, and nearly superhuman power. On the other, they are not concerned with the welfare of these athletes beyond their performance on the field or court and, once they leave the sporting context, may have attitudes toward them characterized by indifference, contempt, or fear. These apparent contradictions are constitutive features of the mascotting relationship, which demands and celebrates a powerful, conquering black hypermasculinity that is both vivid enough and empty enough to be appropriated as a symbol of the community it is supposed to represent. These contradictions illustrate the adaptability of white supremacy to changes in sports fandom. Here I want to build on this argument to show how whiteness continues to reproduce itself as normative even when the mascotting relationship breaks down and the former "mascot" comes to be seen as dangerous.

To make this argument, I draw an analogy to Foucault's discussion of "normalization" in his later work,[8] which is less concerned with the minutiae of individual lives (as disciplinary power was) and more interested in the management of a population, in an effort "to bring the most unfavorable in line with the more favorable" (2007, 63). This form of normalization, which is the goal of what Foucault calls "mechanisms of security," attempts to regulate the circulation of those "favorable" and "unfavorable" elements of society, so as to reduce the danger that the unfavorable elements pose to society as a whole. The aim is thus not the *elimination* of danger (of, say, a contagion) but its management and containment within acceptable limitations. While Foucault's account of security mechanisms is focused on epidemiology, I want to draw an analogy from it to the power relations governing race and white supremacy in the contemporary United States. Though the elimination of black masculinity (or nonwhiteness more broadly) is, for the most part, no longer a goal of white supremacy, and outright prohibitions on race mixing are no longer viable, the movement within and valorization of black men in white society is subject to social mechanisms that are invested in their management and containment. Mascotting is one of these mechanisms, insofar as it allows for the ascension and valorization of black men within sharply circumscribed limitations, and for purposes that benefit white society. This effect is a normalizing one to the extent that it is successful in bringing a wide range of racial interactions and identities closer to the norm of white supremacy. This is not to say that mascotting accomplishes a literal limitation on the proliferation of blackness—as was achieved by, say, the sterilization of black women—but rather, that it functions to enact a limitation on the possibilities of blackness's influence, valorization, or social status. Whiteness and white supremacy are normalized here in the sense that blackness is allowed to continue to exist, as long as it is kept within sharply circumscribed social limits.

When the mascotting relationship becomes untenable, however, as when James, Sherman, and Vick violated norms in ways that exceed the acceptable limitations on black masculinity, they became subject to a special kind of scrutiny, disapprobation, and haterade. There are at least two reasons for this shift. The first is that the violation is so salient, alienating, or otherwise disruptive of the fantasy of identification that fans are no longer able to treat the athlete who committed the violation as a lusory object. To put it simply, the athlete in question becomes too much of a full human being—one who is decidedly unlike the fan in some substantive way—to function as an object of fantasy onto which fans may project themselves. This is what some commentators may have had in mind when they suggested that Sherman and Vick had rendered themselves "too black" for mainstream football fans.[9] Such a lack of identification on its own, however, might not necessarily result in haterade or heightened scrutiny.

For an explanation of the relationship between lack of identification and haterade, we require a second movement, which I will again explain by analogy to Foucault. Although normalization's object is the population, or the social body as such, this does not imply that its power is never directed at individuals. In certain cases—when, for example, it becomes possible locate an individual as the source of a contagion, who not only exhibits symptoms outside the norm, but who *is*, him or herself, "the carrier of a danger to" the group—the goal of broad social defense requires the *means* of identifying, fearing, and (sometimes) segregating specific individuals. This does not necessarily mean that we need an antecedently clear legal or medical standard for their identification. Rather, Foucault suggests, the ability to pinpoint or scapegoat certain individuals as abnormal, dangerous, or degenerate "essentially functions as social defense"—that is, as a means of shoring up and bolstering the identity of the social body over against those who are identified as dangers to it (2003, 317). According to this logic, the active rejection of particular individuals as abnormal, as not belonging, and as threats to the future of society is itself a highly effective means of reinforcing and defending the group's identity—regardless of whether such threats are "real." The figuration of a particular individual or group of individuals as a scapegoat for perceived threats to the stability of a given identity thus has precisely the effect intended—the preservation of the social body—but not for the reasons intended. It is, instead, the mechanism of scapegoating itself that is most responsible for the reidentification of the group.

If mascotting is like a form of normalization, which functions by attempting to bring outliers closer to the norm of white supremacy, scapegoating is the alternative strategy adopted in the face of its failure. The breakdown of mascotting reveals the tenuousness of the relationship between white fans and athletes who are men of color, as it moves, at times overnight, from adoration to loathing—and often for comparatively small infractions. Although this breakdown may appear on the surface as a shift of seismic proportions, closer analysis suggests that mascotting and scapegoating—and the haterade that comes with it—are of a piece as normalizing mechanisms. Each can function both as a means of reproducing and re-creating communal identity and, as I will argue, as a means of racial normalization whose effects exceed the identity of fans and players. Indeed, the breakdown of mascotting not only reveals the antiblack racism characteristic of mainstream sports fandom; it is also instrumental in the broader criminalization of black masculinity.

The Dangerous Individual('s) Dog

In this final section, I want to return to Michael Vick, in part because his is the most difficult case in which to demonstrate the operation of racial normalization (since it involves apparent dis-identification with legal violations and animal cruelty), and in part because his case marks another instance in which the invocation of animals and animal symbols in conjunction with sports fans is not what it appears.[10] The sentiment of dis-identification with Vick on the part of (mostly white) NFL fans and reporters was striking for two reasons: first, it vastly overshadowed any comparable sentiment toward another—white—quarterback who was also beset by public legal troubles at the same time. Ben Roethlisberger, quarterback for the Pittsburgh Steelers, was arrested before the start of the 2010 season for raping a woman in the restroom of a bar. While the prosecution ultimately dropped the charges out of concern that there was not enough evidence to secure a conviction— Roethlisberger acknowledged having sex with the woman in the restroom but maintained that it was consensual—the league found the charges disturbing enough to suspend Roethlisberger for six games (subsequently reduced to four). While there was some discomfort expressed by fans and commentators after Roethlisberger returned to play, often via allusions to "off-the-field issues," it did not rise nearly to the level of the disgust expressed toward Vick. Indeed, although there were off-season reports of fan anger at Roethlisberger's having engaged in behavior that would result in the city of Pittsburgh's "image [being] tarnished" (Netter 2010), Roethlisberger's return to play was marked by an overwhelmingly warm welcome of fan cheers and team support (Battista 2010). One might, of course, suggest that the comparison of these two incidents reveals much about the extent to which covert racism makes white audiences more sympathetic to white people who break the law while concomitantly demonizing people of color who do so or the extent to which violence against women is easily swept aside as run-of-the-mill indiscretion. However, as I will suggest, media and fan concern in such cases is less with the ostensible "victims" of these crimes than with what the crimes do or do not indicate about those who commit them. I am concerned, then, with the extent to which the Vick case illustrates the distinctly racialized character of mainstream sports fandom's response to violations of the social order by previously mascotted athletes. Second—and just as importantly—I am interested in this particular case because of the intensity of the public loathing and the specific quality of the disgust expressed toward Vick, of whom one reporter from his hometown wrote, "The reason prisons exist is because of guys like [him]" (Markon 2007).

Complicating matters in this case is the figure of the victimized animal— the "pit bull"—that at once excites such fervent sympathy *and* fear of danger. The image of the dogfight is fraught with meaning that goes beyond an interest in treating animals ethically. Indeed, examination of animal cruelty law and policy would suggest that the welfare of individual dogs is not, on the whole, the primary object of concern: as Colin Dayan points out (2010), such policy routinely calls for the extermination of even those dogs that *resemble* fighting ones. And, as I will explain, even organizations ostensibly devoted to animal welfare routinely describe those suspect dogs as menaces to society comparable to Vick himself. Fan dis-identification, in this case as in others, does not appear reducible to a concern for the welfare of any specific group of individuals or aversion to individual legal transgressions or violence or even cruelty. On the contrary, the object of this sentiment is more nebulous—as is hinted at in the reporter's choice of words: *prisons exist . . . because of guys like him.*

I will argue in this section that fan and media reception of Vick figured him as an incurable deviant—the sort of person that Foucault refers to in his lectures on security as "the dangerous individual" from whom the healthy body of society must be defended. My interest, in so doing, is to show that the discourse around Vick—and, concomitantly, around pit bulls themselves—is bound up with the criminalization of black masculinity that cannot be mascotted. This claim, as I will explain, has two important features: first, it depends upon a rereading of Foucault's notion of "the dangerous individual" (2003, 34) as a racist and racialized concept, which I will argue for by extending the supporting ideas of "degeneracy" and "heredity" to include a kind of heredity by association or contagion. Second, this implies that the effects of fan discourse around Vick and his figuration as a "dangerous individual" are not limited to the sporting context but reinforce a broader white supremacist view of black masculinity as inherently criminal and dangerous.

The concept of "criminality," according to Foucault, arises in the nineteenth century to identify individuals by a hybrid juridico-medical discourse as "dangerous." Importantly, this label was not equivalent to labeling someone a lawbreaker. This is not to say that "dangerous individuals" did not commit crimes at all. On the contrary, they often did—but such violations were, according to the concept of the dangerous individual, figured as the *manifestations* of an inner essential deviance, which was then purported to be visible in all manner of prior transgressions, from childhood tantrums to dispositions to "nastiness," which could subsequently be understood as causally connected to some particular criminal violation (Foucault 2003). The upshot of such discourse is that it conceptualizes crimes not merely as individual legal violations to be punished. Rather, once we have identified certain types of persons as criminally deviant and dangerous, we can use our knowledge of such unsavory elements to protect the health of "good society." These identifications are instrumental in the consolidation and reproduction of society in normalizing terms.

Ellen Feder has persuasively argued that the identification of dangerous individuals continues in earnest in the contemporary United States through federal programs whose aim is to identify individuals "at risk" for violence. Such initiatives, she claims, are crucially instrumental in the "production of race" in America (2007, 62). In this view, the pathologization of young poor black men as "at risk" for violent behavior positions them as criminal deviants who constitute a threat to good society. In the contemporary United States, as in nineteenth-century France, Feder argues, the "healthy" or "normal" (white) population is maintained by abandoning these supposedly "dangerous" elements to exist in confined spaces that will—ideally—assist in their own self-destruction. Indeed, the discourse around "the ghetto" as a racialized space linked with criminality and deviance further illustrates the pathologizing of blackness today. Beyond Feder's analysis of the demonization of so-called welfare queens as carriers of poverty-cum-violence (70), the discourse around Michael Vick's dogfighting conviction stands as another example. "They move out of the ghetto," the *Atlanta Journal-Constitution* reports, "but the ghetto is still in them" (quoted in Laucella 2010, 47).

Such discourse, as Foucault suggests, both calls attention to the criminal act or legal violation itself and locates or establishes the *source* of criminality in order to contain its threat of contagion. The perceived importance of this enterprise is visible perhaps most clearly in the NFL's extensive investigation of recruits' backgrounds and "character"—measured in a battery of tests, including intelligence and psychological evaluations, in addition to individual surveillance and interviews with others acquainted with players' habits and associates—which is regularly assumed to be risky in the cases of black recruits but not in the case of white recruits (Grano 2010, 256). That these racialized practices are so seamlessly operative in the NFL (an organization that nevertheless employs African Americans at a much higher rate than the wider US work force) is indicative of the extent to which "the ghetto" as racialized space is pathologized as a zone of danger. This danger is not only the "danger" of the so-called bad neighborhood through which white folks avoid walking or driving (Mills 1997) but a danger of criminalized contagion that, it is suggested, infects its inhabitants, making of them potential criminals or deviants. In the case of Vick, the individual crime of financing a dogfighting ring is posited not merely as a mistake or even serious legal or moral violation but as proof of a preexisting danger that ought to have been detected and to which a narrative of deviance can be retrospectively drawn. Indeed, that narrative of criminal deviance grew to include a leaked photo of the quarterback smoking what appeared to be a "blunt" and accusations by a woman that he was responsible for infecting her with a sexually transmitted disease (Laucella 2010, 51).

Here, as in Foucault's discussion, the simple identification of particular "dangerous individuals" is not the only or even primary goal. Rather, as Foucault puts it, insofar as this knowledge is to be mobilized in the protection of "good society," it becomes necessary to identify and consolidate the *sources* of that danger. Foucault puts the problem thus:

> What kind of body can produce a condition that definitively marks the whole of an individual's body? This gives rise to the need to discover the background-body, so to speak, that by its own causality confirms and explains the appearance of an individual who is the victim, subject, and bearer of this dysfunctional state. . . . What is this background-body, this body behind the abnormal body? It is the parents' body, the ancestors' body, the body of the family, the body of heredity. (2003, 313)

The point here is that heredity-based explanations for deviant behavior are instrumental in larger projects of social normalization—that is, once we can pinpoint where danger comes from, we can contain it and regulate it to ensure that the social body takes a more desirable shape. Both Feder and McWhorter (2009) have persuasively argued that similar logics operate in biopolitical regulatory mechanisms such as antimiscegenation laws and differentially distributed access to reproductive technologies and that these have been centrally instrumental in the reproduction of whiteness and racial hierarchizing in North America. I would suggest, however, that this direct, biological understanding of "heredity" as the mechanism of the transmission of danger or abnormality ought to be supplemented by a broader notion of heredity that can account for the more nebulous uses of this concept in our present context—a context in which, as sociologist Ann Morning reports, popular conceptions of race are (even if ontologically incoherent) less and less likely to be purely biological (2009). This broader understanding of heredity as contagion will enable us to make sense of both the discourse around Vick and the concomitant treatment of pit bulls, which are figured at once as pathetic victims and dangerous potential threats.

"Heredity," in Foucault's view, is already a slippery concept. He writes, "The causal permissiveness of heredity makes it possible to establish the most fantastic or, anyway, the most supple hereditary networks. Finding a deviant element at any point in the hereditary network will be sufficient to explain the emergence of a condition in an individual descendant" (2003, 314). Such "causal permissiveness" is demonstrable in contemporary pseudoscientific genetic explanations, in which everything from alcoholism to xenophobia can be "gotten from" one's grandparents, uncles, and cousins. But it is also, I submit, evident in claims about environmental heredity such as those made about Vick: "The ghetto is still in him." There are the less direct statements as well, made by people from league psychologists to sports commentators: some athletes are "unable or unwilling to put distance between themselves and the thug life" (Williams 2007), having "unsavory associates" (Judd 2007), often from childhood, who are dangerous. These friends from their former lives, the story goes, should really just be "cut . . . loose" (Williams 2007) because, while "no one is saying athletes should forget where they come from . . . as a sports star's fame and wealth increase, so does the number of people watching his every move. If he's not careful, it can all fall apart" (quoted in Laucella 2010, 58). The implicit claim, then, is that the contagion of criminality one can inherit from growing up in the "ghetto" results in the pathologizing of all those associated with it, through a kind of proximity transmission. It thus becomes crucial, according to this racist discourse, to separate oneself from one's former life, lest contact with the zone of dangerousness result in infection of the rest of the social body.

This logic becomes comprehensible if we read Foucault's account of the heredity of dangerousness in light of Charles Mills's claim that the racist structure of the social body "races space" itself, such that everything from individuals to music is racialized (1997, 41–52). The zone of dangerousness thus may be carried not only in the bodies of individuals or populations but in the environments, artifacts, practices—and animals—associated with them. Thus, we learn from reports surrounding the Vick case both that dogfighting constitutes "one of the lowest forms of savagery in modern society" (Rhoden 2007) and that the dogs victimized by such "savagery" are themselves "*bred as killing machines*" (*USA Today* 2007; emphasis mine). In pointing this out, however, I do not wish to claim here that the practices involved in dogfighting are not cruel—on the contrary, I would suggest that the starving, drugging, or beating of dogs to incite them to fight is reprehensibly cruel. I am, however, concerned to point out the difference between our registering of this cruelty versus the (equally horrific) cruelty of, say, the force-feeding of ducks through metal tubes in their gullets until their livers become enlarged, which is necessary to make foie gras. Foie gras is routinely served as a delicacy in high-end North American restaurants, and though it is officially banned in some locales, this ban is almost never enforced. More importantly, the cruelty involved in its production is never met with the level of outrage on the part of the general public produced by the Vick dogfighting case—indeed, it is often not registered as cruelty at all. As geographers Elder, Wolch, and Emel have pointed out, this apparent inconsistency is all too common: "Specific human-animal interactions that are legitimized and rationalized over time, become accepted as civilized behavior. Those who do not stay within this repertoire, however, fall over . . . into the netherworld of savagery" (1998, 195). It is not surprising, then, that the making of foie gras is not on the whole met with the suggestion that those involved—whether humans or ducks—are dangers to society. Foie gras is a delicacy associated with the wealthiest members of white American culture.

This is in stark contrast to the general social comportment of the parties involved in dogfighting rings. Dogs confiscated from fighting operations—or even those suspected of being part of a fighting operation, often because of their breed—are figured as such a threat that they are routinely (and often summarily) euthanized, often without investigation or due process. This includes such egregious cases as the seizure and killing of fifty-seven pit bulls, including nineteen puppies, by the Louisiana Society for the Prevention of Cruelty to Animals in 2005 as part of a sting operation involving a kennel that turned out *not* to be a dogfighting ring (Dayan 2010). In the Vick case, both the Humane Society and People for the Ethical Treatment of Animals (PETA), organizations whose mission is animal welfare, recommended that all of the fifty pit bull dogs confiscated from Bad Newz kennels be euthanized (Gorant 2008).

But it is not only those dogs immediately caught up in suspected fighting operations that are figured as carrying the contagion of criminality. The specter of the pit bull looms large in the discourse around dogfighting: this breed is, as major news organizations sensationally put it, a "killing machine" and a "time bomb on legs" (Brand 1987). Indeed, according to the American Kennel Club, the pit bull as such is not a registered breed; most dogs known in the popular consciousness as pit bulls are American Staffordshire Terriers, or Staffordshire Bull Terriers, or just some combination of canine genetics that resembles an ideal pit bull. As Marjorie Garber puts it, "'Everyone knows' and 'no one knows' what a 'pit bull' is. Everyone knows, and no one knows, that 'they' are dangerous" (1997, 194). Because of the difficulty of isolating this "they," many of the growing number of local governments issuing breed-specific pit bull bans include language indicating that the law covers any dog thought to embody the physical characteristics of a pit bull, regardless of pedigree.[11] An anti–pit bull ordinance in Dade County, Florida, for example, specifies that any dog that "substantially conforms" to a set of characteristics associated with the aforementioned breeds will be counted as a pit bull and that the affirmative expert testimony of "a veterinarian, zoologist, animal behaviorist, or animal control officer" that an animal is a pit bull will constitute a "rebuttable presumption" of this fact (194–195). Interestingly, as Colin Dayan points out, this "breed"-specific danger is a comparatively recent development, as Staffordshire Terriers were, in the early twentieth century, depicted as prototypical American pets, appearing everywhere from RCA and Buster Brown ads to *The Little Rascals* (2010). It was not until reports surfaced in the 1970s and 1980s connecting dog-bite attacks by pit bulls to gangs of lawless adolescents in "urban jungles" (Huemer 2000; Applebome 1987; Sager 1987) that the dogs themselves began to be figured as carriers of the contagion of criminality. This image was, it seems, propped up at least in part by the association of pit bulls with the hip-hop music scene[12]—itself a strongly racialized genre in the United States and, arguably, abroad: a law passed in France in 2000 created canine police units whose primary responsibility was to monitor the behavior of pit bulls and other "attack dogs" in French housing projects occupied primarily by nonwhite people (particularly of Arab descent); the popularity of the "dangerous" dogs in these sectors was ascribed to the influence of the culture of "urban ghettos" and "Afro-American lifestyles" in the United States through the transatlantic influence of hip-hop music (Aidi 2004).

It is important to note, moreover, that while the "causal permissiveness" of the concept of heredity is quite saliently exploited in the case of the pit bull, this is made possible by the notion of a breed as such. As John Borneman famously demonstrated in his comparative analysis of American and continental European light-horse breeding, breed classifications in general are contingent human categories masquerading as natural ones: breed names are "first taken from human categories and then projected onto animal classifications" (Borneman 1988, 48). Thus their primary function is revealed in "naturalizing and legitimating the social order about which they speak" (47). Breed designations, sometimes requiring the documentation of lineage, sometimes the "correct" physical features or gait—but *always* requiring investigation and certification by an authorized credentialing body—thus purport to signify heredity as simply *given* but do so through a complex system of knowledge production. The fact that the pit bull is not a recognized breed but a generic "type"—which one presumably knows when one sees it—makes the pit bull, as a hereditary figure, even more malleable, subject to various forms of knowledge production, both within and without authorized governing bodies.

As the specter of the monstrous pit bull is reiterated and reinforced, association with the dogs themselves comes to mark its owners as sociopathic deviants. One study of every *New York Times* article on pit bull owners published over twenty years, for example, found that they consistently portrayed such individuals as thuggish and unsympathetic (Cohen and Richardson 2002). Perhaps unsurprisingly, then, a 2000 study found that some pit bull owners intentionally misrepresent their dogs' "breed" in order to avoid the stigma associated with it (Twining, Arluke, and Patronek 2000). Interestingly, during the same period as the uptick in media reporting on pit bulls and their owners, journalists popularized the use of a new term, "wilding," to describe the criminal violence of "packs" (or sometimes, "wolfpacks") of black and Latino youth (Welch, Price, and Yankey 2002). A metonymic feedback loop thus comes to characterize the relationship between pit bulls, blackness, and the perception of criminality—a relationship that, if Robin James (2011) is correct, functions at least in part to set these dogs up as a proxy for the black men that municipalities would *like* to legislate against but cannot. The contagion that makes this relationship possible works not through traditional heredity but proximity and association. This will not surprise critical race theorists, who have long suggested that the scientific untenability of biological explanations of race poses no real threat to racist thinking. Summing up the content of racist ideology in the racing of space—particularly "the ghetto"—Charles Mills writes, "You are what you are in part because you originate from a certain kind of space, and that space has those properties in part because it is inhabited by creatures like yourself" (1997, 42). We could aptly apply a variation on Mills's account to precisely this relationship: "You are what you are in part because of your dangerous dogs, and those dogs have that property in part because they are kept by creatures like yourself."

With this broader notion of heredity or contagion in mind, Foucault's analysis of the normalizing functions of the dangerous individual—or, we might add, of the dangerous individual's dog—are chillingly prescient in the case of Michael Vick. Insofar as the concept of criminal deviance is deployed in the service of mechanisms of security, it functions, as Foucault puts it, "to justify the existence of a sort of protective continuum throughout the social body ranging from the medical level of treatment to the penal institution strictly speaking, that is to say, the prison and, *if it comes to it, the scaffold*" (2003, 38). It is not altogether surprising, then, that at least one national news anchor suggested that Vick ought to be executed for his crimes (Zirin 2010). We ought, then, to take seriously the relationship between claims like those of PETA director Ingrid Newkirk—"we can only stop killing pits if we stop creating new ones" (Huemer 2000, 32)—and the suggestion that "prisons exist . . . because of guys like Michael Vick," not because unethical treatment of dogs is analogous to racist treatment of humans, but because the racist function of normalization pathologizes and criminalizes them both.

Contrary to the recommendations of some fans, Tucker Carlson, PETA, and the Humane Society, both Vick and most of his dogs are, today, alive and well. In contrast with typical practice, most of Vick's dogs were not killed but were "rescued" by two organizations dedicated to rehabilitating the pit bull's image: BADRAP (Bay Area Doglovers Responsible about Pitbulls) and Best Friends Animal Society. Having been granted permission by the judge in Vick's case to attempt to rehabilitate and rehome the majority of the dogs, BADRAP and Best Friends have relocated and worked to resocialize them into mainstream human and dog society (Gorant 2008; Wittenauer 2008). By all accounts, they have been successful, and many of the dogs are, today, kept as pets in individual homes.

What does this mean for the analysis of Vick and his dogs as paradigmatic dangerous individuals? It means, most importantly, taking seriously the "causal permissiveness" of the notion of heredity as contagion, or heredity through the association of racialized space. It is significant that Vick's dogs had to be removed from their associated locales, taken across the country by animal-rescue organizations—founded and staffed primarily by middle- to upper-middle-class white people—to rural Utah and San Francisco in order to be cleared of the contagion of danger. Similarly, it is significant that, after his release, Vick was castigated for attending "a birthday party in his honor in Virginia Beach [near his hometown] that he should never have attended, given the guest list, [where] a former co-defendant got shot" (Bissinger 2010). In each case, the contagion of dangerousness can be escaped only through dissociation with its supposed hereditary origins, which may, nevertheless, threaten to reemerge. A constant vigilance in the opposite direction, and a performance of significations indicating that the danger has been excised, is called for. Surveillance of those suspected of being carriers of dangerousness—unlike mere perpetrators of individual criminal acts, like Roethlisberger—extends to that which would otherwise appear mundane or insignificant. Most telling, then, is the case of Hector, a former Vick dog rehomed in San Francisco, whose foster owner proudly told the Associated Press, "I put on Yo-Yo Ma one day, and he cocked his head, laid down, and listened to the cello next to the speaker. . . . He's turning out to be a man of high class and culture" (Wittenauer 2008).

Haterade and White Supremacy

When fans hate individual players, they do more than express dislike, moral judgment, or solidarity with the victims of athletes' violations. Fan antipathy for players on the basis of extra-athletic character flaws serves to mark out the limits of one's community and to explicitly dissociate oneself from those who fall outside its bounds. Rooting against such players positions them as *the them* that must be symbolically overcome on the field or court, an "other" whose rejection and (hoped for) defeat is an integral part of shoring up a clear sense of *us*. Haterade is, in short, a crucial instrument in the production and reinforcement of sports fans' identities.

Moreover, the three cases examined here illustrate the extent to which haterade is deployed in racist and racializing ways. Fan hate of individual players is particularly acute—in some cases, clearly disproportionately so—when the players involved in social violations are black men who had previously enjoyed widespread acclaim. The breakdown of the mascot relationship between fans and players in these cases is characterized by two movements: on the part of the players, refusal or failure to subordinate their own interests to those of the team and, by extension, the fan community that they represent; on the part of fans, anxiety and anger at this movement, which is perceived as a threat to the well-being of the community. The frequency with which fans express this anxiety in "think of the children"–style rhetoric, despite their clear exclusion of certain children from the realm of concern, shows that the "threat" posed by the players who excite this anxiety is their potential to destabilize the white supremacist social order. The style of player hate that emerges when players who were formally mascots become objects of vigorous fan antipathy reveals the tenuous nature of white fans' relations with black athletes and a deep suspicion of unconstrained black masculinity. Black men who do not play by the social rules expected of them are portrayed as thugs, villains, and menaces to society—in short, as dangerous individuals from whom good society (and its children) must be protected. Player hate in these cases, emerging as it does as either a disproportionate response to a comparatively minor infraction or as unaccompanied by concern for the victims of more serious infractions can be understood as symptomatic of white supremacy. For what is at issue in each case is not so much a judgment of moral disapproval—if it were, we would expect to find consistent fan reactions in comparable cases—but, rather, discomfort with and rejection of black masculinity that exceeds the bounds and purposes set for it by mainstream sports fandom.

More than a symptom, though, haterade and its accompanying discourse of dangerousness is, in the cases of James, Sherman, and Vick, an instrument of white supremacy's reinforcement. The figuration of these highly visible men as dangerous individuals—and the policies, laws, and attitudes that such images support—has effects that exceed sports fans and contribute to larger mechanisms of security that position black masculinity as deviant, threatening, and in need of containment. The reiteration of white supremacist norms that was covert in mascotting reaches full flower in these cases of player hate, as fans reject, loathe, and wish harm or failure upon those black men who will not be mascots. In the most extreme cases, like those of Vick and Sherman, fan antipathy exceeds the sporting arena, spilling over indiscriminately to anything associated, however loosely, with black masculinity: teams, music, dogs, and even political enemies. In these cases, player hate functions not only to reiterate a particular sense of fan identity but also to contribute to the suspicion, othering, and perceived criminality of black masculinity and its associations in the popular imagination. In this way, the individually directed haterade of sports fans—particularly white sports fans—is both symptomatic of the white supremacist norms quietly underlying typical fandom in the United States and instrumental in their reinforcement.

Women on the Margins of Sports Fandom

My son gets a little jealous, because he says, "Oh, you love [LeBron] more than you love me." And I said, "Oh no, I love you both the same."

GERTRUDE ROBINSON, member, LeBron James Grandmothers' Fan Club

On October 6, 2015, Jessica Mendoza became the first woman ever to call a nationally televised Major League Baseball game during the postseason, as the Houston Astros eliminated the New York Yankees from playoff contention. Mendoza, a regular contributor to ESPN baseball analysis, was no stranger to elite athletic competition: during her NCAA softball career at Stanford University, she was a four-time All-American; she also played twice for the US women's Olympic softball team, winning both gold and silver medals. Throughout the game, though, Mendoza's voice was striking simply in its presence. Though women broadcasters had previously appeared for brief interludes during breaks in the action, the sound of a female voice was simply not a regular feature of a baseball broadcast, much less a nationally televised game of this import. Fans certainly noticed; for any regular spectator of mainstream American sports, it would have been difficult not to. Men are a ubiquitous presence in sports broadcasting—not only as players and coaches but as the voices that narrate fan experience of the game, acting as mediators who parse the play-by-play in real time and as fan representatives who provide commentary on game strategy, weather, or player behavior, like particularly knowledgeable seat companions. Masculinity is omnipresent in the experience of watching a televised game—so much so that it is, for typical fans, not even noticeable. In that context, Mendoza's voice was startling, even distracting. Though many fans voiced support of her, several complained that ESPN should have found a person more qualified to call the game.[1] Another claimed that the mere sound of Mendoza's voice was enough to spoil their experience: "I don't believe when a woman is talking baseball to me in the ESPN booth. It killed it for me, sorry" (quoted in Greene 2015). An Atlanta-based radio broadcaster suggested that ESPN's decision to use Mendoza was indicative that the network was "too frigging cute for their own good" and snidely asked, "Yes tell us Tits McGhee when you're up there hitting the soft-ball you see a lot of 95 mile an hour cutters?" (quoted in Nichols 2015). When asked about these hostile reactions, Mendoza noted that she was more than accustomed to dealing with masculine antagonism in the sporting world: "It's the story of everything I've done" (quoted in Greene 2015).

Though sport is, as I have argued, a highly masculinized arena, sports fandom has always, to some extent, included women. Yet contemporary advertising during sports broadcasts and in the sports section of newspapers (which revolves around the themes of beer, men's clothing, and erectile dysfunction medication) strongly suggests that the prototypical sports fan is—like the prototypical athlete—a heterosexual, cisgender man. The overwhelming masculinity of sports fandom has made it an uncomfortable environment for many women, and perhaps as a consequence, feminist philosophers have had remarkably little to say about it (despite being otherwise willing and capable critics of popular culture).[2] The feminist philosophical work that exists on sports and sports culture is, with good reason, largely critical. But it is also, like most work in the philosophy of sport, largely silent on the question of sports fandom—including women's sports fandom and fans of women's sports. This omission is, I will argue, not insignificant.

Recognizing that sports culture is not exclusively the domain of men will nuance and complicate our understanding of the gendering effects of sports fandom. More than this, attending to the distinct practices of women sports fans can illuminate some underdeveloped resources for critiquing and changing sports fandom in the United States. In what follows, I argue that before we dismiss sports fandom as irrevocably hierarchizing, we should investigate forms of sports fandom that might work to destabilize rigid gender, racial, and sexual norms. Some forms of women's sports fandom, I will argue, involve practices that constitute significant resistance to misogyny, racism, and heterosexism and thus give reason to nuance our analysis of the social functions of sports fandom. Up to this point, I have spent most of my time discussing sports fandom as a domain of masculinity; in this chapter, I shift my focus to investigate women fans of mainstream men's sports and fans of women's sports—especially softball and basketball. I will *not* argue that women's sports fandom is necessarily liberating. I will, however, suggest that some instances of women's sports fandom, like the example of professional "fan" Jessica Mendoza, show that sports fandom *may* work differently than it has and that it can be deployed to reshape subjectivity or remake identity categories.

I will first consider cases of the practices and experiences of women fans of mainstream (men's) sports, with a view to analyzing the hostility that such fans often meet. I will argue that such fan practices disrupt of the hyper-masculinity of the sporting context by undercutting the homosocial environ-ment in which men "safely" experience emotions otherwise forbidden them. Nevertheless, it is not clear that the simple inclusion of women in main-stream practices of sports fandom is necessarily liberatory. Yet some women's fandom of men's sports—including that of a group calling themselves the "LeBron James Grandmothers' Fan Club"—succeeds in valorizing the very forms of subjectivity that are typically excluded from or denigrated by main-stream (white, masculine) sports culture. To support my claim, I will address an objection to sport once commonly leveled by feminists, namely, that sport is inherently masculinist by virtue of its commitment to competition. If this is true, the participation of women in sports fandom would not constitute a disruption to masculine values but an acceptance and reinforcement of them. I will argue, however, that this objection is not persuasive.

Second, drawing on Iris Young's influential essay "Throwing like a Girl," I will argue that fandom of women's sports is significant for its potential to reshape women's and girls' phenomenological experience as bodily agents. Moreover, I will suggest that because women's sports have occupied a sig-nificant communal space for women's queer communities, and because they create opportunities for the proliferation of images of women—particularly queer women of color—that are explicitly agentic, powerful, and not reduc-ible to typical portrayals of women in mass media, women's sports fandom can constitute a major site of resistance to sexist, racist, and heterosexist op-pression. This is not to say that women's sports fandom is perfect—it still, as I will argue, holds the potential for racialized mascotting. Yet the subversive character of (some) fan practices around women's basketball and softball sug-gest that sports fandom need not be complicit in the retrenchment of existing hierarchical social norms. Rather, sports fandom may in some circumstances be instrumental in the production of subjects and communities that reject gender, racial, and sexual oppression.

Despite the problems of much contemporary sports fandom, I will argue, we must not reject it without attending to its margins—which are dispropor-tionately feminine. To accept without question that sports fandom is thor-oughly and straightforwardly masculine is to reproduce a problematically reductive view of it, which accepts the very normative framework it seeks to criticize. Women's sports fandom may not be "typical," but this is precisely the point. Women fans and fans of women's sports *do* fandom in ways that give us reason to hope that for sports fans, all may not yet be lost.

In a Man's World

As we saw in chapter 2, women who enter the realm of sports fandom—
especially those who do so in a serious way, whether as sports media analysts or merely as persons who care about and have opinions on the execution of games—regularly report experiencing hostility as a result. Sometimes
this hostility is brought by other women, from whom women sports fans
feel alienated when discussing sports. More often, however, the hostility in
question is directed at women fans by men. Some forms of fandom, notably
participation in "fantasy" sports leagues,[3] are overtly hostile to women and
"even less welcoming . . . than traditional, enacted sport" (Davis and Duncan 2006; Ruihley and Billings 2012). Other examples of hostility are the fans
who claimed that their experience of watching the American League wild-
card game was "ruined" by the sound of Jessica Mendoza's voice, the men
who subject their fellow women fans to knowledge tests, and even the advertising directed primarily to men during live sporting events.[4] Each of these
practices, intentional or not, convey a clear message to women fans: you don't
belong here.

Such messages of nonbelonging need not be overtly exclusionary; more
often they function by positioning women as second-class fans or "outsiders"
who are permitted entry so long as they remain unobtrusive. This more insidious, less overt form of delegitimation is on display in the rise of "educational"
events explicitly directed at women fans—usually called something like
"Football 101 for Women."[5] Though these events serve the ostensible purpose
of bringing women into the fold of football fandom, they do so by explicitly
positioning women as novices, perpetual outsiders whose only explicit inclusion takes the form of entry-level education. Some of these programs market
themselves by offering women the opportunity to "impress your man"[6]—
assuming not only heterosexual coupling but also that the woman is so ignorant of the content of "her man's" fan practices that he will be "impressed"
by her acquisition of rudimentary knowledge of the workings of the sport.
Although some such programs actually provide discussion of fairly advanced
football strategy—such as, for example, the "Football 101 for Women" program at the University of Colorado, which includes film study and "complex
topics such as the advantage of a Cover 2 defense" (Kuta 2014)—their marketing as "101" classes conveys an image of women fans as specifically in need
of basic introductions to the sport. The "101" label also requires that women
interested in learning more accept the novice designation in order to access
that knowledge. Interested women, in other words, must position themselves
as outsiders to be granted provisional acceptance—the very designation they

must repeatedly fight in normatively masculine fan spaces. That women are welcome in these "permitted outsider" or "special guest" contexts but are met with hostility when they position themselves as full fans or legitimate sports knowers suggests that masculine domination of the sporting arena is de rigueur and that women who exceed the acceptable limits of participation constitute a threat to this masculine norm.

Why, though, does women's full participation in sports fandom constitute a threat to normative masculinity? There are several ways to conceptualize this. First, as Iris Young points out, sport occupies a particularly important place in contemporary performances of masculinity. In her essay "The Exclusion of Women from Sport," she writes,

> In contemporary society sport appears to carry nearly the full weight of the meanings of masculinity. Most masculinist societies contain a number of institutions in which a man can show himself a "real" man, and from which women are excluded. In contemporary society, however, sport remains one of the few institutions which explicitly serves this function, and hence is overburdened with a masculine image. (1979, 50)

Whereas gender-exclusive arenas were previously widely available for men to prove their manhood—including the "public" political sphere, the military, the leadership of the church, the academy, and so on—gender integration has made such spaces less hospitable as mechanisms for the demonstration of masculine dominance. This is not to say that gender hierarchy is no longer characteristic of at least some of these spaces, but it is to point out that there are fewer and fewer zones of explicitly masculine homosociality today; sport (perhaps because it is "only a game") is one of the few arenas in which gender segregation is explicitly sanctioned and valorized. As a result, some form of participation in sport has come to hold outsized significance as a practice of normatively masculine subjectivization. Since the vast majority of men do not possess the physical capability to use athletic participation to prove their manhood, sports fandom—particularly in its knowledge-acquisition forms—takes on special masculine significance.

Masculine significance is attained in sport partly through the performance of social dominance and exclusion, as I suggested in chapter 2. Fandom gives fans—particularly men—the opportunity to enact multiple self-affirming dichotomies: us versus them, insider versus outsider, "real" fan versus bandwagoner/fake, expert versus novice. Fans who are men can affirm their masculinity to the extent that they demonstrate their membership in the privileged side of such dichotomies, and this is often accomplished by distinguishing themselves from the subordinate class of women fans. However, it is worth considering what sports fandom gives male fans beyond the opportunity to prove themselves as superior knowers. In her essay "Football and Feminism," Jan Boxill surprisingly suggests that "sports are the one place men can allow their emotional side to be displayed, where they can be complete. . . . [M]en are supposed to be in control; it is unmanly for them to let their emotions to be shown. . . . [In sports] there is bonding—something women are permitted to do every day and openly" (2006, 117). Traditional, misogynist gender norms figure women as "emotional" or "irrational" and concomitantly require men's emotions to be strictly contained. However, Boxill suggests, the norms around gender-appropriate displays of emotion take on even greater significance as women gain independence and liberation. Increasingly lacking social control, men must turn to sharp control of their own emotions to develop a full sense of normatively masculine subjectivity. Although outward displays of emotion, particularly love for one's friends and those feelings associated with vulnerability, are not permitted in the rigid norms of heterosexual masculinity, the sporting arena constitutes an exceptional space, perhaps by virtue of its homosociality. Just as the homosociality of sports culture permits touching among men that would otherwise be forbidden by heterosexist norms, men are permitted emotional vulnerability within the masculine arena of the sporting context. Within the (presumably) "safe" space of exclusively masculine heterosexuality, men can allow themselves to experience and express love, joy, disappointment, heartbreak, and social bonding. As women become harder to control, such spaces are fewer, meaning that men grow more emotionally stifled. Thus, Boxill suggests, borrowing a phrase from Mariah Buron Nelson, "the stronger women get, the more men love football" (116).

Boxill's analysis is primarily directed at the experience of *playing* football or directly participating in it as a member of a team. She argues, for example, that football "is a place of safe love, where men can share in each other's successes, because each person is essential for any one person's success." Unlike other practices of normative masculine subjectivization, the cooperative nature of team sports allows for connection and celebration of other men's successes. What is interesting, however, is how unusual it seems to describe team sports in these terms, which sound rather more stereotypically feminine than the affect that one might imagine as characteristic of athletes in a locker room. The reason for this, according to Boxill, is that people "don't want to acknowledge the love and the emotions that accompany" teamwork or cooperation. So rather than openly recognizing the importance of such feelings, athletes in homosocial masculine environments engage in misogyny and hyper-heterosexuality. "By denigrating women," Boxill posits, athletes "show it's not the love or emotion of the weak: so rather than show love, they show violence toward those who do" (2006, 120). In this analysis, then, misogynist attitudes and actions make possible the experience of necessary emotions that make players fully human but are forbidden by the norms of heterosexual masculinity.

Extending this analysis to the case of sports fans makes good sense, particularly because most men sports *fans* do not even have the actual experience of physical competition to provide a legitimating context for their emotion. Whereas athletes can point to their physical dominance on the field or court as the "real" object of competition, to which passionate connection to one's teammates might be accidental, fan experiences of "dominance" are purely vicarious. Moreover, the vicariousness of such experiences renders fans emotionally dependent upon the actions of others and at best minimally in control of game outcomes—and then only if they happen to be in attendance. This means that the avenue through which most men experience sport, one of the primary arenas in which they permit themselves to experience unrestrained emotion, feelings of connection to their friends and family, and feelings of affection for their team, hometown, or associated fantasies of identity, is an arena in which they are doubly vulnerable. They are vulnerable to their own passions and vulnerable to the actions of others, which they simply cannot control. With this in mind, the exclusion or subordination of women is even more explicable in the case of sports fandom than in the case of hypermasculine athletes, since athletes can at least use their performance on the field to shore up confidence in their own masculinity. For male fans who depend upon sports fandom to provide both a stable sense of normatively masculine subjectivity *and* an emotional outlet, such direct athletic performances are not possible.

Because women's encroachment into the realm of sports fandom as anything other than mere novices constitutes a threat to the homosociality of the discipline, it has the potential to destabilize sports fandom as a safe means of access to these emotions. This destabilization occurs because the space of fandom is "contaminated" by femininity, rendering it unworkable as a zone of homosociality or hypermasculinity for at least two reasons. First, the stereotypical figuration of women as emotionally vulnerable or incapable of controlling their passions has the effect of holding an unwelcome mirror to the otherwise masculine display of emotion in the sporting context. When the passions indulged in are shared by women, sports fan emotions lose their potential to constitute an acceptable display of masculinity. Second—and perhaps more importantly, given the role of knowledge in masculine sports fandom—the presence of women fans makes salient the social elements of sports fandom, belying its pretensions to being a realm of "hard" facts and knowledge. In their study of women sports fans in the United States, Markovits and Albertson suggest that women fans know less about sports than do men, in the sense of having less propositional knowledge about the history of teams and so on. However, Markovits and Albertson also found that typical women fans are much more likely than men to report that they valued attending games and following a particular team because of the social import of those events.[7] Given what we have seen about the subjectivizing and normalizing effects of sports fandom, and its import for developing a sense of regional or otherwise collective identity, I would argue that it is not quite correct to say that typical male fans "know more" about sports. Rather, it would be more accurate to say that they know sports differently than typical women sports fans do— since women do know something quite significant about sports and sports fandom. Namely, women tend to know sports fandom as a means of social bonding, as a set of practices that increase feelings of love, connection, and community. Whereas men know the details of the histories of games, which they take to be the crux of fandom, women often recognize the larger set of social practices—the rituals, the traditions, the means of cultivating family and group identity—as meaningful, and perhaps as the underlying reason for participating in the spectacle of the games at all. This knowing, it seems, becomes a threat to homosocial and hypermasculine sports fandom: women's knowing of sports fandom in this way not only throws light upon the emotional needs of fans but also threatens (paradoxically) to trivialize fandom by making it feminine. In the face of that trivialization, men who are fans often react with hostility and knowledge tests. If they can prove that such women are not "real" fans on the metric of masculine legitimation, then their knowledge of fandom will apply only to themselves, insulating masculine fandom from this 'feminized' version.

Resistance or Complicity? Women Fans of Mainstream Men's Sport

If women's fandom of mainstream men's sports destabilizes a key site of the reproduction of homosocial, normative masculinity, does this entail that such fandom is an act of resistance to oppression? The presence of women sports fans does seem to pose a threat to masculinity as a performance that dominates or excludes women, but it is not clear that this means that women fans' mere involvement necessarily constitutes a liberatory action. Some forms of women's participation (namely, those adopting the position of perpetual novice) are perfectly compatible with sports fandom as a domain of hypermasculinity. Moreover, as feminists have argued, the mere fact that women begin to occupy roles or accept values once reserved for men is not sufficient to resist oppression. It may very well be that sports fandom remains ineluctably masculinist and that women gain admission to the realm of sports fandom by accepting and internalizing misogyny. Moreover, if sports fandom, as I have argued, often functions as a mechanism of the perpetuation of white supremacy, the situation of women's involvement may be even more worrisome than typical feminist concerns suggest. In this section, I will argue that although women's fandom can and does reproduce existing social hierarchies, certain forms of this fandom trouble those patterns and imbue sports fandom with new and different meanings.

First, as I argued previously, it is entirely possible for women's sports fandom, particularly white women's sports fandom, to reproduce racial hierarchy through the phenomenon of mascotting. The white women who used Kenyan Drake as a prop to demonstrate their football connections at the University of Alabama did not do anything particularly subversive. Similarly, women fans are just as capable as men of imaginatively identifying with black men conceived as symbols of hypermasculinity, dominance, or hyper-heterosexuality. Beyond the reproduction of white supremacy through mascotting, mainstream sports fandom's exclusive focus on *men's* sport contributes to normalization of masculinity and—it would seem—the concomitant subordination and objectification of women. But how might women be plausibly affected (or "objectified") by focus on specifically men's sports? In "Throwing like a Girl," Iris Young famously argues that women are "objectified" by the attendant phenomena of gender-segregated athletics because such segregation has significant effects on girls' and women's subjectivity and agency. Young's argument is that the teaching of boys and young men to play sports from a young age, and the concomitant failure to teach girls and women such skills, results in masculine subjects who view themselves as agents capable of effecting change in their material world, and contributes to the constitution of the feminine subject as an object—that is, as a subjectivity that views itself always from the outside. I argue, extending Young's argument from athletic participation to sports fandom, that this sort of subjectivity-attenuating effect is also a consequence of women's fandom directed exclusively at men's sport. To make this argument, it will be necessary to look more closely at Young's account of the effects of sports participation (or the lack thereof) on female body experience.

In "The Exclusion of Women from Sport," Young argues that women's exclusion from sports culture "symbolizes our exclusion from humanity itself, and . . . contributes in a basic way to a sense of weakness, body-objectification and physical timidity among women" (1979, 50). The reason for this is two-

fold: first, given sport's deep cultural significance, the fact that women are
not featured as active participants on the field or court conveys the idea that
women's activities do not have the same cultural import as those of men. Just
as women's exclusion from history books, religious texts, mainstream fiction,
and politics conveys the insignificance of women's lives, so too does the exclusion of women from sport. Second, and more importantly for individual
subjects, Young argues that the prevention of women and girls from engaging
in sport inhibits their development of a robust bodily agency, which contributes to the phenomenological experience (reinforced by broader social
practices of the constant evaluation of women's bodies) of objectification.
Young develops this argument in "Throwing like a Girl" (1980). Girls throw
"like girls"—moving only their arms, rather than by using the force of their
entire bodies—because they have been trained to take up as little space as
possible in the world and to be conscious of the appearance of their bodies to
outside observers. Whereas boys will use the entire force of their bodies when
throwing, twisting their trunks and extending their limbs fully to maximize
the likelihood of reaching their intended target, girls tend to hold back—
meaning that their physical execution of the action is acutely limited. The root
of this difference, for Young, is in the location of each one's object: boys' attention is focused outward, whereas girls' attention is always to a certain extent
inward, taking their own bodies as objects. This self-objectification results in
a severely attenuated sense of agency, as consciousness of their bodies first as
objects rather than subjects renders women both hyperaware (and fearful)
of potential dangers to it and convinced of their inability to physically act in
the world. So, for example, when most girls and women (who have not had
significant athletic experience) go to catch or throw balls, they tend to think
of themselves as the object rather than the subject of motion. In practice, this
means thinking of the ball as something coming toward me that might hurt
me rather than thinking of myself as moving to catch, throw, and act on the
ball. This form of objectified subjectivity is detrimental to women's athletic
performance, but it also, as Young points out, has effects that carry over into
all features of women's lives. The social practice of keeping girls and women
from participating in sports thus has significantly negative consequences for
women's agency—their first thought when confronted with physical or spatial
challenges is "I can't."

Young's argument is also useful for conceptualizing the effects of hypermasculinity and feminine exclusion from mainstream sports for women
sports fans. The identification with athletes who are exclusively men, in
games that are explicitly masculine, has similarly objectifying effects on the
subjectivity of girls and women. To understand why, it is useful to recall our

discussion of heroes and the lusory attitude—the attitude that enables ordinary objects and persons to take on special significance in the sporting context (Feezell 2013, 149). As fans with the lusory attitude, "we project ourselves into [the athletes'] stories, and we make them our own" (150). Athletes thus become both symbols of our own values and also our means of vicariously experiencing the action of sport. Both features of this identification have important consequences for the experience of women fans because they involve subjectively adopting a masculine perspective in order to participate in the lusory attitude of fandom. Though one might suggest that this is not particularly worrying, given that the lusory attitude requires making a break from "reality" by entering the space of the game, it is significant for two reasons. First, as I have suggested, even if the game itself is a specially demarcated space, the sporting context is never entirely divorced from the broader social world; the two arenas affect one another. Second, and more importantly, this adoption of masculine perspective simply is *not* limited to the sporting context but is consistent with the broader social milieu that treats masculinity as normative.

Considering Simone de Beauvoir's discussion of this broad-based masculine normativity is instructive here. In *The Second Sex*, Beauvoir argues that one of the primary ways girls "become" women is by learning to understand themselves as "other," or as secondary objects to masculine subjects, and that a crucial mechanism for creating this understanding is repeated exposure to and identification with masculine subjectivity. From the beginning of her consciousness, Beauvoir suggests, the little girl's "historical and literary culture, the songs and legends she is raised on, are an exaltation of the man. . . . [T]he little girl discovers the world and reads her destiny through the eyes of men" (2011, 302). From fairy tales to religious and historical texts, girls are exposed to heroes and protagonists who are men. It is striking to see, in fact, just how accurate her account continues to be today: "If the little girl reads newspapers, if she listens to adult conversation, she notices that today, as in the past, men lead the world. The heads of state, generals, explorers, musicians, and painters she admires are men; *it is men who make her heart beat with enthusiasm*" (303; emphasis mine). This description is particularly apt when applied to girl and women sports fans: not only do men run the world; it is the actions of men on which females' fandom, and all its attendant significance, depends. If a woman or girl is to "bask in reflected glory," it is the glory of men; if she is to know herself through the disciplines of fandom, it is through acquiring knowledge about and supporting the actions of men. This knowledge, moreover, must always be acquired to some extent in the third person: women and girls who do play sports do not play the same sports that men do, as women's football does not exist, women play softball rather than baseball, and the rules for the women's versions of basketball and hockey differ from those of the men's games. Women fans, then, face a built-in knowledge deficit, lacking the benefit of playing the games they follow, and are thus reliant to varying degrees on the testimony of broadcasters, male family members, and male athletes to learn. The women who appear in the symbolic drama of the athletic competition appear on the margins—the literal sidelines of the game around which all is organized—supporting, analyzing, cheering on the actions of the men at its center. This perpetually peripheral status has the effect of reinforcing feminine subjectivity as secondary and dependent upon men for its meaning.

Such secondary status is not merely disappointing; it contributes to the production of subjects whose consciousness is characterized by internal contradiction, "a conflict between the fundamental claim of every subject, which always posits itself as essential, and the demands of a situation that constitutes her as inessential" (Beauvoir 2011, 17). What this means, for Beauvoir, is that women's situation is fundamentally dehumanizing and objectifying, in the sense that it reduces women from the human state of for-itself (subject) to in-itself (object). Young's description of "throwing like a girl" is a concrete example of the individualized effects of this form of objectified subjectivity. The perpetual identification of women sports fans with athletes who are men contributes to the same kind of effect, which can occur *despite* the existence of some women athletes. The normativity of masculinity and the importance of identifying with it via the practices of mainstream sports fandom contribute to the perpetuation of a social order in which women find themselves as "others," or as objectified subjects. Though women fans may, like Jessica Mendoza, achieve comparatively elite status, their situation is necessarily restricted by the masculine normativity of the sporting context. For American women sports fans, it is today as Beauvoir describes the situation of girls in France in the 1940s: "The sphere she belongs to is closed everywhere, limited, dominated by the male universe: as high as she climbs, as far as she dares go, there will always be a ceiling over her head, walls that block her path. Man's gods are in such a faraway heaven that in truth, for him, there are no gods: the little girl lives among gods with a human face" (311).

Insofar as women's fandom of men's sports is freely chosen, it constitutes a complicity with masculine normativity and the concomitant othering or objectification of women. Indeed, it is striking to consider that the "gods with a human face" that make women sports fans' hearts "beat with enthusiasm" are dependent for their meaning and value upon the identification and valorization of fans themselves. This is not to say, however, that such women are morally culpable or that they are solely responsible for their own objectified subjectivity. Sports fandom, as I have suggested, is not isolated from the wider social world in which women's objectification and secondary status is daily reinforced. Moreover, given the significance with which fandom is imbued in the contemporary United States, the usefulness of fandom as a mechanism for social and familial bonding, and the concomitant devaluation of traditionally "feminine" activities, there is more than enough incentive for women to engage in it. The complicity of women sports fans with masculine normativity must be understood in this context, and as of a piece with women's complicity in other social practices—like religious practices—that offer, in exchange for their subordination, social significance, connection to community, and a clear sense of identity in a world that demands that they know who they are.

Yet, it is not clear that all women fans of men's sports are *simply* complicit with the masculinity (or whiteness) of mainstream sports fandom or that all forms of women's fandom have the same effects. As I have argued, women fans' acceptance of a perpetual-novice position in sports fandom is rather different than their practice of the full-blown disciplines of sports fandom. There are some forms of women's fandom, moreover, that eschew many of the traditional elements of fandom and, in so doing, render its subjectivizing effects more complex. I turn now to one particularly striking example.

In 2006, Alder Chapman founded the LeBron James Grandmothers' Fan Club (LJGFC) in Akron, Ohio. At the time, James, a native of Akron, was beginning his third season for the Cleveland Cavaliers. Chapman and her fellow LJGFC members—who are, to be clear, grandmothers who are fans of James, not fans of James's grandmothers or fans who are also James's grandmothers—maintain the club through the present day, gathering regularly to watch James's basketball games, to socialize, and to volunteer in the local community. Composed of more than two hundred grandmothers, the majority of whom are women of color, the LJGFC has been featured in both local and national media.[8] The grandmothers perform their fandom in some familiar ways—they wear T-shirts in team colors, watch all of James's games and must not be disturbed when they do so ("when the game is on, don't call Grannie," one member advised),[9] collect memorabilia in scrapbooks, and cheer for James's team. In other ways, however, their fandom diverges from typical fan patterns, as the official LJGFC cheer demonstrates: "GRANNIES RISE UP! GRANNIES RISE UP! FOR L-B-J!" (LJGFC 2015). The grandmothers' fandom is team-located (insofar as they root for the success of James's teams) but individually motivated; it also specifically centers the women's identity as grandmothers in their performance of fandom.

The specificity of their fandom as grandmothers turns out to be important in one of the most nontraditional features of the LJGFC's fan allegiance. Significantly, when James infamously left Cleveland to "take [his] talents to South Beach," the LJGFC, unlike many Cavaliers fans, remained loyal to him. As one member put it in an interview with ESPNW, "When LeBron went to Miami, I was hurt, but I went with him. I followed him, I cheered for him, and he had to make that move in order to better himself" (quoted in Olszowy 2015). Subsequent to the Miami move, the LJGFC transferred its fandom from the Cavaliers to the Heat and penned a poem—which members had printed on their new Heat T-shirts—to explain their shift in loyalties. After opening with a meditation on the love that grandmothers have for grandchildren, the poem concludes:

> The latest kid that touched our hearts
> And bring us so much joy
> Is 6 foot 8 and could be known
> As Akron's Golden Boy
> So rise up grannies everywhere
> He makes our hearts tick
> Who is this child of Akron
> Now wearing number 6
> He has a dream to follow
> But knows from whence he came
> He is the King of every court
> His name is LeBron James!!!
>
> (LJGFC 2015)

Members explain their loyalty to and love for James by appealing to their status as grandmothers, who love their grandchildren unconditionally. Though they bear no relation to him, these women conceive of James as a symbolic grandson precisely because he comes from Akron; insofar as he is a "child of Akron," James bears a relation of kinship to them as progenitors and nurturers of that local community.[10]

This explanation of loyalty significantly transforms typical modes of fan identification. Though fans very often express allegiance to teams and individuals on the basis of regional or local geography, this allegiance often functions by subsuming the individual to the locality or collective, such that the fans' love for and identification with that locale takes precedence—this is what enables fans to identify with changing team personnel over time and what makes both hero worship and mascotting possible. In the case of the LJGFC, however, allegiance to the local community does not trump individual loyalty; it is able to coexist alongside loyalty to the individual. This coexistence is indicated even in differences in the LJGFC's pronoun usage: whereas fans typically refer to their teams as "we," indicating first-person collective identity, the grandmothers often refer to James individually and put greater emphasis on his individual status in "our" hearts, community, etc. Though many in the LJGFC clearly understand James as a representative of their community, in the sense common to hero worship, their explicitly maternal concern for him is not entirely reducible to hero worship. Though the first-person collective is still significant in their discourse—Akron clearly looms large in the group's rhetoric—it does not subsume James to a part of the "we," as simply "one of us" but maintains him in is individuality. Indeed, the LJGFC website is replete with references to the details of James's life, including his wife and children, as well as his off-the-court activities. The relation these fans bear to James is, in short, not merely that of a lusory object; the symbolic kinship relations nurtured by the LJGFC enables their care and concern for James as a human being. As a result, it is not surprising that the LJGFC maintained its loyalty to James in the face of the wave of fan antipathy from northeast Ohio during the years of his move to Miami.

Given the larger context of fan hate for James, including the racialized scapegoating I discussed in the previous chapter, the loyalty of the LJGFC is even more significant. Rather than disband or join with other Cavaliers fans in burning James jerseys, members of the LJGFC couched James's move to Miami in terms common to discourses of racial and individual uplift: "He had to make that move in order to better himself." Their insistence on treating and valuing James as a full human being, not just as an athlete or as a symbol of their community, constitutes a clear resistance to both mascotting and scapegoating. This resistance is especially important, given fan tendencies to reduce black men to their athletic status and the larger white supremacist social milieu that envisions blackness as deviant and cut off from "normal" kinship relations. Though the women may not have had such intentions when forming the group or when standing by James during his time with the Heat, their fandom established a counternarrative to the dominant one suggesting that James owed fans something and that his concern for his own interests amounted to culpable disloyalty. It also, by extension, constituted a resistance to the white supremacist ethos that demands black male athletes stay "in their place." James is valorized not as a mere symbol, token, or mascot but as a young black man who has made his community proud through his incredible accomplishments.

The LJGFC, moreover, explicitly celebrates the community of women who support Akron and one another, using their love for basketball and James to position themselves as a "we" with value—as fans, as community members, and as older women. Their self-descriptions are striking: "If you want to see a real Cavs fan, come to one of our game watches"; "We have a motto of 'love and fun' . . . our love for LeBron, and having fun with each other"; "The grandmas are a team! They are a LeBron James team"; "We realize as Grandmothers each one of us must try and be a living example to our youth" (LJGFC 2015). The LJGFC enables its members to use the presumptively masculine space of basketball to cultivate and valorize aging femininity—which, as Beauvoir and others have pointed out, is so culturally devalued that older women are treated as though they have no more reason to exist. That they valorize aging femininity primarily as black women is also significant, for doing so pushes back against the narrative, popular since the Moynihan report of the 1960s, that lays blame for problems within black communities on the "matriarchal" structure of black American culture and black women's supposed emasculation of black men. These grandmothers are deliberately and unabashedly maternal *and* agential: they are a force for change in the Akron community, in the lives of their own children and grandchildren, and in the usually hypermasculine realm of sports fandom. Despite being fans of a mainstream men's sport, then, it is simply false that their fandom constitutes more complicity with masculine or white normativity. Their performance of sports fandom has the effect of destabilizing the most entrenched oppressive features of mainstream fandom in the United States and gives us reason to hope that sports fandom might not, in every case, function as a mechanism of oppression or the reinforcement of racial and sexual hierarchy.

Women's Sports and Their Fans

In the years since the passage of Title IX of the Education Amendments of 1972, which forbids gender discrimination in educational institutions receiving assistance from the US federal government, women's athletics has seen a sharp increase in participation and quality of competition. As Title IX required more equitable distribution of funds between men's and women's athletics in higher education,[11] more women had the opportunity to compete, to excel athletically, to earn scholarships, and even to play sports professionally. The founding of the Women's National Basketball Association (WNBA) in 1996 increased opportunities for elite women's athletic competition, forming the only women's professional team sports league in the United States having exposure or fan following anywhere close to the mainstream men's leagues. Though average game attendance is comparatively low, average television viewership in 2013 was 231,000 per game, higher than the average game viewership for (men's) Major League Soccer in the United States—though still considerably lower than average game viewership for the NBA, which was between two and four million per game during the previous season.[12] There are also significantly fewer teams in the WNBA than in the NBA, resulting in a smaller fan base overall. Nevertheless, women's sports in general has grown in scope and significance over the past forty years—and for this reason, bears discussing in our analysis of the subjectivizing effects of sports fandom. If women's athletics are not normatively masculine arenas, might they offer a means to counter the hypermasculinity of sports fandom? Moreover, given that women's athletics has been historically associated with lesbian culture and is increasingly populated by high-profile queer women of color, might it constitute a venue in which sports fandom is used specifically to resist oppression?

EMULATING MEN?

In order to argue that fandom of women's sports might be liberatory, it is crucial to address a pressing objection: namely, that by engaging in competitive sports, women athletes do not trouble masculine normativity but rather embrace it and consequently simply reiterate the very values that denigrate femininity. A version of this objection—that women's engagement in traditionally masculine activities does not disrupt masculine normativity but rather reinforces it by accepting its values—has been circulating in feminist circles since at least the 1960s, when consciousness-raising groups called into question any activity aimed at producing hierarchy, including competitions. Academic feminists of the 1980s[13] linked the practice of competition with war and the desire for domination, both of which they conceived as irrevocably masculinist and oppressive. Such feminists argued that the cultural import placed on competition was evidence of the normalization of masculine values, which were harmful to a wide range of people, and thus, that we ought to eschew competition entirely in favor of cultivating more (feminine) nurturing habits. Competitions in general constitute "mini-wars," which foster an antagonistic, warlike mind-set, if not outright hatred (Davion 1987). If this view is correct, no form of competition will succeed in avoiding the evils of masculinism or violence—meaning that women's athletic competition would be equally as problematic as mainstream men's sports.

In her 1999 book *The Rites of Men*, Varda Burstyn puts forth a similar set of worries about athletic competitions. Specifically taking up the question of women's professional basketball, she asks, "To what extent does accepting the values and behaviors of hypermasculine men's culture, embodied in the core men's sports, strengthen or weaken women and society? There will be no social gain if, through learning the mind set and morality of hypermasculinity, women in effect lend their efforts to its broader perpetuation in the name of gender-neutrality or gender equality" (266). Despite the advent of the WNBA as a venue to showcase and celebrate women's athletic achievements, and the apparent increase in social acceptance of androgyny, Burstyn argues that such changes are not true indicators of progress. Rather than an expansion of the liberty of femininity, Burstyn argues, women's turn to mainstream, mass-marketed athletics constitutes an

> unquestioning emulation of hypermasculinity . . . the triumph of hypermas-culinism, its inherent sado-masochistic attitudes to the body and its affirma-tion of domination. This so-called androgyny does not represent the "femini-zation" of culture—that is, the restoration to their rightful place of principles and values long suppressed—even when women voluntarily seek it. While as-serting their right to be physically active and strong and socially instrumental and influential, women should, nevertheless, be transforming physical culture into one that validates the expressive and cooperative dimensions of existence. Women need to continue to value those qualities in themselves and in cultural life, rather than abandon them to the hierarchism and violent instrumentality of the dominant sport culture. (267)

It is because mainstream sport culture is fundamentally about "intermale ranking" (271), according to Burstyn, that women's basketball and softball (for example) are devalued and denigrated in mainstream sports fandom. By adopting the values and practices of men's sports, women do not succeed in transforming their meaning but, instead, simply fail to be men and are yet again positioned as deficient—occupying a position even below those at the bottom of the intermale ranking. Moreover, acceptance of a "physical culture" whose goals are competitive rather than collaborative simply reiterates mas-culine values that can serve only to harm those who do not come out "on top."

In views like Burstyn's, "contemporary sports are . . . rejected *tout court* because playing sport is to be seen as 'selling out'" (Edwards and Jones 2007, 349), insofar as it is inherently masculine. Similar implications would seem to follow for sports fans: if anyone who plays the sport is engaged in a contest of masculinist values, those who watch, identify with, root for, and organize social practices around the athletes and outcomes of those contests would surely be lending similar support to its continuation and significance. One might even argue that because the social significance of the sporting contest depends upon the agreement of fans, that they bear an even *greater* responsi-bility than athletes for the reiteration of masculinist values. Whether one ac-cepts this further conclusion, however, the original objection seems to retain its force: if the rise of women's athletics is tantamount to the acceptance of masculinist values and the emulation of hypermasculinity, then fandom of women's sports cannot constitute an effective means of resistance to the oppressive effects of mainstream sports fandom.

Though this objection might seem plausible on its face, it is not, ultimately, convincing. There are at least three reasons to reject this view, which is problematic not only for its embrace of an untenable gender essentialism but also for its misunderstanding of sport as such. I will discuss the latter problem first. Mainstream sport certainly is competitive, which means that winning is achieved at the expense of someone else's loss. Yet the embrace of competition does not entail that sport is entirely adversarial in structure, nor that it necessarily involves a problematically masculinist or warlike quest for dominance. As Victoria Davion points out, many forms of competition require significant antecedent cooperation in order to render the competition itself possible, and this is particularly true in the case of sport (1987, 57). We can see the significance of cooperation in competition when considering some of the most classic formulations of the nature of games in the philosophy of sport literature. Bernard Suits, for example, famously refers to sport as "the voluntary attempt to overcome unnecessary obstacles" (2005, 55). That is, the goal of sport cannot be made sense of apart from the voluntary agreement to abide by particular rules, which make the achievement of a particular outcome more challenging than it would otherwise be. If my goal, for example, were *only* to get a puck into a net despite the counterefforts of others, there are other ways to do this than to slide it across the ice using a hockey stick, some of which would make the task quite a bit easier. I could, for example, cut a hole in the back of the net and slip it in while no one was looking, or I could set off an explosion that would send my opponents running for cover, leaving the net open for me to place the puck in with my hands. In neither case, however, would I be playing hockey. Playing hockey, like playing any game, requires my opponents and me to agree to abide by certain constraints and to count on one another to try to achieve our goals within those constraints. We must, in other words, cooperate in order to be able to play together—and this cooperation is markedly absent in *actual* warlike engagements. Moreover, the fact that competitors in sports desire opponents who are, as previously discussed, worthy of their competitive efforts, suggests not only cooperation but also at least a threshold amount of goodwill. The pleasure of competition requires an opponent who is skilled enough to pose a plausible threat to my own success; genuine competitors, then, hope for an opponent who does reasonably well. No such necessity exists for the pure and simple desire for violence or domination or for those who are simply engaging in warlike behavior.

More importantly for our present purposes, even if we grant that athletic competition involves *some* measure of the quest to dominate, or (minimally) to be better than others, it does not follow that this behavior is necessarily masculine. Although the assertion of dominance—and particularly, the domination of women—is used by (some) men to assert and cultivate masculinity, this does not imply that physical dominance or control is equivalent to masculinity. We might just as easily explain the linkage of physical dominance and masculinity by appealing, like Young, to the long-standing social practices that enforce the gender binary by expecting and cultivating physical dominance and athletic control in boys and discouraging it in girls. To accept the claim that women who seek to excel athletically or dominate on the court are emulating masculinity, we would have to believe that such characteristics are, as such, essentially masculine and contrary to femininity, regardless of the agent performing them. That is, given that many women actually *do* engage in such competitive athletic behaviors, maintaining that these behaviors are essentially masculine and contrary to femininity requires that we stipulate the classification of such behaviors as masculine or feminine in advance. In the absence of such stipulation, the claim that the numerous women who engage in athletic competition are emulating masculinity is nonsensical. Such a stipulation, however, is question begging: the women who are competitive athletes are emulating masculinity because they are rejecting femininity, and we know this is true because they have embraced competitive athletics. To avoid begging the question, we might reformulate the claim to suggest that athletic competition is more frequently associated with masculinity than femininity—an empirical claim that is plausible, not a universalizing claim that requires the exclusion of counterexamples. As an empirical claim about gendered tendencies, however, this point loses its normative force. It is simply true that more men than women value athletic competition and that more men than women compete athletically—but these facts give us no reason to believe that athletic competition is inherently masculinist or that women ought not embrace it for fear of rejecting their femininity. As an analogy, we might suggest that the fact that more men than women hold public office and value public political discourse gives little reason to believe that engaging in politics is inherently masculinist or that women seeking to assert the value of femininity ought to avoid the political arena.

There have been, and continue to be, fewer opportunities for women and girls to engage and excel in athletic competition than men and boys, and this fact, as feminists have forcefully argued, has resulted in subjects with different sets of values, bodies, and talents. But that things have been so does not tell us that they must be or that they ought to be. Additionally, cultural variance in which endeavors or sports are appropriately "masculine" or "feminine" speaks against the plausibility of considering certain physical activities obviously masculinist. Whereas soccer in the United States is not typically considered hypermasculine, and the women who participate in it are not viewed with the same kind of homophobic suspicion as women who play the more "masculine" sports of basketball or softball, "in Europe and Latin America, it is the exact opposite: Soccer-playing women are seen as butch and exist under the constant suspicion and derision of being lesbians, whereas basketball-playing women are not. The minute women enter any of the male-dominated areas of the hegemonic sports culture, they are immediately . . . construed as unfeminine" (Markovits and Albertson 2012, 107). Rather than some sports or endeavors being inherently "masculinist," it appears that whatever is culturally significant is male dominated (and vice versa), requiring the exclusion of women to ensure the perpetuation of that male dominance.

Moreover, to insist upon a universalizing distinction between "masculine" and "feminine" endeavors is to accept the very norms that have functioned both to denigrate gender-nonconforming individuals and to restrict women's bodies and behaviors. Feminists should be just as wary of accusing women athletes of buying into hypermasculinity as they were of the early restrictions on women's athletic participation on the grounds that such activities would be damaging to their reproductive health or produce "angularity" in their bodies (Hargreaves 1994, 48). Both purport to be saving a "femininity" in peril, but they do so by assuming that femininity must take a specific form— meaning that, ironically, individual women are a danger to their own femininity if they make the "wrong" choices. Feminist efforts to preserve the value of a femininity that is not open to transformation by women are as ethically troubling as they are philosophically misguided.

The concern that fans of women's athletics are valorizing the embrace and imitation of masculinity by women athletes is built upon two primary assumptions: (1) that there is a clear essence of "femininity" or feminine values as such and (2) that competition, particularly athletic competition, is antithetical to that essence by virtue of its embrace of violence, domination, and masculinity. Neither of these assumptions is tenable, and the first has consequences that, more often than not, have the effect of oppressing women and gender-nonconforming individuals. We do not have good reason to believe that such an essence exists; if it did, as Beauvoir points out, we would have a difficult time explaining why "femininity" is so often perceived to be in danger of disappearing. Though we might very well raise concerns about why the sports in which men tend to outperform women are more highly valued— why, for example, football tends to attract more attention than gymnastics, volleyball, or figure skating—such concerns do not imply that those sports are inherently masculine or that women who defy the odds to become elite competitors in them necessarily emulate masculinity. Finally, even if some women *do* consciously embrace performances of masculinity (as many queer women do), there is little reason to believe that in so doing, they denigrate femininity or other women or that their fans do so by valorizing them. The opposite is arguably the case, given the long history of oppressive restrictions on women's bodily presentation. As I will argue in the next section, the explicit presence and celebration of lesbian and (otherwise) queer women in women's basketball and softball, including those women who flout the norms of traditionally feminine gender presentation, has made fandom of these sports an important site of antioppressive resistance.

QUEERING SPORTS FANDOM

In her important historical analysis of homophobia in US women's sport, Susan Cahn shows that although women's athletics has long been marked by stereotype-motivated homophobic suspicion, it also provides an important space of expression and support for women who do not embody the ideals of traditionally heterosexual femininity. She writes, "Paradoxically, the association between masculinity, lesbianism, and sport had a positive outcome for some women. The very cultural matrix that produced the pejorative image [of women athletes as mannish lesbians] also created possibilities for lesbian affirmation" (1993, 344). Cahn documents the transformation in rhetoric surrounding female athletes through the twentieth century, which, though consistently concerned with sexual propriety, does not express that concern in terms of "homosexual panic" until the postwar forties and fifties.[14] The emergence of the stereotype of women athletes as butch lesbians came to be deployed in mainstream discourse as an instrument of ridicule and oppression. This was the case, for example, in the 1952 yearbook at the University of Minnesota, which declared, "Believe it or not, members of the Women's Athletic Association are normal," and that "at least one . . . of WAA's 300 members is engaged" (351), and in the myriad regulations on women athletes' hair, dress, and leg shaving that cropped up during the mid-twentieth century as "an attempt to secure the heterosexual image of athletes" (355). Despite these efforts, queer women were able to use women's athletic spaces as sites of community building, both as athletes and as fans. Importantly, "the athletic setting provided a public space for lesbian sociability without naming it as such or excluding women who were not lesbians" (358). Through oral histories, Cahn shows that for many queer women negotiating their sexual identities in a hostile world, this athletic space was crucial, even for those who might not have been sports fans otherwise. As one interview subject recalled, she went to her first women's softball game despite the fact that "I wasn't the least interested in sports, but it gave me a chance to meet other gay girls," confirming Cahn's analysis that "women's softball provided public space for lesbians to gather when there were few gay bars or other social institutions" (358). Paradoxically, then, the stereotypical figure of the "mannish" lesbian athlete "was not only a figure of homophobic discourse but also a human actor engaged in sexual innovation and struggle . . . us[ing] the social and psychic space of sport to create a collective culture and affirmative identity" (364).

Contemporarily, women's collegiate and professional athletics continues to provide a site for the cultivation of queer women's communities in public spaces. This is particularly true in the case of fans of women's basketball and of the WNBA in particular. In her 2005 study of lesbian and bisexual WNBA fans, Susannah Dolance found that such fans use WNBA games as a special site of "the construction of lesbian community" that is "qualitatively different" than other such venues, insofar as it allows queer women to foster a sense of connectedness and pride in a public space that is not explicitly "for" lesbians (Cahn 1993, 74). As in other cases of sports fandom, lesbian fans construct community through a variety of practices, including congregating with other queer women. Fans in this case make use of a type of we discourse similar to that of other fan bases, but with the slight difference that the "we" is indicative primarily of the fan community itself, rather of fans' identification with the teams that represent them. For example, a repeated trope in the fan discourse Dolance documents is the idea that the WNBA *as an institution* belongs to lesbians, insofar as they constitute the core of its fan base. As one fan of the Washington Mystics put it, "I mean we so support *our* women's sports, it's nice to see them all cheering." Another fan concurred: "This is our sport, and we're women and we're lesbian women in particular, and we need to get out there and support women's sports" (quoted in Cahn 1993, 77). The "we" in both cases is the community of lesbian and queer women, who are taken to have a particularly important relationship to the league and its teams. This is not to say that queer women who are WNBA fans do not identify with "their" teams or with specific players. Rather, fans develop this additional, fan-centric "we" because of the special status of WNBA fandom within heterosexist culture.

The stereotypical association of women's athletics with lesbianism makes possible the identification and valorization of a queer women's community among fans. Interestingly, for fans of the WNBA, a key means of reproducing, celebrating, and valorizing lesbian identity is a fantasy of identification similar to that of hero worship, but which acknowledges the full human person beyond the lusory object. Whereas in hero worship, fans take individual players to be symbolically representative of some feature of their community or identity, lesbian and bisexual WNBA fans regularly participate in what Dolance calls "speculating"—that is, speculating about the sexual identities of individual players, coaches, or other fans, in order to determine whether they are "one of us" (2005, 78). This is important not only because not all queer coaches or players are publicly "out,"[15] but also because this practice of specu-lation about other women in the space of the arena allows fans to cultivate "a sense . . . of a *large* lesbian presence" and to engage in "a kind of 'queering'—making the WNBA more lesbian and more queer through fantasy" (78). This fantasy (which often, to be clear, relies on fan adoption and recirculation of stereotypical images of lesbianism) enables fans not only to play out the sym-bolic victory of their values through the on-court contest, as in the case of hero worship. It also enables fans to imagine themselves as part of a larger community to which both "sides" of the contest belong and through which they are united, despite their competitive context. As one fan put it, the idea of "a whole stadium full" (79) of lesbians coming together was particularly powerful and affirming. Such imaginative practice should not be understood as delusional or "imaginary" in the pejorative sense. Fans routinely make use of such imaginative practices to cultivate a sense of community through the sporting contest. Here, WNBA fans speculate about the sexualities of those around them in order to reproduce their sense of an "I" that bears a clear rela-tion to a robust and valuable, queer, feminine "we."

Beyond speculating on the sexual identities of those around them, queer WNBA fans make use of the space of the arena to publicly perform their col-lective identity, in much the same way that geographically displaced fans use their sports fandom to perform markers of their original regional identity and to gain a sense of connection and rootedness in a location that is not their "home." Although such fans are not displaced, the larger cultural context of homophobia and heterosexism creates a sort of perpetual-outsider status, which heightens the importance of "owned" spaces in which queer women can be metaphorically "at home"—that is, to avoid, at least for a time, being the "other." The importance of WNBA games as settings for these performances is highlighted by the league's fraught relationship with its lesbian fan base and the fan protests that have ensued as a result. In 2002, for example, New York Liberty fans protested the franchise's failure to participate in New York City's annual gay pride activities by staging a "kiss in—standing up and kissing each other during every time out" during a particular game (Kort 2002). In 2009, the Washington Mystics eliminated the "kiss cam" during games, apparently out of concern about the consequences of broadcasting women fans kissing one another (Wise 2009). In more recent years, however—particularly since some of the league's most prominent stars have come out—the WNBA has shifted its response to queer fans. Since 2014, the WNBA has officially celebrated gay pride week, decorating courts with rainbow pride signage during nationally broadcasted games, selling official WNBA pride T-shirts, and making official team appearances in local pride parades (WNBA 2015b). Some have suggested that this shift by the league was the result of financial desperation (Van Riper 2014)—and indeed, it is difficult to imagine that the WNBA would have participated had it not anticipated financial benefit from doing so. Regardless, however, it is telling that such efforts receive fan uptake and that fans actively participate in making WNBA fandom a more explicit venue for the safe, affirming performance of queer identities. Even if we grant that the league is capitalizing on a marketing strategy by connecting itself explicitly with queer identity—just as the Steelers organization markets itself via connection with markers of western Pennsylvania identity—this does not change the fact that fans actively use this medium as a subjectivizing practice, participating in the rituals and disciplines of WNBA fandom to reproduce and affirm core features of their individual and collective identity.

Of particular interest in the case of WNBA fandom is the extent to which it functions to trouble rather than to shore up existing patterns of gender and sexual normalization. Whereas mainstream forms of sports fandom function to valorize hyper-heterosexual masculinity, WNBA fandom is often used by queer women fans explicitly to reject the normativity of both heterosexuality and masculinity. The group Lesbians for Liberty summed up the meaning of this type of fan usage in the "Thank you, Lesbians," cards it distributed on the New York Liberty's Fan Appreciation Day, which proclaimed that the Liberty's queer fans deserved recognition for "supporting women's basketball since its beginnings," for "showing us there are many ways to be a woman," and "for [demonstrating] courage and strength even through adversity" (Kort 2002).

NEW HEROES

In 2013, average WNBA game viewership dramatically increased, from 180,000 viewers per game to 230,000. The difference, it seemed, was attributable to the arrival of a single athlete: Brittney Griner, a six foot eight center taken first in the 2013 draft by the Phoenix Mercury. Griner was (and is) an exceptional athlete: she was the first NCAA basketball player—man or woman—to score two thousand points and record five hundred blocked shots, held the overall NCAA record for number of blocked shots and the women's record for number of slam dunks, and was the national player of the year for the 2012 and 2013 seasons (WNBA 2015a). Her astounding skills

and extraordinary physical frame—in addition to her much-above-average
height, her hands are wider than LeBron James's and her arms longer than
many NBA players'—led many to speculate that she could play against professional men. Prior to her WNBA start, in fact, (NBA) Dallas Mavericks
owner Mark Cuban suggested that he would give Griner a tryout, though
this never materialized. In addition to her star power as an athlete, Griner
made headlines for nonchalantly coming out once she left college, for becoming a spokesmodel for Nike's menswear line, and later, for her (short-lived)
marriage to Tulsa Shock player Glory Johnson. Griner is unquestionably a
star and the object of a significant fan following. Her increasing visibility and
popularity as an athlete—along with that of other queer women of color—is
significant, for it indicates additional complications in the effects of sports
fandom. Some forms of fandom, directed as they are toward unconventional
or unlikely heroes, give us reason to believe that fandom might not necessarily be a bastion of hypermasculinity, homophobia, or white supremacy.

The rise of women's sports, particularly basketball, challenges the typical
subjectivizing effects of sports fandom in at least two ways. It offers, for all
fans, a shift in what it means to identify with athletic agency, disrupting the
equation of normative masculinity and individual heroism; it also has significant potential to change the way girls and women understand themselves.
I will explain both of these effects with reference to the work of Iris Young.

First, it is important to note that lesbians are not the only fans of the
WNBA. Though lesbian fans make up a sizable percentage of WNBA season
ticket holders, the majority of fans who watch the WNBA on television and
follow the league regularly are men (Ourand and Karp 2013). Analysts suggest
that this is because the WNBA appeals primarily to persons who are committed basketball fans; because it is not (yet) a mainstream league, it does not
tend to attract casual fans. As noted previously, the population of fans deeply
committed to a particular sport as such (rather than to individual teams)
and to acquiring knowledge of that sport in all its forms tends to skew more
male than female. The prevalence of masculine fandom even in the case of
women's basketball might, then, appear to be business as usual. Yet I think we
have good reason to believe that the rise of WNBA fandom has importantly
counteroppressive effects, regardless of the gender makeup of its fan base. If
it is true that, as Young suggests, the "exclusion of women from sport" both
indicates and enacts the exclusion of women from the realm of cultural significance, then WNBA fandom constitutes the explicit inclusion of women in
this realm, resisting previously entrenched patterns. Even if—as is likely—a
majority of male fans of the WNBA do not have any sort of feminist commitment, attention to women's sport as a phenomenon worth following affirms

the relevance of feminine action in a world that typically relegates such action to insignificance, or of interest only to "niche" audiences. The increase in attention to women's sport contributes, in other words, to the revaluation of femininity and feminine agents as more than "other," as objects, or as valuable only insofar as they are sexually desirable to men.

Additionally, the rise of the WNBA makes new forms of fan identification possible for fans who are women and girls. The replacement of typical male athletes as lusory objects with women heroes like Griner, Diana Taurasi, Sheryl Swoopes, or Seimone Augustus is important because it allows women and girls to imaginatively project themselves into the sporting narrative without requiring the subjective identification with masculinity that characterizes mainstream sports fandom. When we recall the work of Young and Beauvoir, this shift in identification is important, for the long-standing equation of subjectivity with normative masculinity contributes to the notion of woman as "the second sex" and women's experience of subjectivity as object. The normalization of masculinity, and the perpetual representation of women as objects, contributes to the reproduction of feminine subjectivity that imbues women with the sense of being objects, not subjects, and contributes to a comportment to the world that says, first, "I can't." In contrast, increased exposure to representations of women as athletic agents, and the lusory identification with such women as sports heroes, has the potential to counteract this trend. This theoretical inference is supported by empirical research. A 2009 study, for example, found that adolescent girls and college-aged women are more likely to describe themselves in terms of their physicality—what they can *do* as bodily agents—when exposed to images of women athletes in states of athletic performance (Daniels 2009). In contrast, girls and women exposed to sexualized images of female models or athletes are more likely to describe themselves using statements about their own beauty—and with more negative than positive tone. In other words, exposure to "portrayals of women athletes-in-action, that is, performance athletes . . . trigger[ed] less self-objectification in female viewers" (415). The identification with women athletes as agents and heroes is important not only because it rejects the dominant discourse of femininity as unimportant apart from women's appeal as sexual objects but also because it offers girls and women a means of cultivating a more robust sense of bodily agency—to, in other words, imaginatively inhabit the world as a subject who says, "I can."

One worry for such an argument is that the sex segregation of athletic competition in the United States necessarily limits the effectiveness of the valorization of women athletes. Sex-segregated competition is troubling both because of the questionable gender binarism it presumes and because it is built upon the presumption of the athletic inferiority of women. As philosophers like Torbjörn Tännsjö (2000) have pointed out, similarly justified segregation would be completely unacceptable in any other analogous case: although commitments to evenly matched competition entail the splitting of competitive groups between skill levels (professionals play other professionals, weight classes are separated in boxing, etc.), none of these distinctions is made on the basis of predetermined characteristics with such dubious relevance to an individual's athletic abilities. We would not, for example, countenance racially segregated competition on the grounds that one racial group's athletic abilities were naturally greater than another's. Moreover, Tännsjö suggests, even if it is true that women today are, on average, less athletically gifted than men, on average, this does not imply that any individual women are worse athletes than any individual men, and it does not tell us anything about the *intrinsic* abilities of either sex, since women have, on the whole, lacked the opportunities to develop their athletic talents that men have had. It is thus likely the case not only that sex segregation of sport as a rule is unjustified—we do not know in advance whether any individual person has the capability to compete with another purely on the basis of gender—but also that athletic sex segregation contributes to the perpetuation of women's secondary status, insofar as it denies women the possibility of competing against men and potentially improving in their athletic abilities. We might also add that the normalizing effects of gender segregation are particularly oppressive to gender-nonconforming women, whose bodies are viewed with suspicion and who are therefore subjected to denigrating "gender tests" in competition order to prove that they do not have an unfair advantage over "normal" women.[16]

Though I agree that Tännsjö is correct to argue that sex-segregated competition is not ideal, the valorization of women's athletics is nevertheless a step in the right direction. The institution of women's athletics programs has made competition accessible to women where it would not otherwise exist; most women in collegiate programs are not currently capable of competing against most men in collegiate programs, so the separation of leagues for women ensures that they have the opportunity to develop their abilities. Over time, increase in the opportunities for and standards in women's competition will make more women competitive at higher levels, which should make women athletes more evenly matched competitors in the future. Given the limited opportunities to this point, even "lesser" leagues are better than no leagues at all. Space does not permit me to address fully the question of "gender testing" in competition or the deplorable treatment of intersex and transgender athletes. For now I will say only this: given that the goal of women's leagues is the cultivation of women's athletic talent and greater inclusiveness in athletic competition—and in turn, sports fandom—we ought to eschew such tests and err on the side of including, rather than excluding, interested women from competition, no matter the specifics of their biology or gender presentation.[17] The important thing, for our purposes, is that women's competition, and in particular the WNBA, lays the groundwork for elite athletic competition by women and people who do not fit the hypermasculine mold of mainstream sport. This inclusiveness, however limited it may be at the moment, opens the gender field of sports fandom and has the potential to make that fandom even more significant as a medium for cultivating forms of gendered subjectivity that do not simply reiterate entrenched hierarchies of masculine normativity.

Beyond making possible the identification with feminine athletic subjects, the WNBA proliferates images of black women that stand as an explicit rejection of their figuration as objects of sexual exchange, so prevalent in American popular culture. During the 2015 season, over 70 percent of the WNBA's players were women of color—and in contrast to the NCAA, these players are surrounded and directed by coaching staffs and franchise administrators who are also women and people of color (Lapchick and Nelson 2015). In contrast with cases like the Louisville Cardinals, where the athletic efforts of a black male starting lineup are directed by older, wealthy white men, for the benefit of overwhelmingly white audiences, and in which black women serve primarily as the sexual outlet for mascotted players, the WNBA features black women as agentic, strategic, and powerful. Moreover, it offers a space in which black femininity need not demonstrate heterosexual respectability in order to be worthy of emulation. There is, perhaps, no other cultural practice with such wide appeal today in which affirming images of queer black life are so prevalent. Beyond Griner, out black women occupy positions of prominence in the WNBA, including star players Seimone Augustus, Cappie Pondexter, and Angel McCoughtry, as well as Chicago Sky head coach Pokey Chatman. Significantly, though these women are open about their sexualities, they are not treated as anomalies or mascots by their fans but as world-class athletes and coaches. Fan identification with these women as new kinds of athletic heroes works against the normalization of white heterosexual masculinity that characterizes so much of sports fandom. As Chatman put it in a recent interview, in the WNBA, Pride Day is "just another day at the office" (Evans 2014). In a cultural context that treats both blackness and queerness as suspect, the everyday visibility, appreciation, and celebration of black queer feminine excellence is itself radical.

LADY BEARS AND THE FEVER:
A FINAL IRONY OF MASCOTTING

Given that the visibility and apparent appreciation of black masculinity in mainstream sports fandom often functions to mask a deeper white supremacy in the practice of mascotting, one might reasonably worry that the apparent valorization of WNBA athletes involves the same sort of exploitative, subordinating relation. To make the argument that WNBA fandom avoids repetition of the entrenched patterns of sexual and racial hierarchization that characterizes much mainstream sports fandom, it is necessary to show that fan relations are not similarly characterized by mascotting. My claim is that although it is impossible to ensure that WNBA fandom is completely free of mascotting, the irony of the masculine normativity of mainstream sports culture is that the very femininity that results in the WNBA's dismissal and denigration *also* at the same time provides a shield against most mascotting.

First, it is fairly straightforward that women's basketball players are not subject to mascotting in the sense associated with the vicarious experience of hypermasculinity. This is largely, of course, because women players, according to the binary logic of traditional gender norms, do not afford access to such a phenomenon—because they are women, and because they are not as physically massive, strong, or dominant. One can see the perceived impossibility of mascotting WNBA players in this sense in the criticisms of women's basketball leveled by those who ridicule it. The claim that women don't dunk the basketball, for example, is an oft-repeated reason for finding the women's game boring or unworthy of attention (Rubinstein 1999). Dunking, importantly, not only requires that one jump high enough to bring one's hand above the rim of the goal and (often) hang onto it after slamming the ball through directly; it also constitutes a display of pure physical force in a game often characterized by finesse and strategy. The slam dunk is thus a symbolic enactment of physical dominance—dominance of the material apparatus of the game and the other players one physically towers over, and a break in the flow of the game, which ordinarily prioritizes passing to teammates, skillful shooting, and the utilization of the backboard to maximize the number of positions from which one can reasonably score. The lack of this perceived physical dominance in the women's game (due to the fact that most women are not tall enough to dunk) offers a particularly salient example of its "failure" to provide fans the ability to vicariously indulge in the physical dominance and hypermasculinity that so much of men's sport provides.

The team mascots and symbols associated with the WNBA and women's intercollegiate teams, moreover, avoid the evocation of masculine, animalistic dominance, offering a major departure from the mascots and iconography of mainstream men's teams. On the collegiate level, typical practice is to append the "regular" school mascot with the prefix "Lady." Thus we get the "Lady Bears" and "Lady Tigers," in addition to some more curious examples, like "Lady Knights." In these cases, the other-ing of the feminine team has the effect of rendering the mascot symbolically defanged or diminutive. "Ladies" do not dominate, after all. In the WNBA, not only do very few team mascots evoke fearsome entities (the Minnesota Lynx have the only animal mascot in the league) but nearly all mascots are entirely nonagential. Of the remaining teams—the Sky, the Mercury, the Sparks, the Fever, the Liberty, the Shock, the Stars, the Sun, the Storm, the Wings, the Dream—almost all evoke natural forces or ideals. Such forces do constitute the sort of powerful symbols that can symbolically draw a team together, but they lack the imagery of intentional agency and are decidedly not symbols of violence or domination. Considering the frequency with which natural forces are used as mascots in the women's game as opposed to the men's, it is difficult not to recognize the long-standing feminization of "nature." As feminists have pointed out, the metaphorical treatment of nature as feminine suggests that while it is undoubtedly a powerful force, it is also one that we hope and expect to bring under our control. In both the WNBA and women's collegiate athletics, we see, in varying degrees, the symbolic feminization of mascots, which functions both to symbolically position these teams as nonnormative in the sporting world and to provide fans with something other than what is afforded by mainstream men's teams.

This feminization of mascots, and the concomitant avoidance of symbols of violence and dominance, coheres with the general unavailability to women's sports fans of at least one form of mascotting. The irony, then, is this: the denigration and dismissal of feminine athletic efforts by the equivocation of masculinity and athletic dominance has the side effect of allowing women athletes to avoid mascotting—at least of the hypermasculine type. This avoidance comes at significant cost to the league, since it is likely that the appeal of this form of mascotting draws fans. But it does render individual WNBA athletes less likely targets for the dehumanizing exploitation of mascotting.

The other form of mascotting—the treatment of persons like pets who exist for one's own amusement (and thus requiring them to conform to fan expectations, not to exceed their "place," and to be subject to discard when they are no longer useful)—is more difficult to address in the context of the WNBA. There is less evidence that WNBA fans conceive themselves as a "we" symbolized by a particular team and, consequently, fewer indications that fans think of acquired star players as "ours" in the sense of a community-owned commodity. Yet the strong sense among lesbian groups that the WNBA as a whole is "theirs" still gives reason for pause. There are, I think, good reasons to be concerned about the contrast in racial demographics between the lesbian communities who use WNBA fandom to cultivate a sense of community—which are, at least in some cities, mostly white—and the women whose athletic excellence forms the backdrop of this fan practice. Here, mascotting analogous to that of white fans who perform important white cultural rituals against the backdrop of black bodily sacrifice is arguably engaged in by some fans, at least on a smaller scale. The effects, however, are less obvious here than in the case of (say) Ole Miss fans, both because queer fans of the WNBA are often explicitly interested in the lives beyond the court of the women they cheer and because the smaller scale of the league and its following means that fan expectations of individual players are generally less demanding. If the WNBA grows significantly in popularity—and particularly if increasing numbers of mainstream fans redirect their fandom toward WNBA teams, such that fandom of them comes to carry the same sorts of regionally identifying import as fandom of NFL, MLB, or NBA teams—it is quite likely that this form of mascotting will increase. As things currently stand, however, the devaluation of feminine activity has the ironic effect of mitigating the perniciousness of mascotting.

Women and the Diversity of Sports Fandom

Does women's sports fandom of either sort constitute an example of sports fandom that offers resistance to, rather than complicity with, entrenched patterns of racially and sexually oppressive subjectivization? I have argued that key features of at least *some versions* of women's fandom of mainstream (men's) sport and fandom of women's sports do resist masculine normalization, white supremacy, and heterosexism. Nevertheless, women's sports fandom is by no means a cure-all for the ills of contemporary American sports. Problems remain with the rigid gender segregation of sports, and, as Iris Young points out, the problems of gender in sport are part of such a deeply entrenched cultural problem with gender that women's sports are often dismissed as "not real" sports or the women who compete in them dismissed as "not real" women (1979, 46), meaning that the effectiveness of their subversions is limited. We should not expect that fans cheering for the athleticism of Brittney Griner, taking seriously the baseball analysis of Jessica Mendoza, or self-consciously performing their sports fandom as grandmothers invested in community uplift will, on their own, constitute a solution to the oppressive effects of mainstream sports fandom. Yet the variety of practices of women sports fans—both of mainstream men's sport and of women's sports—give good reason to believe that sports fandom as a practice of subjectivization is not *simply* oppressive.

Sports fandom is a vast constellation of disciplines, habits, and rituals engaged in by an incredible variety of people. Though sport is perhaps the single most masculinized cultural arena in the contemporary United States, when we seek to understand how it works, what it does, and what it gives fans, we simply cannot ignore the femininity at its margins. To do so would be to accept the very masculine normativity that mainstream sports fandom attempts to naturalize and reinforce. But more importantly, it would also be to offer an incomplete picture of sports fandom's effects and the internal conflict that characterizes it. Sports fandom is pleasurable because it offers clear identity and a sense of valuable belonging—and offers them in abundance, to people who, increasingly, live lives disconnected from or marginalized by the communities around them. But, as some forms of women's sports fandom illustrate, it need not do so by encouraging violence, masculine domination, or reproducing the ills of racism, exploitation, or heterosexism. In at least some cases, women's sports fandom is already overcoming those ills, and more besides—offering reason to hope that the "we" of sports fandom may not be too far gone, after all.

Acknowledgments

It is impossible to overstate the importance of others' support and involvement in the creation of this book. I have wanted to write this book for years, but it would not have happened without the generosity and support of my institution, Emory University, and Emory's Oxford College in particular. This book was completed as a result of a generous grant from Emory's University Research Committee and of the gracious support of my academic dean, Kenneth Anderson, and of my chairs, Adriane Ivey and Christine Loflin, who made it possible for me to use that grant to take a pretenure teaching leave.

I must say, as well, how very important my students at Oxford—all undergraduates—have been in the process of writing and researching this book. My Philosophy of Sport class in the spring of 2015 was a daily inspiration and an important venue for talking through my ideas about sports fans and racial and gender identity. My students in Philosophy of Sport were engaged, careful, and creative thinkers and helped me to think in new ways about the problems of collegiate athletics, the appeal of football in the United States, and the possibilities for women's sports.

Beyond my Philosophy of Sport class, two students in particular deserve special recognition. Jocelyn Hong and Kevin Kilgour both worked with me as research assistants through the Pierce Institute's Oxford Research Scholars program, which pairs excellent first- and second-year undergraduate students with faculty members to work one-on-one in disciplinary scholarship. They both displayed research acumen and conversational insight far beyond their years, and this book would be less rich without their work.

I would like to thank, as well, the individual scholars who read and commented on pieces of the book, or whose feedback at conferences or in our offices was particularly important in my thinking and revising. Some of them are anonymous, including the extraordinarily helpful reviewers for the University of Chicago Press, *Critical Philosophy of Race*, and *Culture, Theory, and Critique*. Others I am happy and grateful to mention by name: Elizabeth Branch Dyson, Robin James, Joshua Mousie, John Stuhr, Richard Lee, Gus Skorberg, Mark Sanders, Kevin Quarmby, and Molly McGehee. I must also say that I am indebted to Sarah Bankston and Ellen Neufeld, whose work in the Oxford College library has been superb, and who have always managed to find whatever resource I needed, no matter how obscure.

Finally, I offer special thanks to my friends in "Chicks on Football," who inspired me to think of sports fandom differently, and to my family, who have supported my work throughout this long and difficult process. My parents taught me to love sports and to be loyal to my team—and to ask critical questions even (or especially) about those things that I love. They were my first introduction to sports fandom and to philosophy, and this book would not have been possible without them. My partner, Joshua Mousie, read drafts of the manuscript, put up with my obsessive sports fandom, and offered continual encouragement. More than this, he has been the brightest spot in all my days, and the reason I was able to continue this work after the illness and death of our beloved Dewey. I will never be able to express how grateful I am for him or to account for all of the ways in which he has touched my life and this work.

Notes

Introduction

1. I am using "spectatorship" differently here than it is commonly used in performance studies, according to which spectatorship takes a variety of forms, some of which are quite active. In distinguishing fans from spectators, I have in mind a distinction similar to Schechner's integral audience versus accidental audience distinction: "an accidental audience comes 'to see the show' while the integral audience 'is necessary to accomplish the work of the show'" (1988, 220).

Chapter One

1. Rowe also held the dubious distinction, during his playing days, of pitching a game in which thirty-five runs were scored (twelve on errors) (Baseball-Reference 2015).

2. This "football" is the football of the United Kingdom—or "soccer," as it is known in the United States.

3. As I argue in chapters 2 and 7, the demand for knowledge acquisition is particularly gendered and is used to exclude women from the status of "real" fans.

4. The Tool Race is Turner Field's version of a "mascot race," a common between-innings act at baseball games. Mascot races feature runners costumed as characters with oversized heads, often bearing some relation to local culture (e.g., the "Sausage Race" at the Milwaukee Brewers' Miller Park, the "Racing Presidents" at the Washington Nationals Park). For more, see Fox Sports 2011.

Chapter Two

1. The record of this responsibility is sharply dichotomous: if, in the judgment of the official scorekeeper (in the contemporary game this person is notably anonymous and unseen), a runner reaches base not because of the excellence of his play but because of some failure on the part of the defensive fielder, the play is recorded as an "error," assigned to the offending fielder; if, on the contrary, he reaches base because he hit the ball in such a way that it could not be reasonably expected to be successfully defended, the play is recorded as a "hit" for the offensive team. There are no further options, and following particularly difficult plays, fans and players alike anxiously await the news: "How will they score it?"

2. It is worth noting here that Chadwick developed the box score around the same time that Bentham developed the panopticon. I would argue that this is no accident, as the shift to disciplinary techniques in power became particularly popular during the Victorian period in England—the home of both Bentham and Chadwick.

3. Rayman attributes the origination of this shift to Branch Rickey, the manager of the Brooklyn Dodgers who recruited Jackie Robinson to become the first black athlete to play in major league baseball (2005, 105).

4. See, for example, Deadspin.com, whose slogan is "Sports News without Access, Favor, or Discretion."

5. See for example Code 1991 and Medina 2013.

6. Though propositional knowledge is typically taken as the paradigm case of knowledge in epistemology ("*S* knows that *P*"), it is important to remember, as feminists such as Lorraine Code (1991) have pointed out, that knowing *how* to do something is also knowledge, as is *knowing a person*. Neither of these are necessarily expressible in propositional form, and so they are less easily quantified than propositional knowledge. Thus, even if men who are sports fans have more propositional knowledge about sports, it does not necessarily follow that they have "more knowledge" as such, particularly when we consider the import of knowing *how* to properly participate in other fan rituals, to which I will return later in the chapter.

7. I use "normalization" here in the sense derived from Foucault's early work on disciplinary practices: as a set of practices that both trains individual bodies to conform to norms and, at the same time, in McWhorter's words, "homogenize[s] the group by enabling all differences among its members to be understood as deviations from the norm and therefore as essentially related to it" (1999, 156). This is distinct from the normalization Foucault describes in his later work, including *Security, Territory, Population*; there, such disciplinary practices are referred to using the "barbaric word" "normation" (2007, 57).

8. See for example Deegan and Stein 1978 and Bain-Selbo 2012.

9. Though market capitalism is surely involved in sports fandom; I will return to this in the following chapter.

10. University of Mississippi fans are far from the only group of southern white fans whose fandom has racializing (or racist) effects, though the specifics of their traditional fan practices make them a particularly vivid example. I will return to the question of race and majority-white fan bases in subsequent chapters, where I will look more closely at other white fans in the South and beyond.

11. Throughout, I use "white supremacy," following Charles Mills, to refer to the taken-for-granted "system of domination by which white people have historically ruled over, and, in certain important ways, continue to rule over non-white people," which is so common as to be unnoticed by most whites (1997, 1–2).

Chapter Three

1. Quoted in Silva 2007. Emphasis mine.

2. Although the data on college sports are also fascinating, they are much more unwieldy, as colleges more frequently change mascots and are themselves less stable institutions. The relative stability of professional sports teams in the United States will be important for comparative purposes later in the chapter, as I undertake a historical analysis of professional sports mascots from the mid- to late nineteenth century through the present.

3. See King and Springwood, *Beyond the Cheers: Race as Spectacle in College Sport* (SUNY 2001), 55–56. Although this is an otherwise brilliant book, to which I am significantly indebted, this claim is simply false.

4. The Browns pose a particularly interesting case: in 1996, Browns owner Art Modell moved his franchise to Baltimore, where it became the Baltimore Ravens. Fan anger in Cleveland was so great that Modell's move of the team was the subject of a lawsuit, the settlement of which involved the concessions that (1) Cleveland would be able to reinstitute the Browns at a later date under a new franchise and (2) Modell would *give the history of the Browns* to this new franchise. The law, in this case, had to be bent to accommodate fan belief.

5. Indeed, as Grano and Zagacki (2005) suggest, the rhetoric of sports fans suggests that winning and losing of "their" teams is precisely a matter of the community's honor and sense of itself.

6. I focus here on professional baseball and football because these sports have the longest history of professional league competition in the United States and thus offer a larger range of data. I am restricting this historical investigation to professional teams in order to provide a legitimate basis for comparison with the contemporary team mascots represented in table 1.

7. For additional arguments that Native American mascots require the stereotyping of Native Americans, see Black 2002, Springwood 2000, and Spindel 2000.

8. See table 3. Ironically, the Redskins were the last NFL team to reintegrate, in 1962.

9. For more on the idea that Native American mascots reveal more about whiteness than "redness," see King and Springwood 2005 and M. Taylor 2013.

Chapter Four

1. For more on my use of the term "white supremacy," see the section in chapter 3 on terminological clarifications.

2. I am following the emerging convention of using "Latinx" as the "inclusive, gender-neutral way to identify people with Latin American roots of any kind" (Weiss 2016). Whereas "Latino/a" tacitly assumes a masculine/feminine gender binary, "Latinx" allows for a spectrum of gender identities.

3. These were "Great Men and Their Environment"(1992a) and "The Importance of Individuals" (1992b). Neither is focused specifically on athletic heroes, but the point remains the same. Interestingly, several of James's contemporaries *did* attempt to extend the type of argument he makes for hero worship to sports fandom—specifically, by arguing that watching young men exert themselves on the football field would inspire fans to be great themselves. Josiah Royce issues a scathing response to such arguments in his essay on football, in which he claims that football fandom encourages fans to do nothing but get riled up and passively watch others.

4. "Tebowing" involves dropping to one knee while holding one hand clenched to a bowed head in mock prayer in an inappropriate public place. Fans and celebrities alike were photographed Tebowing in increasingly ridiculous places, including actor Robert Downey Jr. at the 2011 Academy Awards. Tebow has since trademarked the act of Tebowing (Associated Press 2012).

5. Harvard oarsmen were studied in an effort to prove that athletics would improve the white race. The study found that "men who had rowed for Harvard were on the average more likely to get married and to have more than their share of children." They were thus "'superior in the matter of perpetuating the best elements of the American race,' especially in matters relating to 'the question of race decline'" (Townsend 1996, 99).

6. For images of James Ivy, see Southern Documentary Project 2010 and Colonel Reb Foundation 2015.

7. I discuss the case of Tyrann Mathieu in detail in chapter 5.

8. MLB has grown particularly concerned in recent years about its failure to attract black fans. A recent sociological study suggests that black fans perceive baseball as being "white" and "not for us" (Brown and Bennett 2015).

9. There are also a not insignificant number of Asian players in MLB, though their numbers in 2015 make them slightly less than 2 percent of all MLB players (Lapchick and Nelson 2015).

10. These recruiting operations are a significant cause for concern, as they are premised upon a grotesquely exploitative system that (among other things) normalizes the signing of (usually impoverished) boys at the age of sixteen and pays players significantly less if they are signed any older than this. For more, see the documentary film *Pelotero* (Makuhari Media 2011).

11. In addition to mascotting Martínez, this fan makes use of the normative masculinity of the sporting context to position Dominican women fans as sexual objects, thereby reiterating the normativity of both the whiteness and the heterosexual masculinity of the "we" of Boston sports fandom.

12. Thanks to Robin James, who pointed out to me that the jingle itself is a "Disney-meets-Paul-Simon version [of] Afropop" (personal communication).

Chapter Five

1. The original viral honey badger video ("The Crazy Nastyass Honey Badger (Original Narration by Randall)") is here: https://www.youtube.com/watch?v=4r7wHMg5Yjg; the Mathieu honey badger video ("TM7 Honey Badger") is here: https://www.youtube.com/watch?v=N5pIZ9lJuWk.

2. Many have argued that the current system is exploitative of the very players the NCAA ostensibly exists to protect. Others have suggested that it is at odds with the missions of those academic institutions on which it financially depends.

3. Royce argues that while football players themselves might exhibit "loyalty," a virtue that he calls "the very central moral ideal," spectators do not seem to do much at all. He caricatures them thus: "Yet one persists in saying: 'How loyal their [the players'] devotion makes me, by reason of the contagion of their noble example! See the results. I cheer, I wave my flag. In the tumult and passion of my loyalty I lose my wits. How noble all this makes me! See how I rage and exult'" (2009, 218–219).

4. There was a "question of whether a man *not* of the decent sort should properly be *allowed* to be an athlete. . . . The 'amateur' athlete was pure in mind, spirit, and body, 'uncorrupted by material considerations.' . . . [T]he scions of the Yankee elite had appropriated to themselves the definition of what it meant to be a man playing college football, this most manly and violent of sports. A mere game had become the touchstone of the nation's larger debate about white male American identity, masculinity, education, leadership, status, and moral character" (Buford 2010, 52–53). As a result of concern about the potential of football to corrupt such character, President Theodore Roosevelt (a Harvard alum) was involved in the creation of the governing body that became the NCAA, which, among other things, restricted eligibility to exclude nonamateurs—that is, men "not of the decent sort."

5. See for example Kaelin 1968 and Loland 2002.

6. I will return in the final chapter to the question of gender-segregated competition and its foundational presumption that women are athletically inferior to men.

7. In this context, it is interesting to note the outsized devotion of southern football fans to collegiate teams over professional ones. Though this preference is no doubt partially explainable as a simple matter of chronology—professional football did not come to the South until much later than the rest of the country—it is telling that fan devotion to professional teams tends to be strongly racialized in the region, with fans who are people of color much more likely to primarily support professional teams and fans who are white much more likely to support collegiate teams as their primary allegiance.

8. My focus is on black athletes because of the demographic makeup of intercollegiate athletics. Even baseball, which, at the professional level, is nearly one-quarter Latino and 2 percent Asian, lags in recruiting players of color who are not black (Brennen 1997).

9. The tone of online discussions of those who watched footage of Ware's injury ranged from morbid curiosity to gleeful disgust. For example see Cliffe 2013.

10. The video has since been removed from Alpha Phi's official page, but it remains accessible on YouTube: https://www.youtube.com/watch?v=KudwS5U90uA.

11. For more on how the Greek system is used to transmit elite social status, particularly through "maintaining sameness," see DeSantis 2007.

12. One example is the University of Kentucky's men's basketball team. In such cases, athletes need not be concerned with grades, since their limited time at the institution mitigates the academic eligibility problem.

13. Hawkins 2010, 37, 131; New 2014; Weinstein 2013; B. Ley 2002.

14. See for example Tomasson 1994, Nomura 1995, Weiler 2014, and former Notre Dame coach Lou Holtz's comments on Fox News at https://www.youtube.com/watch?v=TlNGFlJnxXQ.

15. For discussion of the scientific repudiation of race as a natural kind and the subsequent evolution of "race thinking," see P. Taylor 2013.

16. A popular argument against the payment of athletes in the "revenue sports"—men's football and basketball—is that the profits they bring to the institution financially subsidize women's athletics programs. If these players were paid, the story goes, universities would not be able to fund athletic opportunities for women to play volleyball or basketball, which would jeopardize their Title IX compliance.

17. Examples of fan comments taken from ESPN's Facebook page: https://www.facebook .com/ESPN/?fref=nf.

18. See for example J. Butler 1995, P. Collins 2004.

19. University of Michigan coach Jim Harbaugh explained the proper placement of the quarterback's hands under center thus: "You take that knuckle right there on your finger, that pointer finger, should go squarely right in the middle of his asshole. Right in the middle of it. Find the asshole, that's where . . . that knuckle goes. . . . [H]e sets the top hand in, and lets the center sit on it, so the center's got pressure on him, he knows where the hand is. The knuckle's in the center of the asshole" (quoted in T. Ley 2013).

20. George Bush Sr.'s infamous "Willie Horton" presidential campaign ad made implicit use of this justification. See Wacquant 2002.

21. This trope is employed by the country song "Where I'm From," which Tim Tebow sings on *Everything in Between*, as mentioned in chapter 4.

22. See Crossett et al. 1996, Frintner and Rubinson 1993, Sønderlund et al. 2014.

23. Nothing in the video contradicted what the NFL already knew of Rice's case, which had already been addressed by the league with a comparatively minor punishment.

Chapter Six

1. Vick was recently released from a federal prison sentence for dogfighting charges; Woods was recovering from the revelation of his extensive infidelity to his wife, which seriously tarnished his public image.

2. When the action is directly related to a player or team's performance, outcomes are quite different. Allegations of performance-enhancing drug use, for example, can result in permanent damage to fans' willingness to identify with an athlete.

3. *Urban Dictionary* defines "haterade" as "a figurative drink representing a modality of thought," and as "a fictional beverage, parodying the popular sports drink 'gatorade,' purportedly consumed by individuals who are jealous of others, supposedly fueling their ability to be jealous of, or 'hate on,' others." For an example of its use in sports media, see ESPN 2010.

4. One might account for this by noting, as feminists have previously, the widespread acceptance of the view that domestic violence is a "private" matter, distinct from the "public" sphere. Because fans are accustomed to such compartmentalization of violence against women, it may be easier for them to distinguish it from the "public" world of competition than other sorts of social violations.

5. Socrates expresses a similar line of thought in his argument for the censorship or expulsion of poets in the ideally just city in Plato's *Republic*.

6. Notably, rumors indicate that Bird's ire in such cases was particularly high when a white player was assigned to guard him (Simmons 2014).

7. On the day following the interview, *Deadspin* reports, there were 625 mentions of the word "thug" on American cable television—more than any single day in the prior three years (Wagner 2014).

8. Here, as in chapter 2, I do not purport to offer a strictly Foucaultian reading but to describe this phenomenon using Foucault's work as a useful starting point for an analogy.

9. Matthew Schneider-Mayerson (2010) makes a similar argument about the NBA's decline in popularity with white fans beginning in the 1970s, which corresponded with an influx of black players.

10. For analysis of the potentially misleading appearance of animals and animal symbols in sports fandom, see chapter 3 on mascots.

11. Nashville, Tennessee, is one example, banning dogs who resemble "pit bulls" in public parks. The province of Ontario likewise bans the breeding of pit bulls and prohibits any dog classified (presumably by border guards) as a pit bull from being brought into the province.

12. Pit bulls have figured prominently in music videos and albums released by several major hip-hop artists in the past twenty years, including Jay-Z, DMX, and Bow Wow.

Chapter Seven

1. Notably, Mendoza appeared as a replacement for Curt Schilling, a former MLB pitcher, who was suspended from ESPN for sharing an Islamophobic tweet: "It's said only 5–10% of Muslims are extremists. In 1940, only 7% of Germans were Nazis. How'd that go?" (Almasy 2015).

2. A search of the *Hypatia* archives, for example, turns up only a handful of articles centrally engaged with sports and not many more that even mention sports.

3. In "fantasy" sports, fans compete against one another by creating "fantasy" rosters of real-life players from a variety of teams—usually through an online platform that tracks the performance of these individual players on a weekly basis, and tallies those players' collective

scoring and performance. A fan whose collection of real-life players scores more than or out-plays the fan she is matched up against wins the game that week. Fantasy sports participation is disproportionately masculine.

4. The masculinity of advertising during sporting events is even more striking when one considers that professional leagues' own market research indicates that mainstream sport fan bases are nearly half women (Harwell 2014).

5. The Tennessee Titans, Jacksonville Jaguars, University of Tennessee, University of Colorado, and University of North Carolina at Charlotte have all hosted events of this type.

6. An entire morning news segment on Charlotte, North Carolina's, WCNC was devoted to this goal in its coverage of the Carolina Panthers' 2014 Football 101 clinic. See http://www.wcnc .com/videos/entertainment/television/charlotte-today/2014/06/23/10230414, accessed December 15, 2015.

7. See especially Markovits and Albertson (2012), chapter 4, "Fandom and the Typical Female Sports Fan." For more on women fans and explicitly social reasons for sports fandom, see also Dietz-Uhler et al. 2000 and Hall and O'Mahony 2006.

8. I learned of the LJGFC when members appeared on the Cooking Channel show *My Grandmother's Ravioli*, but it has also been featured on local Cleveland news programs and on ESPN's website marketed to women, ESPNW.

9. Throughout this section, quotes are from the ESPNW video profile of the LJGFC unless otherwise noted. That video is accessible at https://www.youtube.com/watch?v=QKqG _w3HeKo.

10. The LJGFC's volunteer work in the local community (and in particular, its emphasis on encouraging children to finish secondary school) is significant not only as an instance of philanthropy but in reinforcing this kinship relation.

11. Compliance with Title IX does *not* require that institutions spend an equal amount on men's and women's athletics; the vast majority of collegiate athletics programs still spend considerably more on men's athletics than women's. Rather, an institution may demonstrate compliance by showing that it (1) provides athletic opportunities for men and women students proportionate to their respective enrollments, (2) accommodates the "interests and abilities" of the underrepresented sex, or (3) has a "history and continuing expansion" of the athletic programs for the underrepresented sex (Reynolds 2003).

12. See Ourand and Karp 2013 and Karp 2015 to compare average viewership. Exact time comparisons are difficult for the NBA and WNBA, since the NBA season runs across two calendar years, whereas the WNBA regular season runs from June to October in a single year.

13. For example, Yudkin 1982, Gearhart 1982, Love and Shanklin 1984.

14. Prior to this period, the concern was more about athletics encouraging sexual aggression in general, still thought to be masculine, but presumptively heterosexual (Cahn 1993, 347).

15. At the time of Dolance's interviews in 2002, there were no "out" players or coaches in the WNBA, despite widespread speculation.

16. The most famous case of such testing in recent years was that of Caster Semenya, a runner from South Africa who was required to undergo "gender tests" to continue competing internationally after some of her competitors at the 2008 Olympics accused her of looking like a man. There has been speculation that Brittney Griner will have to submit to a "testosterone test" to play for the 2016 US women's basketball Olympic team (Abraham 2013).

17. The NCAA includes transgender student athletes in the teams of their self-identified gender. For the official NCAA position, see NCAA Office of Inclusion 2011.

References

Abbott, Henry. 2010. "LeBron James' Decision: The Transcript." TrueHoop, ESPN.com. July 8. http://espn.go.com/blog/truehoop/post/_/id/17853/lebron-james-decision-the-transcript.

ABC News. 2015. "Alabama Sorority Alpha Phi Yanks Recruitment Video after Internet Uproar." *Good Morning America*. August 17. http://abcnews.go.com/US/alabama-sorority-alpha-phi -yanks-recruitment-video-internet/story?id=33127022.

Abraham, Laurie. 2013. "How Slam-Dunking, Gender-Bending WNBA Rookie Brittney Griner Is Changing the World of Sports." *Elle*. November 4. http://www.elle.com/culture/career -politics/interviews/a12606/brittney-griner-profile/.

Aidi, H. 2004. "'Verily, There is Only One Hip-Hop Umma': Islam, Cultural Protest, and Urban Marginality." *Socialism and Democracy* 18 (2): 107–126.

Almasy, Steve. 2015. "Curt Schilling Suspended by ESPN after Controversial Tweet." CNN. August 26. http://www.cnn.com/2015/08/25/us/curt-schilling-insensitive-tweet/.

American Psychological Association. 2005. "Resolution Recommending the Immediate Retirement of Indian Mascots, Symbols, Images and Personalities by Schools, Colleges, Universities, Athletic Teams, and Organizations." Reprinted in *The Native American Mascot Controversy: A Handbook*, edited by C. Richard King, 209–216. Lanham, MD: Rowman and Littlefield, 2010.

Anderson, Benedict. 1991. *Imagined Communities: Reflections on the Origin and Spread of Nationalism*. New York: Verso.

Anderson, Eric, and Mark McCormack. 2010. "Comparing the Black and Gay Male Athlete: Patterns in American Oppression." *Journal of Men's Studies* 18 (2): 145–158.

Andrews, David L. 1996. "The Fact(s) of Michael Jordan's Blackness: Excavating a Floating Racial Signifier." *Sociology of Sport Journal* 13: 125–158.

Angelo, H. 1876. "The Base Ball Fever." Sheet music. Philadelphia: Marsh and Bubna.

Applebome, P. 1987. "Series of Pit Bull Attacks Stirs Clamor for New Laws." *New York Times*, July 12, 16.

Arens, William. 1975. "The Great American Football Ritual." *Natural History* 84: 72–80.

Associated Press. 2009. "Chancellor Wants Song Halted." ESPN.com. November 10. http://www .espn.com/college-football/news/story?id=4643111.

———. 2012. "Tim Tebow Prevails in Trademarking 'Tebowing.'" *USA Today*, October 19. http://www.usatoday.com/story/sports/nfl/2012/10/19/tim-tebow-trademarks-tebowing/1645333/.

Bacon, P. 2010. "Obama Weighs in on Michael Vick, and Other Cultural Issues." *Washington Post*, December 28.

Bain-Selbo, Eric. 2012. *Game Day and God: Football, Faith, and Politics in the American South.* Macon, GA: Mercer University Press.

Barnhart, Robert K., ed. 2002. "Fan (2)." *Chambers Dictionary of Etymology*. New York: Chambers.

Barr, John. 2015."Katina Powell to Turn Over Documents to NCAA Investigators Next Week." ESPN.com. November 12. http://espn.go.com/espn/otl/story/_/id/14113128/katina-powell-speak-ncaa-investigators-next-week-allegations-louisville-cardinals-men-basketball-team.

Barr, John, and Jeff Goodman. 2015. "Former Louisville Recruit about his Visit: 'It Was like I Was in a Strip Club.'" ESPN, October 20.

Bartky, Sandra. 1990. *Femininity and Domination: Studies in the Phenomenology of Oppression.* New York: Routledge.

Baseball-Reference. 2015. "Dave Rowe." Accessed November 30, 2015. http://www.baseball-reference.com/players/r/roweda01.shtml.

Battista, J. 2010. "For Roethlisberger, Feelings of Anxiety Fade with the Sound of Cheers." *New York Times*, July 31.

Beauvoir, Simone de. 2011. *The Second Sex.* Translated by Constance Borde and Sheila Malovany-Chevallier. New York: Vintage Books.

Benedict, Jeff. 1999. *Public Heroes, Private Felons: Athletes and Crimes against Women.* Boston: Northeastern University Press.

Ben-Ze'ev, Aaron. 1992. "Anger and Hate." *Journal of Social Philosophy* 23(2): 85–110.

———. 1993. "Another Look at Pleasure-in-Others'-Misfortune." *Iyyun: The Jerusalem Philosophical Quarterly* 42 (July): 431–440.

Bissinger, B. 2010. 'Time to Forgive Michael Vick." *Daily Beast*, December 23. http://www.thedailybeast.com/articles/2010/12/23/michael-vick-why-its-time-to-forgive-him.print.html.

Black, Jason E. 2002. "The 'Mascotting' of Native America: Construction, Commodity, and Assimilation." *American Indian Quarterly* 26 (4): 605–622.

Boeringer, Scot B. 1999. "Associations of Rape-Supportive Attitudes with Fraternal and Athletic Participation." *Violence against Women* 5 (1): 81–90.

Borneman, J. 1988. "Race, Ethnicity, Species, Breed: Totemism and Horse-Breed Classification in America." *Comparative Studies in Society and History* 30 (1): 25–51.

Borucki, Wes. 2003. "'You're Dixie's Football Pride': American College Football and the Resurgence of Southern Identity." *Identities* 10: 477–494.

Boxill, Jan. 2006. "Football and Feminism." *Journal of the Philosophy of Sport* 33: 115–124.

Brand, D. 1987. "Time Bomb on Legs." *Time*, July 27.

Brennen, Ed. 1997. "Latinos en Beisbol; Forum Scouts the Territory." *Hispanic Outlook in Higher Education* 8 (8): 6.

Brown, Brandon, and Gregg Bennett. 2015. "'Baseball Is Whack!': Exploring the Lack of African American Baseball Consumption." *Journal of Sport and Social Issues* 39 (4): 287–307.

Buford, Kate. 2010. *Native American Son: The Life and Sporting Legend of Jim Thorpe.* New York: Knopf.

Burstyn, Varda. 1999. *The Rites of Men: Manhood, Politics, and the Culture of Sport.* Toronto: University of Toronto Press.

Butler, Judith. 1990. *Gender Trouble: Feminism and the Subversion of Identity*. New York: Routledge.

———. 1995. "Melancholy Gender / Refused Identification." In *Constructing Masculinity*, edited by Maurice Berger, Brian Wallis, and Simon Watson, 21–36. New York: Routledge.

Butler, Mike. 1997. "Confederate Flags, Class Conflict, a Golden Egg, and Castrated Bulls: A Historical Examination of the Ole Miss–Mississippi State Football Rivalry." *Journal of Mississippi History* 59 (2): 123–139.

Butterworth, Michael L. 2013. "The Passion of Tim Tebow: Sports Media and Heroic Language in the Tragic Frame." *Critical Studies in Media Communication* 30 (1): 17–33.

Butterworth, Michael, and Karsten Senkbeil. 2015. "Cross-Cultural Comparisons of Religion as 'Character': Football and Soccer in the United States and Germany." *International Review for the Sociology of Sport*, May 28.

Cahn, Susan. 1993. "From the 'Muscle Moll' to the 'Butch' Ballplayer: Mannishness, Lesbianism, and Homophobia in U.S. Women's Sport." *Feminist Studies* 19 (2): 343–368.

Callais, Todd M. 2010. "Controversial Mascots: Authority and Racial Hegemony in the Maintenance of Deviant Symbols." *Sociological Focus* 43 (1): 61–81.

CAPA (College Athletes Players Association). 2014. "What We're Doing." College Athletes Players Association website. Accessed December 5, 2015. http://www.collegeathletespa.org/what.

Carroll, Jason Michael. 2009. "Where I'm From." *Growing Up Is Getting Old*. Arista Nashville. Sony Music Distribution. Compact disc.

Cavicchi, Daniel. 2014. "Fandom before 'Fan': Shaping the History of Enthusiastic Audiences." *Reception: Text, Readers, Audiences, History* 6 (1): 52–72.

Césaire, Aimé. 2001. *Discourse on Colonialism*. Translated by Joan Pinkham. New York: Monthly Review Press.

Chase, Chris. 2011. "Pittsburgh-Area Hospital Wrapping Babies in Terrible Towels." *Yahoo Sports*. January 30. http://sports.yahoo.com/nfl/blog/shutdown_corner/post/Pittsburgh-area -hospital-wrapping-babies-in-Terr?urn=nfl-314361.

Churchill, Ward. 2003. *Acts of Rebellion: The Ward Churchill Reader*. New York: Routledge.

Cialdini, Robert, et al. 1976. "Basking in Reflected Glory: Three (Football) Field Studies." *Journal of Personality and Social Psychology* 34: 366–375.

Cincinnati Commercial Gazette. 1883. "Total Eclipse. The Champions' Fourth Successive Victory over Louisville." Vol. 43, iss. 280: 3.

Cliffe, Nicole. 2013. "The 23 Fold Path to Successfully Watching Kevin Ware Break His Leg." *Hairpin*, April 3. http://thehairpin.com/2013/04/the-path-to-successfully-watching-kevin -ware-break-his-leg/.

Coates, Ta-Nehisi. 2014. "Richard Sherman's Best Behavior." *Atlantic*, January 20. http://www .theatlantic.com/entertainment/archive/2014/01/richard-shermans-best-behavior/283198/.

Code, Lorraine. 1991. *What Can She Know? Feminist Theory and the Construction of Knowledge*. Ithaca, NY: Cornell University Press.

Cohen, J., and J. Richardson. 2002. "Pit Bull Panic." *Journal of Popular Culture* 36 (2): 285–317.

Collins, Patricia Hill. 2004. *Black Sexual Politics: African Americans, Gender, and the New Racism*. New York: Routledge.

Collins, Randall. 2004. *Interaction Ritual Chains*. Princeton, NJ: Princeton University Press.

Colonel Reb Foundation. 2015. "'Blind Jim' Ivy." Accessed December 5, 2015. http://www .colonelreb.org/news-clips.

Corlett, J. Angelo. 2013. "Economic Exploitation in Intercollegiate Athletics." *Sport, Ethics and Philosophy* 7 (3): 295–312.

Cottingham, Marci D. 2012. "Interaction Ritual Theory and Sports Fans: Emotion, Symbols, and Solidarity." *Sociology of Sport Journal* 29: 168–185.

Cox, John W., and Mark Maske. 2015. "NFL Ally Protests Redskins Name." *Washington Post*, January 19.

Crawford, Anthony, and Bruce Niendorf. 1999. "The Michael Jordan Effect." *American Business Review* 17 (2): 5–10.

Crawford, Garry. 2004. *Consuming Sport: Fans, Sport and Culture*. New York: Routledge.

Croghan, Rosaleen, et al. 2006. "Style Failure: Consumption, Identity, and Social Exclusion." *Journal of Youth Studies* 9 (4): 463–478.

Crossett, Todd W., James S. Ptacek, Mark A. McDonald, and Jeffrey R. Benedict. 1996. "Male Student-Athletes and Violence Against Women: A Survey of Campus Judicial Affairs Offices." *Violence against Women* 2 (2): 163–179.

Crouse, Karen. 2014. "Ray Rice Is an Outlier: Most Domestic Abuse Suspects Play On." *New York Times*. September 11. http://www.nytimes.com/2014/09/12/sports/football/ray-rice-is-an-outlier-most-domestic-abuse-suspects-play-on.html?_r=0.

Curtis, Bryan. 2011. "S-E-C! S-E-C! S-E-C!: That Inescapable Chant and the 'New' Southern Pride." *Grantland*. September 15. http://grantland.com/features/s-e-c-s-e-c-s-e-c/.

Crowley, Michael. 1999. "Muhammad Ali Was a Rebel. Michael Jordan Is a Brand Name." *Nieman Reports* 53 (3): 41–43.

Dalakas, Vassilis, Robert Madrigal, and Keri L. Anderson. 2004. "'We Are Number One!': The Phenomenon of Basking-in-Reflected-Glory and Its Implications for Sports Marketing." In *Sports Marketing and the Psychology of Marketing Communication*, edited by Lynn R. Kahlo and Chris Riley, 67–79. Mahwah, NJ: Erlbaum.

Daniels, Elizabeth A. 2009. "Sex Objects, Athletes, and Sexy Athletes: How Media Representations of Women Athletes Can Impact Adolescent Girls and College Women." *Journal of Adolescent Research* 24 (4): 399–422.

Danielson, Michael N. 1997. *Home Team: Professional Sports and the American Metropolis*. Princeton, NJ: Princeton University Press.

Davion, Victoria. 1987. "Do Good Feminists Compete?" *Hypatia* 2 (2): 55–63.

Davis, Angela Y. 1981. *Women, Race, and Class*. New York: Vintage.

Davis, Laurel R. 1993. "Protest against the Use of Native American Mascots: A Challenge to Traditional American Identity." *Journal of Sport and Social Issues* 17 (1): 9–22.

———. 2002. "The Problems with Native American Mascots." *Multicultural Education* 9 (4): 11–14.

Davis, Nickolas, and Margaret Carlisle Duncan. 2006. "Sports Knowledge Is Power: Reinforcing Masculine Privilege through Fantasy Sport League Participation." *Journal of Sport and Social Issues* 30 (3): 244–264.

Dayan, Colin. 2010. "Dead Dogs: Breed Bans, Euthanasia and Preemptive Justice." *Boston Review*. March/April. http://new.bostonreview.net/BR35.2/dayan.php.

Deegan, Mary Jo, and Michael Stein. 1978. "American Drama and Ritual: Nebraska Football." *International Review for the Sociology of Sport* 13 (3): 31–44.

DeSantis, Alan. 2007. *Inside Greek U: Fraternities, Sororities, and the Pursuit of Pleasure, Power, and Prestige*. Lexington: University Press of Kentucky.

Dickson, Paul. 2011. "Fan." In *The Dickson Baseball Dictionary*, edited by S. McAfee. New York: W. W. Norton.

Dietz-Uhler, Beth, et al. 2000. "Sex Differences in Sport Fan Behavior and Reasons for Being a Sport Fan." *Journal of Sport Behavior* 23 (3): 219–231.

Dixon, Nicholas. 2001. "The Ethics of Supporting Sports Teams." *Journal of Applied Philosophy* 18 (2): 149–158.

Dolance, Susannah. 2005. "'A Whole Stadium Full': Lesbian Community at Women's National Basketball Association Games." *Journal of Sex Research* 42 (1): 74–83.

Dreyfus, Hubert, and Sean Dorrance Kelly. 2011. *All Things Shining: Reading the Western Classics to Find Meaning in a Secular Age.* New York: Free Press.

Dundes, Alan. 1978. "Into the Endzone for a Touchdown: A Psychoanalytical Consideration of American Football." *Western Folklore* 37 (2): 75–88.

Eaton, Diane. 2012. "Our SF Giants Wedding." Pinterest.com. Accessed December 1, 2015. https://www.pinterest.com/dianameaton/our-sf-giants-wedding/.

Eder, Steve. 2013. "Rutgers Officials Long Knew of Coach's Actions." *New York Times*, April 6. http://www.nytimes.com/2013/04/07/sports/ncaabasketball/rutgers-officials-long-knew-of-coach-mike-rices-actions.html?_r=0.

Edwards, Lisa, and Carwyn Jones. 2007. "A Soft Gynocentric Critique of the Practice of Modern Sport." *Sport, Ethics, and Philosophy* 1 (3): 346–366.

Elder, Glen, Jennifer Wolch, and Jody Emel. 1998. "Race, Place, and the Bounds of Humanity." *Society and Animals* 6 (2): 183–202.

Elliott, R. K. 1974. "The Aesthetic in Sport." In *Readings in the Aesthetics of Sport*, edited by H. T. A. Whiting and D. W. Masterson. London: Lepus.

ESPN. 2010. "Mark Cuban Mixes Up a Glass of Haterade." SportsCenter blog. April 21. http://espn.go.com/blog/sportscenter/print?id=46067.

———. 2011. *Tim Tebow: Everything in Between.* Film, directed by Chase Heavener.

———. 2012. *Team Spirit.* Film, directed by Errol Morris.

Evans, Jayda. 2014. "Chicago Sky Coach Pokey Chatman Talks about Elena Delle Donne and Pride Games." *Seattle Times*, June 30. http://www.seattletimes.com/sports/storm/chicago-sky-coach-pokey-chatman-talks-about-elena-delle-donne-and-pride-games/.

Facebook, Inc. 2015. Erin Tarver's Facebook Page. July 6. https://www.facebook.com/erin.tarver/posts/10100935733135138

Feder, Ellen. 2007. "The Dangerous Individual('s) Mother: Biopower, Family and the Production of Race." *Hypatia* 22 (2): 60–78.

Feezell, Randolph. 2013. *Sport, Philosophy, and Good Lives.* Lincoln: University of Nebraska Press.

Fiske, John. 1992. "The Cultural Economy of Fandom." In *The Adoring Audience: Fan Culture and Popular Media*, edited by Lisa A. Lewis, 30–49. New York: Routledge.

Five Civilized Tribes Intertribal Council. 2001. "The Five Civilized Tribes Intertribal Council Mascot Resolution." Reprinted in *The Native American Mascot Controversy: A Handbook*, edited by C. Richard King, 195–196. Lanham, MD: Rowman and Littlefield. 2010.

Foucault, Michel. 1988. *The History of Sexuality.* Vol. 3, *The Care of Self.* Translated by Robert Hurley. New York: Vintage.

———. 1990a. *The History of Sexuality.* Vol. 1, *An Introduction.* Translated by Robert Hurley. New York: Vintage.

———. 1990b. *The History of Sexuality.* Vol. 2, *The Uses of Pleasure.* Translated by Robert Hurley. New York: Vintage.

———. 1995. *Discipline and Punish: The Birth of the Prison.* Translated by Alan Sheridan. New York: Vintage.

———. 2003. *Abnormal: Lectures at the Collège de France, 1974–1975.* Translated by Graham Burchell. New York: Picador.

———. 2007. *Security, Territory, Population: Lectures at the Collège de France, 1977–78.* Translated by Graham Burchell. New York: Picador.

Fox Sports. 2011. "MLB's Racing Mascots Are Off and Running." FoxSports.com. March 27. http://www.foxsports.com/mlb/lists/major-league-baseball-competitive-racing-mascots -gallery-032711.

———. 2014. NFC championship game postgame interview with Erin Andrews. January 19.

Fricker, Miranda. 2009. *Epistemic Injustice: Power and the Ethics of Knowing.* New York: Oxford University Press.

Frintner, M., and L. Rubinson. 1993. "Acquaintance Rape: The Influence of Alcohol, Fraternity Membership, and Sports Team Membership." *Journal of Sex Education and Therapy* 19: 272–284.

Fryberg, Stephanie A., Hazel Rose Marcus, Daphna Oyserman, and Joseph M. Stone. 2008. "Of Warrior Chiefs and Indian Princesses: The Psychological Consequences of American Indian Nicknames/Logos/Mascots." *Basic and Applied Social Psychology* 30: 208–218.

Gantz, Walter, and Lawrence A. Wenner. 1995. "Fanship and the Television Sports Viewing Experience." *Sociology of Sport Journal* 12: 56–74.

Garber, Marjorie B. 1997. *Dog Love.* New York: Touchstone.

Gearhart, Sally Miller. 1982. "The Future—If there Is One—Is Female." In *Reweaving the Web of Life: Feminism and Nonviolence,* edited by Pam McAllister, 266–284. Philadelphia: New Society.

Giulianotti, Richard. 2015. "Supporters, Followers, Fans, and Flaneurs: A Taxonomy of Spectator Identities in Football." In *Sociological Perspectives on Sport,* edited by David Karen and Robert E. Washington, 249–262. New York: Routledge. Previously published in *Journal of Sport and Social Issues* (2002) 26 (1): 25–46.

Gorant, J. 2008. "What Happened to Michael Vick's Dogs. . . ." *Sports Illustrated,* December 23.

Grano, Daniel. 2010. "Risky Dispositions: Thick Moral Description and Character-Talk in Sports Culture." *Southern Communication Journal* 75 (3): 255–276.

Greene, David. 2015. "ESPN's Jessica Mendoza on Being the First Woman to Call a MLB Play-off Game." Interview. NPR, October 18. http://www.npr.org/2015/10/15/448840656/espn-s -jessica-mendoza-on-being-the-first-woman-to-call-a-mlb-playoff-game.

Greenlee, Craig T. 2015. "Integrating the SEC." *Diverse: Issues in Higher Education,* February 12, 14–15.

Hall, Donald. 2006. "Muscular Christianity: Reading and Writing the Male Social Body." In *Muscular Christianity: Embodying the Victorian Age,* edited by Donald Hall, 3–16. Cambridge: Cambridge University Press.

Hall, John, and Barry O'Mahony. 2006. "An Empirical Analysis of Gender Differences in Sports Attendance Motives." *International Journal of Sports Marketing and Sponsorship* 7 (4): 39–51.

Hannity. 2010. Fox News, December 28.

Hargreaves, Jennifer. 1994. *Sporting Females: Critical Issues in the History and Sociology of Women's Sports.* New York: Routledge.

Harris-Perry, Melissa. 2010. "Michael Vick, Racial History and Animal Rights." *Nation,* December 30.

Harwell, Drew. 2014. "Women Are Pro Football's Most Important Demographic. Will They Forgive the NFL?" *Washington Post,* September 12. https://www.washingtonpost.com/business/ economy/women-are-pro-footballs-most-important-market-will-they-forgive-the-nfl/ 2014/09/12/d5ba8874–3a7f-11e4–9c9f-ebb47272e40e_story.html.

Hawkins, Billy. 2010. *The New Plantation: Black Athletes, College Sports, and Predominately White NCAA Institutions.* New York: Palgrave Macmillan.

Hebdige, Dick. 1979. *Subculture: The Meaning of Style.* London: Routledge.

Hendrickson, Robert. 1987. "Fans." *The Facts on File Encyclopedia of Word and Phrase Origins.* New York: Facts on File Publications.

Hognestad, Hans K. 2012. "Split Loyalties: Football Is a Community Business." *Soccer and Society* 13 (3): 377–391.

Howard, Greg. 2014. "Richard Sherman and the Plight of the Conquering Negro." *Deadspin,* January 20. http://deadspin.com/richard-sherman-and-the-plight-of-the-conquering-negro-1505060117

Huemer, A. 2000. "Scapegoats and Underdogs: The Pit Bull Dilemma." *Animals' Agenda* 20 (4): 30–33.

Izod, John. 1996. "Television Sport and the Sacrificial Hero." *Journal of Sport and Social Issues* 20 (2): 173–193.

James, Robin. 2011. "'Killing in the Name': On the Racialization of Pit Bulls and the Politics of Breed-Specific Legislation." Paper presented at the annual meeting of the Association for Practical and Professional Ethics, Cincinnati, OH, March 3–6.

James, William. 1987. "The Moral Equivalent of War." In *William James: Writings, 1902–1910,* 1281–1293. New York: Library of America, Penguin.

———. 1992a. "Great Men and Their Environment." In *William James: Writings, 1878–1899,* 618–646. New York: Library of America, Penguin.

———. 1992b. "The Importance of Individuals." In *William James: Writings, 1878–1899,* 647–652. New York: Library of America, Penguin.

Jones, Janine. 2004. "The Impairment of Empathy in Goodwill Whites for African Americans." In *What White Looks Like,* edited by George Yancy, 65–86. New York: Routledge.

Judd, A. 2007. "Trouble Has Vick's Number." *Atlanta Journal-Constitution,* July 22.

Kaelin, E. F. 1968. "The Well-Played Game: Notes toward an Aesthetics of Sport." *Quest* 10: 16–28.

Kansas City Star. 1888a. "Sporting Proceedings." June 1.

———. 1888b. "Sporting Proceedings." August 13.

Karp, Austin. 2015. "NBA Regular-Season Audience Lower on National Nets, but Teams See Gains On RSNs." *Sports Business Daily,* April 22.

Keown, Tim. 2015. "The Confession of Arian Foster." *ESPN: The Magazine.* August 18. http://espn.go.com/nfl/story/_/id/13369076/houston-texans-arian-foster-goes-public-not-believing-god.

King, C. Richard, and Charles F. Springwood. 2001. *Beyond the Cheers: Race as Spectacle in College Sport.* Albany, NY: SUNY Press.

Klein, Alan. 2000. "Latinizing Fenway Park: A Cultural Critique of the Boston Red Sox, Their Fans, and the Media." *Sociology of Sport Journal* 17: 302–422.

Kort, Michele. 2002. "Hoops and Kisses: The New York Liberty Has a Lesbian Coach and a Lesbian Star Player—But Is the Team Shunning Its Lesbian Fans?" *Advocate,* October 1.

Kraszewski, Jon. 2008. "Pittsburgh in Fort Worth: Football Bars, Sports Television, Sports Fandom, and the Management of Home." *Journal of Sport and Social Issues* 32 (2): 139–157.

Kuta, Sarah. 2014. "Some CU-Boulder Alums Irked by 'Football 101 for Women' Clinic." *Daily Camera,* July 6. http://www.dailycamera.com/cu-news/ci_26088762/some-cu-boulder-alums-irked-by-football-101.

Lacan, Jacques. 1999. *Écrits.* Translated by Bruce Fink. New York: W. W. Norton.

Lake, Thomas. 2013. "The Book of Tebow." *Sports Illustrated Longform*, November 26. http://www.si.com/longform/tebow/index.html#asection-1.

———. 2015. "Unbroken: Kevin Ware Rebuilding His Hoops Career Away from the Spotlight." *Sports Illustrated*, January 20. http://www.si.com/college-basketball/2015/01/20/kevin-ware-leg-louisville-georgia-state.

Lapchick, Richard, and Natalie Nelson. 2015. "The 2015 Women's National Basketball Association Racial and Gender Report Card." TIDES (The Institute for Diversity and Ethics in Sport), University of Central Florida. October 21. http://nebula.wsimg.com/28d57b7b134d9c22a277d36d8ce5d35d?AccessKeyId=DAC3A56D8FB782449D2A&disposition=0&alloworigin=1.

Laucella, P. 2010. "Michael Vick: An Analysis of Press Coverage on Federal Dogfighting Charges." *Journal of Sports Media* 5 (2): 35–76.

Laymon, Kiese. 2015. "How They Do in Oxford." *ESPN: The Magazine*, October 15. http://espn.go.com/college-sports/story/_/id/13842293/the-allure-ole-miss-football.

Leland, John. 1995. "Hoop Dreams." *Newsweek*, March 20, 48–55.

Ley, Bob. 2002. "Outside the Lines: Unable to Read." *Outside the Lines*, episode 103. ESPN. Accessed December 7, 2015. http://sports.espn.go.com/page2/tvlistings/show103transcript.html.

Ley, Tom. 2013. "'Find the Asshole, That's Where That Knuckle Goes': A Young Jim Harbaugh on How to Play Quarterback." *Deadspin*, January 22. http://deadspin.com/5978007/find-the-asshole-thats-where-that-knuckle-goes-a-young-jim-harbaugh-on-how-to-play-quarterback.

Lindsay, Peter J. 2008. "Representing Redskins: The Ethics of Native American Team Names." *Journal of the Philosophy of Sport* 35: 212–213.

LJGFC (LeBron James Grandmothers' Fan Club). 2015. LeBron James Grandmothers Fan Club website. Accessed December 8, 2015. http://www.lebronjamesgrandmothersfanclub.org/Grannies-News.html.

Loland, Sigmund. 2002. *Fair Play in Sport: A Moral Norm System*. New York: Routledge.

Lott, Eric. 1992. "Love and Theft: The Racial Unconscious of Blackface Minstrelsy." *Representations* 39 (Summer): 23–50.

Love, Barbara, and Elizabeth Shanklin. 1984. "The Answer Is Matriarchy." In *Mothering: Essays in Feminist Theory*, edited by Joyce Trebilcot, 275–283. Totawa, NJ: Rowman and Allenheld.

LSU Starting Lineup Video. 2012. Accessed April 5, 2013. http://www.youtube.com/watch?v=9RVOB71pKu4.

Magary, Drew. 2014. "The Hater's Guide to Derek Jeter." *Deadspin*, July 16. http://deadspin.com/the-hater-s-guide-to-derek-jeter-1605937020.

Makuhari Media. 2011. *Ballplayer/Pelotero*. DVD. Directed by Ross Finkel, Trevor Martin, and Jonathan Paley. USA: Strand Releasing.

Malone, Karl. 1993. "One Role Model to Another." *Sports Illustrated*, June 14, 84.

Markon, J. 2007. "Redemption Easier Said Than Done." *Richmond Times-Dispatch*, August 28.

Markovits, Andrei S., and Emily Albertson. 2012. *Sportista: Female Fandom in the United States*. Philadelphia: Temple University Press.

Markovits, Andrei S., and David T. Smith. 2007. "Sports Culture among Undergraduates: A Study of Student Athletes and Students at the University of Michigan." Ann Arbor: Michigan Publishing, University of Michigan Library.

Maske, Mark. 2009. "Vick Is Back. Now What?" *Washington Post*, July 28.

McCreanor, Timothy, et al. 2005. "Youth Identity Formation and Contemporary Alcohol Marketing." *Critical Public Health* 15 (3): 251–262.

McIntire, Mike, and Walt Bogdanich. 2014. "At Florida State, Football Clouds Justice." *New York Times*, October 10. http://www.nytimes.com/2014/10/12/us/florida-state-football-casts-shadow-over-tallahassee-justice.html.

McMahon, Sarah. 2007. "Understanding Community-Specific Rape Myths: Exploring Student-Athlete Culture." *Affilia: Journal of Women and Social Work* 22 (4): 357–370.

McNamee, Mike. 2003. "*Schadenfreude* in Sport: Envy, Justice, and Self-Esteem." *Journal of the Philosophy of Sport* 30: 1–16.

McWhorter, Ladelle. 1999. *Bodies and Pleasures: Foucault and the Politics of Sexual Normalization*. Bloomington: Indiana University Press.

———. 2009. *Racism and Sexual Oppression in Anglo-America: A Genealogy*. Bloomington: Indiana University Press.

Medina, José. 2013. *The Epistemology of Resistance: Gender and Racial Oppression, Epistemic Injustice, and Resistant Imaginations*. New York: Oxford.

Miller, J. 2009. "Vick Divides a Shocked Philadelphia Fan Base." *New York Times*, August 14.

Mills, Charles W. 1997. *The Racial Contract*. Ithaca, NY: Cornell University Press.

Mitchard, Jacquelyn. 1993. "Jordan's Retirement Says Volumes about His Mourning Fans." *Milwaukee Journal*, October 10.

Morning, Ann. 2009. "Toward a Sociology of Racial Conceptualization for the 21st Century." *Social Forces* 87 (3): 1167–1192.

Morris, Peter. 2003. "What It Means to Be a Fan." Paper presented at Society for American Baseball Research Convention, Denver.

Morrison, Toni. 1992. *Playing in the Dark: Whiteness and the Literary Imagination*. New York: Vintage Books.

Mumford, Stephen. 2004. "Allegiance and Identity." *Journal of the Philosophy of Sport* 31 (2): 184–195.

———. 2012. *Watching Sport: Aesthetics, Ethics, and Emotion*. New York: Routledge.

NAACP (National Association for the Advancement of Colored People). 1999. "Resolution in Opposition to Native American Mascots." Reprinted in *The Native American Mascot Controversy: A Handbook*, edited by C. Richard King, 201–202. Lanham, MD: Rowman and Littlefield. 2010.

National Baseball Hall of Fame. 2015. "Henry Chadwick." Accessed November 30, 2015. http://baseballhall.org/hof/chadwick-henry

National Congress of American Indians. 1993. "Denouncement of the Use of Any American Indian Name or Artifice Associated with Team Mascots by Any Professional/Nonprofessional Sports Teams." Reprinted in *The Native American Mascot Controversy: A Handbook*, edited by C. Richard King, 199–200. Lanham, MD: Rowman and Littlefield. 2010.

National Public Radio. 2010. "Is it Time to Forgive Michael Vick?" *Talk of the Nation*, December 28.

NCAA (National Collegiate Athletics Association). 2005. "Statement by NCAA Senior Vice-President for Governance and Membership Bernard Franklin on University of Illinois, Champaign Review." Press release. November 11.

———. Office of Inclusion. 2011. *NCAA Inclusion of Transgender Student-Athletes*. NCAA Handbook Supplement. https://www.ncaa.org/sites/default/files/Transgender_Handbook_2011_Final.pdf.

Netter, S. 2010. "Pittsburg [*sic*] Fans Turn on Ben Roethlisberger." *ABC News*, April 22.

New, Jake. 2014. "Two Decades of 'Paper Classes.'" *Inside Higher Ed*, October 23. https://www
  .insidehighered.com/news/2014/10/23/report-finds-academic-fraud-u-north-carolina
  -lasted-nearly-20-years.

New York Times. 1953. "Jim Thorpe Is Dead on West Coast at 64." March 29.

Newman, Joshua I. 2007. "Old Times There Are Not Forgotten: Sport, Identity, and the Confederate Flag in the Dixie South." *Sociology of Sport Journal* 24: 261–282.

Nichols, Rachel. 2015. "The Sports World Deserves Better Than It Got This Week." CNN, October
  9. http://www.cnn.com/2015/10/08/opinions/nichols-sports-jessica-mendoza-greg-hardy/.

Nietzsche, Friedrich. 1989. *On the Genealogy of Morals.* Translated by Walter Kaufmann. New
  York: Random House.

Nomura, Shawna. 1995. "She Can't Feel Sorry for Scholarship Athletes." Letter to the editor. *Los
  Angeles Times*, April 8.

Nylund, David. 2004. "When in Rome: Heterosexism, Homophobia, and Sports Talk Radio."
  Journal of Sport and Social Issues 28 (2): 136–168.

OED Online. 2015a. S.v. "fan, n.2." Accessed November 30, 2015. http://www.oed.com.proxy
  .library.emory.edu/view/Entry/68000?rskey=Lz420F&result=2.

———. 2015b. S.v. "mascot, n." Accessed November 30, 2015. http://www.oed.com.proxy.library
  .emory.edu/view/Entry/68000?rskey=Lz420F&result=2.

OleMissSports. 2016a. "Traditions." http://www.olemisssports.com/trads/ole-miss-trads.html.

———. 2016b. "Traditions: Songs." http://www.olemisssports.com/trads/school-songs.html.

Oliver, Kelly. 2007. *Women as Weapons of War: Iraq, Sex, and the Media.* New York: Columbia
  University Press.

Olszowy, Lynn. 2015. "LeBron James Has a Legion of Grandmothers Rooting for Him." ESPNW,
  May 28. http://espn.go.com/espnw/athletes-life/article/12970340/lebron-james-legion-grand
  mothers-rooting-him?ex_cid=sportscenterTW.

Orenstein, Susan. 2014. "Bringing Piety Back: Tim Tebow, Sports, and American Culture." In
  Fan CULTure: Essays on Participatory Fandom in the 21st Century, edited by Kristin Michael
  Barton and Jonathon Malcom Lampley, 61–75. Jefferson, NC: McFarland.

Ourand, John, and Austin Karp. 2013. "With Rebound, WNBA Solidifies Spot at ESPN." *Sports
  Business Daily Journal*, November 11.

Pettus, Emily Wagner. 2014. "Ole Miss Taking More Steps for Racial Diversity." *Associated Press*,
  August 1. http://bigstory.ap.org/article/ole-miss-taking-more-steps-racial-diversity.

Popik, Barry, and Gerald Cohen. 1996. "Sports Fan: Its 1880s Origin in St. Louis." *Comments on
  Etymology* 26 (1): 2–12.

Portmann, John. 2000. *When Bad Things Happen to Other People.* New York: Routledge.

Pro Football Hall of Fame. 2013. "Oorang Indians." Accessed June 10, 2014. http://www
  .profootballhof.com/history/decades/1920s/oorang.aspx.

Quinn, Kevin G. 2009. *Sports and their Fans: The History, Economics and Culture of the Relationship between Spectator and Sport.* Jefferson, NC: McFarland.

Rayman, Joshua. 2005. "Discipline and Punish the Ball: Foucault, Metaphysics, and Baseball."
  International Studies in Philosophy 37 (1): 95–117.

Reynolds, Gerald. 2003. "Further Clarification of Intercollegiate Athletics Policy Guidance Regarding Title IX Compliance." *Marquette Sports Law Review* 14 (1): C1–C4.

Rhoden, W. 2007. "The Elusive Vick Takes the Hardest Hit." *New York Times*, July 20.

Rhodes, James. 2011. "Fighting for 'Respectability': Media Representations of the White,
  'Working-Class' Male Boxing 'Hero.'" *Journal of Sport and Social Issues* 35 (4): 350–376.

Roberts, Dorothy. 1997. *Killing the Black Body: Race, Reproduction, and the Meaning of Liberty.* New York: Vintage.

Roelofs, Monique. 2005. "Racialization as an Aesthetic Production: What Does the Aesthetic Do for Whiteness and Blackness and Vice Versa?" In *White on White / Black on Black*, edited by George Yancy, 83–124. Lanham, MD: Rowman and Littlefield.

Rovell, Darren. 2016. "Famed 'Be Like Mike' Gatorade Ad Debuted 25 Years Ago." ESPN, August 8.

Royce, Josiah. 2009. *Race Questions, Provincialism, and Other American Problems.* Enlarged edition. Edited by Scott L. Pratt and Shannon Sullivan. New York: Fordham University Press.

Rubinstein, Julian. 1999. "Slam It, Baby!" *Salon*, September 2. http://www.salon.com/1999/09/02/slamdunk/.

Rudolph, Jennifer Domino. 2010. "The Hit Man from Washington: Place, Marketable Deviance, and Major League Baseball." *Journal of Sport and Social Issues* 34 (1): 62–85.

Ruihley, Brody, and Andrew Billings. 2012. "Infiltrating the Boys' Club: Motivations for Women's Fantasy Sport Participation." *International Review of the Sociology of Sport* 48 (4): 435–452.

Russell, J. S. 2012. "The Ideal Fan or Good Fans?" *Sport, Ethics and Philosophy* 6 (1): 16–30.

Sager, M. 1987. "A Boy and His Dog in Hell." *Rolling Stone*, July, 36.

Schechner, Richard. 1988. *Performance Theory.* New York: Routledge.

Schneider-Mayerson, Matthew. 2010. "'Too Black': Race in the 'Dark Ages' of the National Basketball Association." *International Journal of Sport and Society* 1 (1): 223–233.

Searle, John R. 1995. *The Construction of Social Reality.* New York: Free Press.

Sedgwick, Eve. 1985. *Between Men: English Literature and Male Homosocial Desire.* New York: Columbia University Press.

Segrave, Jeffrey. 1997. "A Matter of Life and Death: Some Thoughts on the Language of Sport." *Journal of Sport and Social Issues* 21: 211–220.

Shulman, David. 1996. "On the Early Use of 'Fan' in Baseball." *American Speech* 71 (3): 328–331.

Silva, Eric O. 2007. "Public Accounts: Defending Contested Practices." *Symbolic Interaction* 30 (2): 245–265.

Silverman, Robert. 2014. "LeBron James Is a Better Leader than Michael Jordan Ever Was." *Daily Beast*, May 15.

Simmons, Bill. 2014. "God Loves Cleveland." *Grantland*, July 11. http://grantland.com/features/god-loves-cleveland/.

Smith, Mychal Denzel. 2014. "The School-to-Prison Pipeline Starts in Preschool." *Nation*, March 28. http://www.thenation.com/blog/179064/school-prison-pipeline-starts-preschool#.

Smith, Thomas G. 2012. *Showdown: JFK and the Integration of the Washington Redskins.* Boston: Beacon.

Snowdon, Paul. 2013. "Sport and Life." *Royal Institute of Philosophy Supplement* 73: 79–98.

Sønderlund, Andres L., et al. 2014. "The Association between Sports Participation, Alcohol Use, and Aggression and Violence: A Systematic Review." *Journal of Science and Medicine in Sport* 17 (1): 2–7.

Southern Documentary Project. 2010. "Blind Jim at an Ole Miss Football Game, 1947." Accessed December 5, 2015. https://vimeo.com/9387535.

Spindel, Carol. 2000. *Dancing at Halftime: Sports and the Controversy over American Indian Mascots.* New York: NYU Press.

Sporting News. 2009. "SEC Football Is. . . ." September 28, 26–33.

Springwood, Charles F. 2000. "Fighting Spirits: The Racial Politics of Sports Mascots." *Journal of Sport and Social Issues* 24 (3): 282–305.

Stuart, Reginald. 1982. "20 Years after Admitting Meredith, Ole Miss Merges Its Old and New

Images." *New York Times*, October 3. http://www.nytimes.com/1982/10/03/us/20-years-after -admitting-meredith-ole-miss-merges-its-old-and-new-images.html.

Suits, Bernard. 2005. *The Grasshopper: Games, Life and Utopia*. 3rd ed. Toronto: University of Toronto Press.

Sullivan, Shannon. 2006. *Revealing Whiteness: The Unconscious Habits of Racial Privilege*. Bloomington: Indiana University Press.

Swanson, Ryan. 2015. "Establishing Proper 'Athletic Relations': The Nascent SEC and the Formation of College Athletic Conferences." *Alabama Review* 68 (2): 168–188.

Tamburrini, Claudio M. 1998. "Sports, Fascism, and the Market." *Journal of the Philosophy of Sport* 25 (1): 35–47.

Tännsjö, Torbjörn. 1998. "Is Our Admiration for Sports Heroes Fascistoid?" *Journal of the Philosophy of Sport* 25 (1): 23–34.

———. 2000. "Against Sexual Discrimination in Sports." In *Values in Sport: Elitism, Nationalism, Gender Equality, and the Scientific Manufacture of Winners*, edited by Torbjörn Tännsjö and Claudio Tamburrini, 101–115. New York: Taylor and Francis.

Taylor, Michael. 2013. *Contesting Constructed Indian-ness: The Intersection of the Frontier, Masculinity, and Whiteness in Native American Mascot Representations*. Lanham, MD: Lexington Books.

Taylor, Paul C. 2013. *Race: A Philosophical Introduction*. 2nd ed. Malden, MA: Polity.

Tomasson, Chris. 1994. "Paying College Athletes Would Be Very Unwise." *Spartanburg Herald-Journal*, July 7.

Townsend, Kim. 1996. *Manhood at Harvard: William James and Others*. New York: W. W. Norton.

Traubner, Richard. 2003. *Operetta: A Theatrical History*. Rev. ed. New York: Routledge.

Travis, Clay. 2015. "Hot Alabama Sorority Enlists Kenyan Drake to Star in Recruitment Video." *Outkick the Coverage* (blog). Fox Sports. August 9. http://www.foxsports.com/college -football/outkick-the-coverage/hot-alabama-sorority-enlists-kenyan-drake-to-star-in -recruitment-video-080915.

Twining, Hillary, Arnold Arluke, and Gary Patronek. 2000. "Managing the Stigma of Outlaw Breeds: A Case Study of Pit Bull Owners." *Society and Animals* 8 (1): 25–52.

US Commission on Civil Rights. 2001. "Statement on the Use of Native American Images and Nicknames as Sports Symbols." Reprinted in *The Native American Mascot Controversy: A Handbook*, edited by C. Richard King, 191–194. Lanham, MD: Rowman & Littlefield. 2010.

USA Today. 2007. "Window on a Cruel World." July 20.

Van Riper, Tom. 2014. "Is It the Beginning of the End for the WNBA?" *Forbes*, May 23. http:// www.forbes.com/sites/tomvanriper/2014/05/23/is-it-the-beginning-of-the-end-for-the -wnba/.

Vascellaro, Charlie. 2011. "Native Americans Significant in Baseball History." MLB.com. Accessed June 9, 2014. http://mlb.mlb.com/news/article.jsp?ymd=20111212&content_id= 26150368&c_id=mlb.

Viroli, Maurizio. 1995. *For Love of Country: An Essay on Patriotism and Nationalism*. Oxford: Oxford University Press.

Wacquant, Loïc. 2002. "From Slavery to Mass Incarceration." *New Left Review* 13 (January– February): 41–60.

Wagner, Kyle. 2014. "The Word 'Thug' Was Uttered 625 Times on TV on Monday. That's a Lot." *Deadspin*, January 21. http://regressing.deadspin.com/the-word-thug-was-uttered-625 -times-on-tv-yesterday-1506098319.

Wann, Daniel L. 2006. "Understanding the Positive Socio-Psychological Benefits of Sport Team

Identification: The Team Identification–Social Psychological Health Model." *Group Dynamics* 10 (4): 272–296.

Washington Post. 2015. "Stubborn Critics of the Team Name." Letter to the editor. January 25.

Watts, Rebecca B. 2014. "Being Tim Tebow: The Rhetorical Construction of a Football Savior-Superhero." *Florida Communication Journal* 42 (2): 1–16.

Watts, Sarah. 2003. *Rough Rider in the White House: Theodore Roosevelt and the Politics of Desire.* Chicago: University of Chicago Press.

Weiler, Jonathan. 2014. "Colin Cowherd's Anti-College Players' Union Rant Gets Everything Wrong." *Huffington Post*, January 29.

Weinfuss, Josh. 2015. "Tyrann Mathieu Accepted LSU Scholarship on the Spot." ESPN, September 30. http://www.espn.com/blog/arizona-cardinals/post/_/id/16513/tyrann-mathieu-accepted-lsu-scholarship-on-the-spot.

Weinstein, Adam. 2013. "Jameis Winston Isn't the Only Problem Here: An FSU Teacher's Lament." *Deadspin*, November 21. http://deadspin.com/jameis-winston-isnt-the-only-problem-here-an-fsu-teac-1467707410.

Weiss, Jessica. 2016. "What the Term 'Latinx' Means." *Univision News*, July 12. http://www.univision.com/univision-news/united-states/what-the-term-latinx-means.

Welch, M., E. Price, and N. Yankey. 2002. "Moral Panic over Youth Violence: Wilding and the Manufacture of Menace in the Media." *Youth & Society* 34 (1): 3–30.

Wilbon, Michael. 1998. "'He Got Game' Shows Life in a Real Disturbing Way." *Washington Post*, May 7.

Williams, M. P. 2007. "Remember Your Roots, Your Worth." *Richmond Times-Dispatch*, August 15.

Wise, Mike. 2009. "Mystics Give Big Issue the Kiss-Off." *Washington Post*, July 27. http://www.washingtonpost.com/wp-dyn/content/article/2009/07/26/AR2009072602357.html.

Wittenauer, C. 2008. "An Underdog's Second Chance." Associated Press, January 27.

WNBA. 2015a. "Brittney Griner." http://www.wnba.com/player/brittney-griner/#/panel-four.

———. 2015b. "WNBA Pride." Accessed December 9, 2015. http://www.wnba.com/pride/.

Wonsek, Pamela. 1992. "College Basketball on Television: A Study of Racism in the Media." *Media, Culture, and Society* 14: 449–461.

X, Malcolm, and Alex Haley. 1964. *The Autobiography of Malcolm X.* New York: Ballantine Books.

Yancy, George. 2004. "Introduction: Fragments of a Social Ontology of Whiteness." In *What White Looks Like*, edited by George Yancy, 1–24. New York: Routledge.

Young, Iris M. 1979. "The Exclusion of Women from Sport: Conceptual and Existential Dimensions." *Philosophy in Context* 9: 44–53.

———. 1980. "Throwing like a Girl: A Phenomenology of Feminine Body Comportment Motility and Spatiality." *Human Studies* 3 (2): 137–156.

Yudkin, Marcia. 1982. "Reflections on Woolf's Three Guineas." *Women's Studies International Forum* 5 (3): 263–269.

Zagacki, Kenneth S., and Daniel Grano. 2005. "Radio Sports Talk and the Fantasies of Sport." *Critical Studies in Media Communication* 22 (1): 45–63.

Zirin, Dave. 2010. "On Dimples and Dog Whistles: Why Tucker Carlson Dehumanizes Michael Vick." *Nation*, blog post, December 30. http://www.thenation.com/blog/157378/dimples-and-dog-whistles-why-tucker-carlson-dehumanizes-michael-vick.

———. 2013. "Man Men: Why Fox News and Former Players Defend former Rutgers Coach Mike Rice." *Nation*, April 3. http://www.thenation.com/article/mad-men-why-fox-news-and-former-players-defend-former-rutgers-coach-mike-rice/.

Index

African Americans. *See* black people
Alabama, University of, 2, 119–23
Albertson, Emily, 35, 178, 213n7
Aldridge, LaMarcus, 99
All Things Shining (Dreyfus/Kelly), 25
Alpha Phi video, 119–23, 131
Anderson, Benedict, 42, 46
Andrews, David L., 106
Andrews, Erin, 144, 156–57
androgyny, 188
animals: abuse of, 144, 160–68; black people and, 81, 99–100, 109, 116, 128, 136, 138; mascots, 57, 61–62, 62t, 67, 81, 201, 212n10 (*see also* mascots); Native Americans and, 53, 61–62; women and, 201, 202
antipathy, for players, 143–70, 212n3. *See also specific players*
Aristotle, 29, 154
Asian Americans, 104, 210n9, 211n8
Augustus, Seimone, 197, 199

Barkley, Charles, 81–82
Bartky, Sandra, 121
baseball, 9–11, 30–31, 77–80, 101–5, 109–12, 179. *See also specific persons, teams, topics*
"Base Ball Fever, The" (song), 13–14
basketball, 81–82, 105–8, 116–18, 182–87, 193–97, 200. *See also specific persons, teams, topics*
Beauvoir, Simone de, 4, 36, 181, 182, 186, 191, 197
Ben-Ze'ev, Aaron, 148–49, 150
Big Al (mascot), 120, 121
Bird, Larry, 155
BIRGing, 26, 29, 51, 52, 97, 99
black people: mascotting and, 115–23 (*see also* mascotting); masculinity and, 3, 6, 115–23, 124, 127, 128, 129, 134 (*see also* masculinity);

normal schools, 112; segregation, 48, 70t, 71t, 114; sexuality and, 54, 55, 138; slavery, 46, 54, 96, 100, 127, 133, 137; white people and (*see* whiteness); women, 6, 123, 139–40. *See also* race; *and specific persons, topics*
Blind Jim (mascot), 96–97
Boston Braves, 76
Boston Red Sox, 62, 104, 147
Boxill, Jan, 176
boxing, 87, 88, 198
box scores, 30, 31, 208n2
Brown v. Board of Education, 114
Burstyn, Varda, 188
Butler, Judith, 9, 37
Butterworth, Michael, 92

Cahn, Susan, 192, 193
Cavicchi, Daniel, 8
Césaire, Aimé, 132, 133
Chadwick, Henry, 30
Chapman, Alder, 183
Chapman, Aroldis, 99
Chatman, Pokey, 199
Christianity, 44, 85–92
Christie, Chris, 135
Cleveland Browns, 62, 209n4
Cleveland Cavaliers, 6, 143, 154, 169, 173, 183–86
Cleveland Indians, 76
Code, Lorraine, 208n6
Cohen, Gerald, 12
Cohn, Linda, 34
Collins, Patricia Hill, 126
Collins, Randall, 26, 131
colonialism, 133
Comiskey, Charlie, 13